The Adult Years

Frederic M. Hudson

The Adult Years

Mastering the Art of Self-Renewal

Jossey-Bass Publishers · San Francisco

THE ADULT YEARS
Mastering the Art of Self-Renewal
  by Frederic M. Hudson

Copyright © 1991 by: Jossey-Bass Inc., Publishers
                     350 Sansome Street
                     San Francisco, California 94104

                         &

                     Jossey-Bass Limited
                     Headington Hill Hall
                     Oxford OX3 0BW

Library of Congress Cataloging-in-Publication Data

Hudson, Frederic M., date.
    The adult years : mastering the art of self-renewal / Frederic M.
Hudson.
        p.   cm.—(Jossey-Bass social and behavioral science series)
(Jossey-Bass higher and adult education series)
    Includes bibliographical references and index.
    ISBN 1-55542-365-5
    1. Adulthood.   2. Adulthood—Psychological aspects.   3. Life
cycle, Human—Social aspects.   4. Life cycle, Human—Psychological
aspects.   5. Self-actualization (Psychology) I. Title.
II. Series.   III. Series: Jossey-Bass higher and adult education
series.
HQ799.95.H83   1991
305.24—dc 20   91-9922
                                                            CIP

Manufactured in the United States of America

The paper in this book meets the guidelines for
permanence and durability of the Committee on
Production Guidelines for Book Longevity of the
Council on Library Resources.

JACKET DESIGN BY FIFTH STREET DESIGN

FIRST EDITION
HB Printing   10 9 8 7 6 5 4 3 2
Code 9172

A joint publication in
The Jossey-Bass
Social and Behavioral Science Series
and
The Jossey-Bass
Higher and Adult Education Series

Contents

Preface

There is one central question that I hear over and over again in my work with adults: What can I count on in a world where little is definite anymore? This book searches for answers. In today's world, few adults know how to chart their lives with confidence. As pervasive change overwhelms self-confidence and social stability, adults are tentative, brooding, and unclear about the future.

The old formulas for mastering adult life are highly unreliable. The prevailing pattern for managing time—to work most of the time, to love some of the time, and to do fantastic things on weekends—leaves people feeling their lives are little more than the shadows of their jobs. Even successful adults with abundant time for living say they feel more vulnerable and adrift than their striving parents and grandparents were. This book is written to help today's adults master the art of self-renewal in our kind of world.

This book is about the experience of adult life in a world of complex change. How can adults find personal fulfillment in the midst of continuous turbulence? How can they find value and human challenge as global chaos stirs up their lives? The thesis is that as adults learn to master the change process within their own lives, they will find new ways to renew their families, workplaces, and culture. Adult mastery of change is critical to the renewal process that our entire society seeks. This book describes how the forces of adult empowerment are also forces for social renewal.

The purpose of this book is to articulate the complex adult process taking shape among educated Americans today, and to identify specific skills that can empower them throughout the life cycle. The book maps out the vast adult territory and provides a framework for how adult life can proceed vitally from age twenty to about age eighty in our kind of world. Through a careful reading of this material, readers should be able to locate where they are in the change process and which skills are critical for designing a fulfilling personal and social future.

Point of View

Most grown-ups know very little about the territory of their fifty to sixty adult years. They often lack realistic expectations and get mired in their own disappointments. They run out of dreams and may lack the ability to envision new ones. Some feel trapped by their early adult decisions regarding life partners, education, and careers. Most lose their way on a long journey they are not trained to take. Life has become more complex and more fragile—all the more reason to master the art of living during our adult years.

Good intentions and hard work are no longer enough to ensure lasting happiness and success. Today's adults need maps for the journey, along with the required human competence. As a nation, we waste our most valuable human resource—adults—because we don't promote their continued learning, development, deployment, and utilization in a systematic way. The relatively young field of adult development has produced much information but little applied knowledge on how adults can sustain self-renewing lives. There is abundant research that describes and explores aspects of adult life, but precious little wisdom for how adults can design and manage their own lives. This book is an effort in that direction. We will explore ways an adult today can establish a life course, construct durable life structures, manage life and career changes and transitions, engage in lifelong learning and training, live an anticipatory life rather than a reactive one, master the art of self-renewal, and contribute to planetary renewal. For too long, Americans have kept the interior life of the self apart from the social adventure. In this book, "psychology" is linked to development of adult lives within their social settings—marriages, work life, leisure activities, adult networks, and social concerns.

A major theme of this book is that today's adults can provide our society with an ongoing source of cohesion and renewal. No one has stated this better than John W. Gardner, whose writings on self-renewal have been a major inspiration for this book: "If a society hopes to achieve renewal, it will have to be a hospitable environment for creative men and women. It will also have to produce men and women with the capacity for self-renewal. . . . We know that men and women need not fall into a stupor of mind and spirit by the time they are middle-aged. They need not relinquish as early as they do the resilience of youth and the capacity to learn and grow. Self-renewal is possible."[1]

Audience

This book is written for American adults who have succeeded in some aspect of their lives and now want to examine their future possibilities. These people have the readiness and ability to master more of the adult journey through new learning and training. These are adults who typically work hard, live busy lives, maintain careers or volunteer roles, manage money, play well, and fear that the yellow brick road ends sometime during the adult years.

These adults are increasingly a pluralistic group of men and women from many ethnic backgrounds, with varying amounts of formal education and career experience. They include single and married adults, those who are divorced or remarried, homemakers as well as careerists, leaders and followers, wealthy and not so wealthy, individuals from varied life-styles, and twentysomethings through seventysomethings. This diverse audience—the emerging dominant minority in an aging America—is looking for ways to fulfill individual dreams while providing leadership to the faltering institutions of our society.

They are *high performing adults:* people who are successful but have not developed autonomous, private lives, professionals who want to rearrange their lives and priorities but don't know how to do so, and midlife adults facing outplacement, job terminations, or new career directions. Some are *disappointed adults:* men and women who feel stuck, bored, or trapped by the routines of their lives, adults who want to find a new beginning for their lives, and people whose lives are unraveling and who are overwhelmed by change or tragedy. Many are *professionals* seeking new ways to manage human and organizational change: leaders and managers who want skills for transition management and human resource directors, educators, career counselors, clergy, physicians and nurses, psychologists, and social workers who work with adults and adult systems. Some are *students* searching for an overview of the adult journey and a basic understanding of the competencies required: undergraduate, graduate, and professional degree students who want to understand the adult life process in the context of contemporary change and renewal.

Organization of the Book

Part One, on the emerging adult of our time, examines the paradox that while accelerating change has unshackled adults from cultural constraints and provided many new opportunities for personal and professional development, it has also disoriented and disempowered them. Chapter One contrasts the new opportunities for adult living with the widespread negative belief that the best days for America are behind us. The chapter concludes with a challenge for personal and social renewal. Chapter Two contrasts linear and cyclical frameworks for understanding adult life. A case is made in support of the cyclical pattern, in which people experience stability in their lives for a period of time, followed by a period of transition and reevaluation, followed by more stability. A chart is provided to illustrate the fundamental differences for adult life between the modular process of cyclical living and linear portraits. Two kinds of cycles, the cycle of change and the adult life cycle, are identified as the critical notions for mastering adult empowerment.

Part Two, which interprets the ongoing cycle of change in our lives, describes the human skills that empower adult life structures and transitions. Chapter Three presents the pattern of adult change, with four phases of change and ten life skills for facilitating adult renewal and empowerment. A map illustrates how the cycle of change works. Chapter Four describes how to build strong adult life structures and how to cooperate with their endings. The chapter explains how adults usually repair and renew dysfunctional life structures. Chapter Five interprets life transitions that occur when life structures cannot be sustained, repaired, or renewed; it defines life transitions and their purpose. The intricate processes of disengagement and *cocooning,* during which adults heal and discover their own self-sufficiency, are interpreted. Chapter Six continues to present the cycle of change as it moves from cocooning to self-renewal and reintegration with the world. This is a time when a person's core values are reevaluated as he or she proceeds with renewed confidence to find a new life structure.

Part Three portrays the life cycle changes that take place in adult life from about age twenty to age eighty.[2] The dominant theme is how adults redefine their life purpose at different points in the life cycle. Chapter Seven explains how adults define life meaning and mission across the life cycle, as basic values are reprioritized within human systems. A map of the adult life cycle is provided, along with a table of adult changes, by decade, in life purpose, values, systems, and tasks. Chapter Eight describes today's twentysomethings and thirtysomethings, including case examples and interpretations of their central life issues. Chapter Nine examines how fortysomethings and fiftysomethings express their life purpose, as self-reliance and interdependence become important focal points in the adult life cycle. Chapter Ten looks at the continuities and changes in sixtysomethings and seventysomethings, as adult life continues to find new orientations and integrity, even as the aging process becomes more dominant. Chapter Eleven presents six principles of life-cycle change. How do adults understand the changes that they go through during the long adult years? What are the principles that guide adult development from adolescence to death? Six very different points of view are described and explored.

Part Four applies the ideas of the book to the self-renewing process in people and society. Chapter Twelve investigates the connections between adult life and global chaos. Six human dimensions of chaos are identified as creative ways adults can move into leadership roles and participation in the world as we have it. Chapter Thirteen outlines the qualities of self-renewing people and then presents an articulation of adult mastery skills. A discussion of

adult learning investigates ways adults can acquire these skills, followed by an exploration of the developmental and transformative
types of adult learning. The book ends with a discussion of the
leadership challenge facing today's adults.

The Epilogue presents a proposed model for a profession of
"adult mentors" to facilitate adult development and transformation.

Background

Robert Lifton, in *The Broken Connection*, says "There is a special
quality of life-power available only to those seasoned by struggles
of four or more decades. . . . The life-power of this stage can be
especially profound."[3] This book grows out of twenty years of
teaching "adult development" and "human systems development,"
mostly at the graduate level, and training adults in the skills presented here in a variety of settings, including corporate, governmental, religious, educational, and national intensive seminars I have
sponsored. The major struggle in the field of adult development, as
in most of the behavioral and social sciences, has been over methodology. How can adults be objectively studied? Examining adult
phenomena is like studying a moving target, touching on genetics,
personal life cycles, family and work systems, the aging process,
political and economic issues, sociohistorical epochs, and environmental conditions. The study of adults is extremely complex, and
the orientations of the various academic disciplines do not seem
adequate for the interdisciplinary or transdisciplinary phenomena
in this field.

Nevertheless, the professional researchers in this field are
high on methodology and low on theory. They are more concerned
with objective ways of knowing than with beliefs about the objects
being studied—adults. They study the parts more than the whole.
Biologists examine adults from a perspective of organicity, chemistry, and evolution. Psychologists study individual behavior moving through a life span. Sociologists see social forces and systems
shaping roles and events that they call "adult life."[4]

Describing how adult life proceeds is difficult. Today's intro-
ductory texts on adult development are litanies of research findings
from hundreds of studies that do not lend themselves to generali-

zations or life applications. Students and laypeople often feel flooded with information and tidbits of knowledge but left with little wisdom they can apply to their own lives. There is no easy way out of this dilemma. We need more theory building *and* more quantitative and qualitative research.

Carl G. Jung has had considerable influence on this field.[5] Although a psychiatrist by training, his orientation is basically spiritual and mythological. Unlike Freud, who viewed human life as shaped through psychosexual stages in the early years of life, Jung portrayed the second half of life as a time of immense growth and development, particularly for personal introspection, reevaluation, and spiritual discovery. Although many developmentalists are not attracted to his mythological and symbolic way of organizing human constructs, he has exerted considerable influence upon Charlotte Buhler and Fred Massarik, David Gutmann, Daniel Levinson, Joseph Campbell, and Robert Bly.[6] I have found that much of the Jungian material speaks to people in midlife and beyond, particularly his theme of individuation, which he viewed as the ripening of the inner, adult self in the second half of life. Many Jungian themes will be endorsed and woven into the material in this book, but these themes need to be related to other theories and modified by research findings in the field.

Erik H. Erikson produced the first systematic scheme of adult development, which was based on a Freudian perspective as it had evolved into ego psychology.[7] Erikson's genius was to stretch the psychosexual stages of human development into psychosocial concepts, bridging psychological and social orientations. Erikson, who has written much more specific material about children and adolescents than he has about adults, pictured life as a series of sequential stages. Two more recent scholars, Roger Gould and George E. Vaillant, expand the perspective of Erikson.[8] Gould identifies adult progressions in relation to gradual transformation of the infantile myth of absolute safety, while Vaillant views adult life as a gradual adaptation of defense mechanisms to the realities of aging. Robert Kegan, a stage theorist from a Piagetian orientation, offers a theoretical model of the stages of adult life based on an ongoing rhythm between a need for independence or separation and a need for inclusion or attachment.[9]

Although "stage theory" is very popular in the public's mind today, partly because of Gail Sheehy's *Passages*,[10] this book will argue against specific stages during the adult years. The lack of conceptual clarity among Erikson, Levinson, Gould, Vaillant, and Kegan is sufficiently disturbing to question the usefulness of this way of thinking. Moreover, the social forces of change are now major sources of personal change and development and can be neither subordinated to normative age periods nor distilled into predictable events. Yet we all need some way of explaining the "sequencing" of our lives from birth to death, and this book will suggest that throughout the life cycle, adults keep rearranging the same basic life issues (such as identity, achievement, intimacy, play and creativity, search for meaning, and contribution) around changing perspectives that our personal development, aging, and social conditions evoke from us. In this book, the contributions of Erikson, Gould, Levinson, Vaillant, and Kegan will be expressed in the context of personal cycles within social change.

The two central concepts of this book, life structures and transitions, originate with Daniel Levinson. He writes with clarity about how adults sequence their way through life using psychosocial periods of coherence and periods of change. I find his descriptions of life structures and transitions very compelling, but I completely disagree that this flow of adult life is tied to the chronology of our years. Although some research supports his claim, most dispute it. In my study and work with adults, I have found that crises and transitions do not necessarily correlate with any particular age.

Most of the current literature on adult development has been written with the assumption that adults live in a world in which order is predominant over change. This book assumes that we now live in a period in which change is predominant over order. Adult life from now on will proceed with multiple options, random opportunities, information overload, lifelong learning, a global orientation, ongoing social upheavals, and a constant need for people to be responsible for themselves as they raft their way along the river of change.

A prominent place is given to human system changes that affect the adult life cycle. The scholar I prefer who explains the impact of social forces on adult development is Marjorie Fiske, who examines adult commitments in the context of social realities.[11] But she is much better at seeing the details of her own research than at articulating the overall flow of adult life. The writings of Matilda W. Riley, Klaus Riegel, Urie Bronfenbrenner, and Gerard Egan have had considerable influence on the social factors in adult life reflected in this book.[12]

This book is meant to provide direct information to the reader, with notes that connect the main text with many further notions and references. A major contribution of this book is helping American adults understand the contours of their lives within the world as it is experienced today. Each of us individually and all of us as we are bound together can and must become responsible for the personal and social realities of our time. The future presents us with more freedom than we have ever asked for and more complexity than we have ever wanted. Yet it is all we have, and more than enough for shaping life paths far beyond the destinations that most of us seek.

Acknowledgments

There are many whom I wish to thank for their contributions to this book: My mentors and guides and the scholars who reviewed my manuscript as it was taking shape: Anne Alonso, Richard Beckhard, Ted Berkman, William Bridges, Robert Farnquist, Rick Flatow, Charlie Garfield, Robert and Mary Goulding, Joseph Handlon, Althea Horner, Morris Keeton, Elaine Kepner, Malcolm Knowles, Judy Long, Lynn Luckow, Jack Murphy, Sam Osherson, John Schuster, Edie Seashore, Robert Tannenbaum, John Vasconcelles, and Jackie Zilbach; my wife, Pamela McLean Hudson, and my children Jeffrey Scott Hudson, John Marshall Hudson, Lisa Sue Hudson, Christopher McLean Hudson, Michael McLean Hudson, and Charles McLean Hudson; the many adult clients with whom I have worked, and my colleagues on the faculty of both the Fielding Institute and the Hudson Institute; and my former students, particularly my doctoral students who researched themes of adult life. My special thanks to my editor, Rebecca McGovern, and the Jossey-Bass staff, who provided me with much encouragement and helpful criticism. I also want to thank those who volunteered biographical material for this book—Marvin Banasky, Marilyn Mosley, Richard Haid, and Larry L. King. Finally, my trusty Xerox 860, granddaddy of the computer world whose life has exceeded its life cycle, but who has been my computer companion for fifteen years—thanks, old buddy!

Santa Barbara, California   Frederic M. Hudson
July 1991

The Author

Frederic M. Hudson is president of the Hudson Institute of Santa Barbara, California. He received his B.A. degree (1956) from Kalamazoo College in philosophy, his M.Div. degree (1959) from Colgate Rochester Divinity School in social ethics, and his Ph.D. degree (1968) from Columbia University in interdisciplinary studies. Hudson was a Rockefeller Fellow and a Danforth Fellow.

For the past twenty years, Hudson has conducted seminars for adults wanting to exercise creative choices in planning their lives. Through consultation, leadership training, transition management, and life-design seminars in educational and corporate settings, he has worked with more than 11,000 adults. His training programs have been effective with executives and managers as well as with adults without careers or wealth. He is most widely known for his work with individuals and organizations "in transition" and has worked with personnel from hundreds of corporations and governmental agencies. The Hudson Institute of Santa Barbara, which he founded in 1986, has hosted participants from a wide range of backgrounds, including political leaders, senior officers of major corporations, work teams, educators, entrepreneurs, public relations and advertising executives, scientists, strategic planners, physicians, religious leaders, and sales executives.

Hudson is a member of the Society for Values in Higher Education, the American Society for Training and Development, and the Organization Development Network. He has served as president of the National Association of Free-Standing Graduate Schools, trustee of the California Family Studies Foundation and the San Francisco Consortium, and institutional representative at the Council of Graduate Schools in the United States (1979–1986), the American Council on Education (1974–1986), the American Association of Colleges (1975–1986), the Western Association of Schools and Colleges (1974–1986), the Council for Adults and Experiential Learning (1974–1986), and the National Council of Schools of Professional Psychology (1976–1982). He has contributed articles to such publications as *Innovations in Counseling Psychology* (1977), *Instant Relief: The Encyclopedia of Self-Help* (1979), *Guidance Bulletin of the Iowa Personnel and Guidance Association* (1979), *Rothman's World Symposium on Human Resources* (1983), the New Directions for Higher Education quarterly sourcebook from Jossey-Bass *Meeting the New Demand for Standards* (1983), and *Redecision Therapy: Expanded Perspectives* (1985, volume 2). His books include *Careers in World Affairs* (1960), *The Reign of the New Humanity* (1968), *Planning Your Life Through 2004* (1979), and *Poems from Midlife* (1982).

Hudson's career has been devoted to leadership roles in experiential education for adults. He has designed learning programs at several collegiate institutes to help students grow and develop as persons and as innovative change agents. He has lectured widely at universities and professional associations on adult learning, social ethics, and the management of change. As a dean and teacher at Stephens College, Columbia, Missouri (1961–1964), he directed off-campus service projects and internships; as assistant professor and chaplain of Colby College, Waterville, Maine (1964–1969), he engaged students in learning projects related to the civil rights movement, the antipoverty program, and the peace movement, and he was a frequent lecturer at universities on human development through participation in social movements. In 1969, he was appointed academic dean of Lone Mountain College, San Francisco, where he developed an external masters degree program in psychology for adults.

In 1974, Hudson became the founding president of the Fielding Institute, a professional graduate school in psychology and organization development. Fielding is a freestanding external degree institution, with headquarters in Santa Barbara, California. Now regionally accredited and widely recognized, it is one of the few graduate schools in the nation designed exclusively to educate adult professional leaders with advanced degrees. At Fielding, Hudson applied his knowledge of adult development and social systems to the graduate training of midlife adults.

In 1986, Hudson left the Fielding Institute to begin the Hudson Institute of Santa Barbara, which offers training programs for adult renewal, empowerment, and leadership. With over 150 trained faculty located throughout the United States and Canada, the Institute provides short-term programs in life planning, life transition management, retirement planning, outplacement, career renewal, and couples' development, as well as long-term leadership programs for community leaders, corporate executives, and professionals who want mastery in the principles of adult life.

This book is dedicated to
my father, Albert F. Hudson, 1907–1990
and
my father-in-law, Percy W. McLean, 1919–1990

Prologue

In August 1943, when I was nine years old, I awakened one morning in silent terror. I was unable to move any part of my body except my eyes. My muscles seemed frozen, and my voice was silenced. Although I had gone to bed as a walking, talking, wiggling boy, I woke up the next day paralyzed with polio. Neither my legs nor my arms would respond to my desperate efforts to move, and my neck and jaw were rigid as rocks. Breathing was panicked and pain was everywhere. In the 1940s, polio was a dreaded epidemic of unidentified origin for which there was no means of prevention, and no real medical treatment. Many who contracted it died; others went through life in braces and wheelchairs.

The next thing I remember was lying on the back seat of my parents' old automobile as they drove me thirty miles from my home in upstate New York to a hospital in Syracuse. That journey was unbelievably painful. I was sicker than I had ever felt in my life, and I knew the seriousness of the journey. I felt a helplessness and fear never experienced before. What will happen to me? Am I going to die soon? Is this my final trip? Will I never see my home or family again? Why can't somebody do something? How much worse can I get and still stand it? It isn't fair. . . . That day remains vivid in my mind, like a screeching siren or flashing red light. I felt I was leaving my family to live my entire remaining life in the next few days, weeks, months—who knew how long?

At the hospital, they placed me on a very hard bed (with no pillow) in a quarantined ward. I spent my waking moments staring upward at the ceiling—my only option—and feeling totally helpless. The main treatment I received was the "Sister Kenny" hot packs administered frequently throughout the day and night, so hot that they scorched my body and smelled like wet, burnt wool—a smell I will never forget.

A wise nurse named Susan spent lots of time with me. Quiet and caring, she visited me frequently and told me many things. Her main message went like this: "Your future, Frederic, is hidden on the ceiling, and you can find it if you look very hard. Look for what you will be doing as you grow up. It's all up there. Will you be a track star, a tennis player, a scientist? Will you be going on trips to faraway places? Will you be making model airplanes and flying your kites? Will you be going to summer camps and swimming? Will you go to college and become someone special? Will you marry and have a family? Frederic, all you have to do is to study the ceiling. When you see your future, it will start to happen!" I spent hours and then days and months searching for my future in the maze on the dirty ceiling above my immobile body. There were many designs discernible there, with cracks in the plaster, shadows, and abundant Rorschachs for me to identify. The first vision I saw had me running and playing and active again. After a while, I had only to lift up my eyes and I would see myself bouncing through the woods, alive with movement. Then I saw myself having friends, and laughing again, and climbing trees. After a few months of ceiling gazing, I pictured myself going to college and becoming a husband and father someday. I envisioned myself as a doctor.

My nurse Susan convinced me that if I would keep rehearsing my vision on the ceiling, sooner or later my body would begin to move again and make it all happen. I never doubted her. I let her coach me toward my highest self when my body was at its all-time low. Knowing my eyeballs were my only moving part, she brought a projector and flashed stories and pictures on the ceiling for me to consider as I pondered my future. She projected a checkerboard and taught me how to play checkers and chess as she learned to intuit my preferences. She would read me books while instructing me to find my life in the patterns overhead. She brought me music to listen to, and I began to feel the world of sound open up before me, as I had never heard it before. She obtained my fourth-grade homework assignments and tutored me without my even knowing I was doing schoolwork.

Before contracting polio, I had not been much of a student. My family was struggling to survive the Depression and World War II, and I was squeezed in between a brother a year older and a sister a year younger. Life was a constant scramble. But during my months in the hospital, in my desperate physical condition, time was all I had, second after second, and I wanted to learn everything I could. I wanted to become everything I could become. And I believed magically that what I envisioned on the ceiling would come to pass. Everything I imagined seemed possible, and what did I have to lose?

One day, as I was entranced in a forest walk along the cracks in the ceiling, I felt a wiggle in the toes of my left foot. It was not much, but it was *everything*. I could move my toes, a little. When Susan made her rounds, she assured me that this was the beginning of my future unfolding—not merely my getting well but my visions being realized. She said my strength would slowly return up my legs, my backbone and arms, and finally my upper neck and chin. "You are now in training," she would say, "so practice moving your legs for the rest of this month, and soon you will walk and then you will run. We will prepare you to be an outstanding runner, okay? You will want to be in good shape for medical school." Susan attached strings to my toes so I could ring a bell if I wanted her, and I remember making so much noise that the other nurses complained royally.

When my legs became somewhat mobile, Susan found a way to have them open and close windows and doors, using ropes joining my legs to them through pulleys that she installed in various places. Pretty soon my room looked like a gymnasium, and I had no intention of ever leaving. This was my learning center, my opportunity to become all that I could be. The last thing to cooperate was my neck and upper chest, and although I still can't touch my chin to my chest, I have been eternally grateful for everything I learned and have become in my recovery. I now walk, run, play tennis, and live without any noticeable deficit.

The hardest thing I ever did was to leave that room. I cried in anguish as my wheelchair left the hospital for my uncle's farm, where I was quarantined to learn to walk again. My loneliness there was punctuated by the deadly, daily visits of an orthopedic nurse who made me exercise, without any of the mentoring that Susan commanded. It was months before I could walk, but when I did, I reentered my family system and my schooling as someone with a vision of where I was going and how I would get there. I had a mission, a life purpose.

I did not fully grasp what Susan had taught me until midlife, when I was struggling mightily with my path and life course. By then I had completed a Ph.D. program at Columbia University, entered the professorial ranks of higher education, and become a husband and father. But in my late thirties, when my youth felt spent, I thought my life was over. I had run out of vision. After much soul-searching, I returned to what I had learned from Susan— to be visionary and responsible for my own future. At midlife I learned, painfully, to gaze at the sky above me and begin again. I found a new world of possibilities.

Thank you, Susan. You taught me some powerful lessons: To listen to those who care about me, as you did. To see how I want my life to unfold. To trust my vision. To take responsibility for my life course. To learn how to learn, and unlearn, and relearn. This book is my effort to return the favor to those paralyzed by the experiences of life in our time.

The
Emerging Adult

1

The
Adult Dilemma

For many Americans the "revolution of rising expectations" may be simply a desire for a larger house and
a second car, but for some it is a growing demand for
the fulfillment of needs which are not basically material but are primarily psychological needs for a larger
and more satisfying life experience.
> —*Angus Campbell, The Sense of Well-Being
> in America*[1]

For years, John and Monica have been comfortable and modestly
successful. They have two active children, good friends, and a home
that they've enjoyed for nine years. John, a manager for fifteen years
with AT&T, is deep into his career. Although he hasn't received all
the promotions he thinks he deserves, he knows he is an effective
leader with his work teams. His evaluations have been positive, and
he believes he is relatively secure. But at forty-four, John doesn't feel
comfortable with his life. He keeps reviewing the same questions in
his head: "I'm worried about me. I'm concerned about Monica and
my kids. How can I feel less scared and more secure, knowing how
fragile the entire world is right now? I know I'm more successful
financially than my parents, but am I better off? Why do I feel
disappointed when I've really done very well? Here I am at my peak,
and I feel less than full. How can I spend more time with my wife

and children? When will I get time to enjoy the life-style I've worked so hard to obtain? When does my own life begin?"

Monica, forty-one, worked her way up to her present position as the director of marketing for a mid-range computer firm. Like John, Monica often finds herself pondering difficult questions: "I like everything I'm doing, but there's not enough of me to go around. How do I deal with that without reducing myself to a puddle of water? I'm off to work each day, scrambling with the house chores, worrying about my kids, and jamming my weekends full of activities. I'm spread too thin, and I keep saying that it is only until the kids grow up, but what will I be like by then? I feel very challenged by my career, and I want to keep going. And that's my problem—I want to focus, but I don't want to give anything up. Should I accept my limitations or try to fulfill my promise? If I'm as wonderful and successful as everyone seems to think, why do I feel that part of me is drowning while another part just wants to break free?"

This book is for people who, like John and Monica, have run a few laps into the adult years, and on the one hand feel they are getting somewhere, but on the other hand feel they are not empowered. They are busy making life work but living only a little. They are gravely concerned about the state of the world and how it may impact their future but unsure what they can do about it.

Six New Adult Realities

Since the beginning of our country, the adult years have been predesigned and guided by our society. No longer. To master our fifty to sixty years as adults we must know how to navigate our own lives through peaks and valleys of an ever-changing territory. Compared with previous generations, our adult prospects are freer from conformity yet more complex, less predictable, and more turbulent. Consider the impact of six new realities upon your life:

Our Entire Society Is Becoming an Adult Culture. What for centuries has been a youth-oriented culture is slowly being transformed by an aging America:[2] (1) In 1984, the number of people sixty-five and over for the first time equaled the number of adolescents in our country. In fact, the number of Americans over sixty-five has more than doubled since 1950. (2) In 1987, there were 25,000 people one hundred years old living in America; in the year 2000, there will be over 100,000. (3) During the past decade, the number of Americans between the ages of thirty-five and forty-four has increased by 42 percent. Today, the median age in the United States is thirty-five; that is, half of all the people in our country are older than thirty-five and half are younger. By the year 2025, the median will reach forty. The twenty-first century will begin with half of the nation in "midlife." The graying of America is our most significant demographic trend. Just as a youth culture characterized the 1960s, an "agequake" describes the turn of the century. (4) More older adults will remain in productive life-styles because the meaning of retirement is changing rapidly from a sudden disconnection from work to a redefinition of work and other life interests.

How will this maturation affect American institutions? What new services and opportunities are required to support the needs of the growing ranks of middle-aged and elderly? Will there be age wars and internal conflicts, or will American leadership become more caring at home and diplomatic abroad? How will the consciousness of the country—its deep-seated values and dreams—change?

We Are Reinventing Adulthood. Our world is not the world our parents knew. Our parents found stability in the social containers of their lives—family, workplace, community, and nation. We find those containers to be in constant flux, sometimes pulling us apart but often allowing us to experience new roles and opportunities. Our parents moved passively through their maturity, believing that the rules and roles for getting older were definite and fixed. We assume that we have fewer rules and more choices for mapping our race through time. Our parents viewed the adult years as a time when the man worked, the woman raised the kids, and the rewards for both were becoming grandparents and reaching an adequate retirement. Invisible rules guided their lives, measured by predictable time points: when to marry, when to have children, when to retire. Cultural expectations were uniform.

For us, the adult years are filled with volatile change and

multiple options. We can design our lives more or less the way we want them, without inviting cultural scorn. At the same time, the social forces that govern our lives are more turbulent, fostering strains on marriages and convulsions in the work world. Through the intensity of our television screens, our lives are related to the international scene as never before, as we vividly experienced with the Persian Gulf war. For us, life is less definite but more flexible, less secure with more options yet blurrier choices. We are altering the way we look at the grown-up years. You can sense it in movies such as *Shirley Valentine* and *Field of Dreams;* in TV shows such as "thirtysomething," "The Cosby Show," "Golden Girls," and "Baby Boom"; in the new rush of magazines like *Lear's, Men's Health,* and *Working Woman;* and in newspaper columns by Ellen Goodman, Daniel Goleman, and Anna Quindlen. All these touch the importance and complexities of the adult years.

At forty-seven, Louise suffered a severe heart attack; in spite of her remarkable recovery, she wondered how many years she really had left. Ever since her illness struck, she had been conducting a silent review of her life, and she was often anxious or depressed. What kind of future could she plan on? As a successful realtor, she reasoned, "If I'm going to be okay, then I want to stay in charge of my work and keep as active as ever. If I'm going downhill and into more heart surgery, I want to cut back and do some personal things with my life." Her husband and two children, both in their teens, were terrified by her brush with death and wanted her to work part-time or retire completely.

Louise decided to work out of an office in her home. She maintained a regular schedule of workouts at the local athletic club and adopted a diet for a healthy heart. Although it took her many weeks to get accustomed to being with the family most of the time, she enjoyed the projects that she was doing with her teenage children. Her work progressed satisfactorily, but she discovered that it wasn't as important to her as she had thought it would be. She was gradually rearranging the direction of her life and feeling good about it.

Today's Adults Are Living a Quarter Century Longer Than Adults in 1900. The life span of men and women has been extended significantly. In 1776, life expectancy was about 35, and the median age of our populace was 16. In 1886, life expectancy was 40 and the median age 21. In 1920, the typical woman lived to be 54; the life expectancy of women born in 1988 is 78; and for women born in the year 2040 it is projected to be 91.5. In 1920, life expectancy among men was 53; today it is 71 and in the year 2040 it will jump to 85.9.

Since 1920, we have added more than a quarter of a century of living. What do we do with it? Where do we turn when we run out of script? What do we do after the first or second plunge into adulthood has plateaued or peaked? How do we sustain passion and a sense of purpose for fifty or sixty adult years?

Mac was eighty-three and confused. His life was blessed with health, sufficient funds, and the ability to take care of most of his needs. But in the previous year, his wife had died, after a lengthy illness. Mac didn't like living alone, and he didn't have much to live for. He figured that he had pretty much done it all. But after participating in a support group for several months, Mac decided to begin a small mail-order business with two of his grandchildren. Using his financial resources for start-up funds, he taught them how to succeed at running a business—something that Mac had done all his adult life until he retired at seventy-five. As the business began to grow, Mac met Gertrude, a widow who had much in common with him. In time, Mac felt like his old self again, but with a future.

Adult Intimacy Comes in Many Forms from Many Sources. There are many ways that today's adults get love and affection in their lives. Until now, adult intimacy in America has been defined largely by unwritten cultural rules for marriage and family life. With the arrival of effective birth control in the second half of the twentieth century, social patterns of intimacy changed more dramatically than at any previous point in history. Adults now have choices not available to earlier generations—to marry or not to marry, to parent or not to parent, to divorce or not to divorce. Gay and lesbian relationships now openly provide patterns of love and affection that earlier generations denied or hid. Adult friendships are another important source of intimacy today, for both sexes. In today's world, intimacy is a series of bonds and attachments, not merely a significant other.

Leisure and Health Are Major Commitments. America has traditionally been a "work-ethic" culture, but a "leisure ethic" has recently evolved as an equally important part of the new breed of adults. In the past two decades, a significant number of Americans have changed the way they think about food, calories, cholesterol, fat, dieting, smoking, exercise, participatory sports, and stress control. Smoking is in social disfavor, and sparkling water has replaced alcohol for many. Compared to adults in 1920, we have leaner bodies, more active life-styles, and a will to manage the aging process instead of merely "getting old." *Health* has become a watchword for self-esteem and longevity. Today's adults see the connection between taking care of their bodies continuously and extending the quality of life well into elderhood.

Adults Anticipate Several Careers in a Lifetime. We used to think of a career as a linear progression throughout the adult years, moving from an apprenticeship to a mentor phase. Now we understand that careers develop in a sea of changing lives and work opportunities. Through multiple careers or jobs, it is possible to explore more parts of the work world and to develop more parts of oneself.

One group that benefits from the new flexibility in career lines is those who reenter the work force at midlife or perhaps begin to shape a career identity for the first time after the children leave home. At fifty-six, Donna felt at a turning point. Her husband, a businessperson in Atlanta, was absorbed in his career. The last of Donna's three children had just graduated from high school and was on her way to college. Donna felt that her world was being torn apart. Even though she was proud of her accomplishments as a wife and mother, she felt abandoned and stripped of her rank. "I say I'm not going to cry about it, but in fact I cry a lot. What's going on with me? I just don't feel complete without my kids in my home. Is that so bad?" The truth was that Donna didn't feel complete with herself. She needed a new agenda for her own life, apart from others. She talked about her options with her women friends and gradually created a plan. In a few years, Donna graduated from her local community college and began her career as an interior designer. She felt competent and challenged again. Her marriage, meanwhile, changed considerably, as her husband became more interested in travel and gardening.

Although most adults spend more of their lives at their workplace than they do anywhere else, a 1990 Roper poll reported that Americans view work as the eighth most important consideration in their lives. Rated higher than the benefits of work were children's education, family life, health, quality of life, friends and relatives, love life, and income and standard of living.[3]

For eighteen years, Donald had been a community leader. He had served on task forces, the city council, and the county administration. He was a dynamic leader who knew how to make strategic moves and empower others. He was often the recipient of generous praise and recognition. At forty-nine, however, he wanted a private life of his own where he could talk about and share something other than politics, crises, and deadlines. To enrich his personal life without endangering his professional success, Donald found a professional counselor who could help him make some fundamental changes. Since he had always wanted to sail, he rented a sailboat for a year and committed himself to weekly sailing ventures, usually by himself. He joined a men's group made up of men a lot like himself and found profound support there. Donald succeeded at growing Donald—the person—through travel, cooking, sailing, new friendships, and a rebirth of passion at home. He became interested in contributing to the Nature Conservancy as a volunteer, so he donated significant portions of time to its work. He felt more relaxed and humorous and less consumed by his public duties. He was the same Donald, yet a better one.

The Decline of Confidence and Hope

The rub is that many adults do not feel emergent. They love their newly acquired freedom, but resent the loss of social protection and safety. A great many capable adults feel vulnerable instead of visionary, trapped instead of empowered. They feel that they are marking time or sliding downhill. The complexities of their lives confine them at the very time when new freedoms and options have arrived. Just when personal options have expanded, making adult life work has become more problematic. Planning the future is more tenuous.

- Leah feels a double bind. "My government job provides me with benefits I simply can't or won't give up—retirement, health insurance, flextime, and frequent vacations. In seven years, my benefits will reach the highest level. I can't risk making a job change. My golden handcuffs control my future, and I hate that."
- Jim loves his engineering job, but his life at home is a disaster zone. Although people call him a workaholic, the truth is that Jim doesn't feel comfortable, challenged, or rewarded anywhere but at work.
- Susan feels that somehow she got off course. "I'm a savvy lawyer, but that's not enough for me anymore. I'm thirty-eight and should have thought more about marriage and children."
- Rodney lives in silent terror as AIDS takes away so many of his friends. "How can I plan my life when I may not have a future?"
- Ralph, a musician, remembers when he was bursting with energy. "Nothing could stop me back then. Now I've lost it, whatever 'it' was. What I need is passion again, a new adventure I can believe in. Maybe a trip to Bali?"

These situations are commonplace today, as more people who entered the adult years with a flurry some time ago now find themselves mired down by changes and complexities that they hadn't anticipated. There are at least five reasons:

Lost in Yesterday's Decisions. We are all ushered into the adult years with great hoopla, but few are prepared for the long haul. "I like the freedom to be me," one midlifer blurted, "but I just don't know how to make me happen anymore." When you trade in your early years for adult ones, few trumpets blow; it feels more like an ending than an arrival. Adult lives are long strings of days and years, lacking demarcation. It's easy to get lost.

Adult life begins as a series of snapshots, which soon take the form of a rather long, repetitive movie. After young adults sort out their life options, they often feel trapped by their early decisions. Some get mired in the specialized roles that they create in career or home life. By the time you're twenty-seven or so, you're pretty much on your own and either accelerating ahead or caught in the under-tow of your early adult decisions. Some people marry young, expecting love and parenthood to make their lives sing. Parenting lasts a very long time. At forty-five, Katie, who has never complained about just being a housewife and mother, wonders what she can really do "outside" the home that can make a real difference and give her a life of her own. Others shape their early adult lives around career decisions, which may not make sense ten years later, when they may be difficult to change. As one dentist put it, "How could I have known at eighteen when I decided to become a dentist that at thirty-eight I would be spending 98 percent of my time repeating simple routines in which I lost interest long ago? How could that eighteen-year-old boy do this to me?" Laurie, a beautician, remembers when going to work made her life sing. "Now it's a real drag, but I'm so far into it that I don't know how to jump ship and still have the money and life-style I've got now."

There are some doors in life that can be entered but can't be opened from the other side. There are some places in adult life that seem to have no exits. Choices have consequences, and even though time is on the side of the young adult, if the youthful dreams are extinguished in one's twenties or thirties, life may proceed as little more than stale routines and bankrupt habits. Creative adult life requires the birth of many new dreams, the possibilities of many new adventures, and the excitement of risk taking.

Betrayed by Our Expectations. Although adults today are increasing their expectations for life options, they often experience a wide gap between dream and reality. There are more options but fewer real choices. By thirty-five or so, a great many feel that what they wanted isn't what they got, and what they got is a world they didn't ask for and don't understand. Although the end isn't in sight, the end of the beginning has arrived, and it often feels as though the future cannot and will not fill the void. The expectations of youth are seldom matched by the experience of later life. No wonder so many hardworking, well-intending adults often say that they feel lost, deprived, or out of synch with their expectations. Should they try harder or lower their expectations? Are there other alternatives?

- At forty-two, Don, a fitness addict, confesses "Although my body is still in great shape, the prospects ahead aren't. I don't see much except a boring downhill ride."
- Mary, who is up to her ears in supporting her family and getting somewhere at work, wonders "Where am I, with my own life? I'm busy all the time, but I don't feel like I'm going anywhere."
- Sandy has tried her best to make her life work, but she hasn't found the key. "I'm divorced, raising a kid alone, still scrambling for a career that fits me, and hurting for money. I am thirty-five and mad."

A significant number of Americans are pondering ways to balance the security achieved in their early adult years with their unfulfilled dreams that linger. The disjunction between expectations and realized experience cannot remain extreme for very long in adult life without a crisis occurring. If we are to enjoy our mature years, our hopes and our common experience need to be ordinary friends. If we experience grandiose expectations alongside ordinary reality, we get *EXPECTATIONS/reality*—a formula for chronic disappointment. Equally disappointing is the opposite equation, which is experienced by a growing number of young and disfranchised adults—*expectations/REALITY,* in which motivation is low while survival issues are overwhelming. The best formula for creative living is *expectations/reality,* in which adults find available resources for their dreams, and available dreams for their resources.

Unprotected by Our Social Systems. The social conditions that have provided us new permission and pathways for our adult lives have also provided us with reduced social stability, predictability, and safety. When the long adult years proceed within ambiguous social containers, such as marriages, families, schools, careers, work organizations, communities, and nation, it takes strong, confident adults to guide the rudders—no easy requirement in today's world. Our cultural containers are themselves going through convulsive changes, setting many adults adrift on an odyssey not of their own choosing.

An even bigger surprise is the extent of global turmoil affecting our lives today. The social context of adult life in America is less stable than previously in this century. Marriages are less secure; careers are in flux; financial security is difficult to manage; corporations are undergoing major upheavals; the future of the natural environment is tenuous; economic cycles are less predictable; and political turmoil is a never-ending global phenomenon. Americans are no longer assured an indefinite future of progress, prosperity, and predictability. Our assumptions about adult life are changing.

The world of my father was very different. In 1934, when I was born, my father went bankrupt, and the Depression detoured his life and mine into survival issues. It took him fifteen years and endless jobs to achieve economic stability for our family. Yet even during the nightmare of personal failure, he felt that he was riding the wave of an immutable promise of manifest destiny. And he was.

My father and his generation believed that our nation had a unique mission, to set a moral example for how life should be lived and how a society should be run. He believed that Americans should cooperate with whatever the president, Congress, and our military forces might decide was right. Although my father did not like President Roosevelt, he viewed the presidency as a sacred role, and he felt that we could depend on the moral and legal integrity of elected officials, judges, members of the professions, and the churches throughout the land. Guiding us all, he used to say, was "the American dream" of liberty, justice, and opportunity for all. Almost all the people I knew when I was growing up felt that they were part of an unstoppable progress. The social institutions of our democracy would provide safety, protection, and expanding opportunities for the development of personal life.

My dad was a pharmacist working in a pharmaceutical manufacturing plant. Even though he believed strongly in individual freedoms, he had no doubts whatsoever about the primacy of the basic organizations of society over all of his personal decisions. During World War II, he worked to fill a medical ship with supplies for the wounded. When the ship was sunk by enemy forces before it reached England, my father rolled up his sleeves and started over.

His career as a pharmacist served as a linear container and definer for his entire adult life. All he wanted, throughout his adult years, was to live out the occupational, marital, parenting, and leadership roles that befell him. He assumed, like those before him, that he was building a better America and that progress toward some new world that his children would inherit was the grand design that would be carried out if he and others just did their best and trusted the cultural flow. His was an ordered world, where heterogeneous people were bound together by common beliefs. Or so he thought.

Until the early 1960s, most Americans similarly constructed their lives in the shadows of our dominant institutions. Government, corporations, businesses, churches, and schools shaped the roles that we assumed and provided reasons for things being the way they were. If "change" or a "crisis" occurred forty years ago, the stable forces of our culture would interpret and assimilate it. Both conservative and liberal forces worked that way: tolerating dissonance while shaping consensus. That is how we rallied as a nation to face external threat in World War II and its aftermath. Today we have no consensus, and crisis is an everyday event.

Even relating this story feels strange to me. Most Americans don't experience the world this way. In a world of chaotic change, what seemed linear in the past seems cyclical today. What felt stable is turbulent; the once permanent is transitory. What we know most of all is that the society around us doesn't seem as safe or dependable or honorable as it used to be. Our institutions are discordant and our global destiny is questionable. As Americans, we are adrift in a sea of change, without an indisputable cultural core. We remain nostalgic for an America that is no more, and we anticipate decline instead of gain.

Compared with my father's generation, the American people have gradually diminished in both self- and social confidence. My dad saw permanent "rules" and "principles"; I experience fluctuating "holding patterns." The containers of my life are no longer dependable repositories for defining my life; they are only temporary vehicles for evolving my life design. While I feel freed from the constraints that restricted his life options, I lack a dependable and predictable environment for the living of my days.

Inundated by Information and Random Choices. When our cultural containers do not measure our lives and filter change for us, the forces of change penetrate us directly as individuals. Individual adults now directly monitor more information, more consumer decisions, and more news than they can possibly want or use. The very forces that provide us new life options also flood us with a sea of imagined choices. If knowledge is power, then information is not knowledge—it is only data. How can adults wade through the flood of data that they receive constantly to get the knowledge that they need for making wise decisions?

A large supermarket has more than 25,000 items to choose from. Cable TV may provide as many as fifty-three television channels. There are now 11,092 magazines and periodicals. Information invades our lives constantly, requiring us to sort out the kernels from the chaff. The information explosion confronts our lives at such a pace that it is difficult to maintain a distinction between trivial and important data. What purports to be news often focuses our attention on issues and events that we have no say over, leaving us feeling powerless as individuals, as with the voluminous reporting of the Persian Gulf crisis. How do we stay informed while not becoming overloaded and overwhelmed? How do we keep a balanced view of the world when the news is by definition alarming and crisis-laden?

Each person must now manage an increasing number of consumer variables. Cars are more complicated to drive, and managing traffic in urban areas takes constant vigilance. Warehouse stores provide us with extensive choices for tools, food, toys, furniture, and clothes, but making the right decisions is taxing and time-consuming. Returning items is frustrating. Getting almost anything repaired is a long and complex process. The adult liberation from societal constraints is often accompanied by an overload of decision points on each individual. While the systems of our lives have loosened their grip on us, the direct decisions required of each individual to make life work have multiplied, leaving many people swamped and stressed.

Bewildered by Complex Change. Change has come in many forms throughout the course of history. Many people have had their lives transformed for the better or wrecked beyond repair by unanticipated change. If change opens doors to human betterment, it is viewed positively as a source of new opportunities. Without change, there would be no growth or development, no creative breakthroughs or discoveries, no becoming. If change diminishes human betterment already in hand, it is considered a threat to the quality of life. The pace and discontinuity of change seem to make experience obsolete. People then become defensive about the past and resistant to the future. What is your experience with change, and how do you view your own human prospects as we approach the twenty-first century? Is change your friend or foe? Consider five basic questions:

1. How has change affected the way you think and feel about your future? How has it affected your motivation and sense of purpose? As you experience more change in your daily experience, are you more optimistic or pessimistic about your life prospects today than you were ten years ago?
2. Have the forces of change increased or decreased your opportunities for living and working and reaching your goals?
3. Have the forces of change increased or decreased your financial security over the past ten years?
4. Have the forces of change increased or decreased your confidence in America's future? In your own future?
5. Has change freed you from the artificial constraints of the past, allowing you to find many new ways to find fulfillment? Or are you swamped by change—unable to maintain constancy and the quality of life you desire?

I have been asking these questions of audiences for more than fifteen years now. The most common answer is that while we feel that our past is less reliable than it used to be as a guide to the future that we deserve, the forces of change are part of the problem, not the solution. Most of us are not change masters; we resist it.

Change takes life away from us, and we don't want to lose the America that was. Like earlier Americans, we remain "isolated" from the world around us and think that the magic of America will somehow keep our past alive no matter how turbulent change becomes. We liked our culture the way it was right after World War II, and a lot of change today intrudes on the life that we had then. We can take in the chaos of the world and make it over into an Americanized order. Or can we? Consider what has happened in the past forty years to our great factories, our automobile industry, our educational system, our control of the dollar, our space mission, our health care system, our influence abroad, our sense of purpose. As a culture, we are reacting to change and not learning very much about the change process itself.

Most of us continue to live as though change were an occasional intrusion, an irritant, in our otherwise organized lives. It is precisely our "organized lives" that complex change is altering, whether we like it or not! Today we get ruffled but not terribly surprised when change makes a new appearance. We expect random intrusions, more and more. We may kick and scream, but we know that it is "just another crisis," requiring us to "adapt" in some new way we wish we didn't have to. Take the rise in gasoline prices a few years ago. When the price of gas first soared as the oil cartel was getting under way, there was a public outcry. We grumbled and drove our cars a little less. Now we take it for granted that the cost of gas will rise again, along with almost everything else. Even after Iraq invaded Kuwait in 1990 and the gas prices leaped, the reaction was nothing compared to the first such crisis. Change is here to stay, accepted as an inevitable intruder that will bother us but not force us to alter how we live and work.

The sociologist C. Wright Mills once made a distinction between problems and issues. When four or five people in a social setting are jobless, that is a "problem," but when huge numbers of people suffer from unemployment, that is an "issue." We treat change as a problem, not an issue. Unfortunately, change is not only an issue; it is the dominant issue for our foreseeable future, and the empowerment of adults in our time depends on finding ways to be friends with change. We keep reacting to change; we have not learned to ride on its waves; we resist taking on a new consciousness anchored in the change process itself. Change brings with it its own kind of organization, like a river flowing, and we do not seem to be learning that. Change. We've grown accustomed to its face, but that's about all. Most of us are not on the inside of the change process, and it is not on the inside of us. Instead of viewing change as a challenge to live as global citizens with new ground rules, we feel angry and sad that our American privileges are being altered or diluted. We feel an intense loss, but we are not grieving and moving on.

America's Failure of Nerve

Our very resistance to change is fundamentally an inability to let go of an unworkable past in exchange for a workable future. Adults have reduced their dreams to personal concerns and acquisitions while finding infinite fault with social structures. We have lost track of the necessary connections between our well-being as persons and the well-being of the social environment around us.

According to Daniel Boorstin, author of *The Image or What Happened to the American Dream,* our dream has devolved from extravagant expectations in the founding years of our country to several types of shrinkage.[4] News gathering is now news making— a flood of pseudo-events. Heroes have become celebrities, and travelers are tourists. With that shrunken dream has come a pendulum swing from a naive endorsement of American ideals to a pervasive pessimism about our future. Consider the impact in the past thirty years of Vietnam and the murders of John F. Kennedy, Martin Luther King, and Robert Kennedy. Consider the ignominy of Spiro Agnew and Richard Nixon and the drawn-out Watergate episode. Consider Jimmy Carter's reactive presidency, with runaway inflation, the oil embargo, the Iranian crisis, and endless unanticipated problems. Our temporary NASA success in outer space and our military blitzkrieg in the Persian Gulf served to ignite our hopes, momentarily. But overall, we have moved from the end of our childlike innocence as an isolated nation to a superpower country marked by disappointment, guilt, and anger over our inability to lead—the old-fashioned way. Now, it seems, the world is leading us. So we cling to our shrinking dream as we back into the future with less and less sense of direction.

Motivation to make life work is disabled by a vicious circle: personal daring and adult empowerment are curtailed by social disillusionment and cynicism; social empowerment is curtailed by reduced personal vision, motivation, and leadership. In forty short years, we have moved from a victorious superpower of dreamers and achievers to a society of whiners.

Recently, I consulted with the entire regional work force of a Fortune 500 company about issues of low worker morale and poor customer service. When I asked hundreds of people to tell me what was wrong, I heard the usual corporate complaints about company leaders and bureaucracy, but the loudest concerns reflected a widespread loss of confidence in our social system itself. In various ways, the broad forces of change had invoked a failure of nerve within the company.

Robert Zinderman, a twenty-five-year employee now serving as vice-president for service and sales, was concerned about the current changes in corporate ownership. "Controlling stockholders of major firms," he began, "are more interested in immediate profits through mergers, acquisitions, and buy-outs than they are in building excellent companies. Do you think my CEO cares about me and my future? I can tell you this: the loyalty of workers to this company has decreased remarkably in the past ten years. The company doesn't stand by us any more. We are all temporary, working at the whim of our investors, waiting for pink slips we don't deserve."

Michael Gideon, a district manager for thirty-six years, lamented that "the quality of life in America will never be as good as it used to be. We don't make things the way we used to. Our engineering, our equipment, our parts—they used to be the best, and today they are only so-so. We are no longer committed to being the best we can be. My workers are less committed to bottom-line results than they used to be. What is most depressing is that I don't know what we can do to change things."

Ann Brydon, the administrative manager, who worked her way up the ladder from a secretarial position during the past twenty-two years, was more concerned with the quality of life issues: "The cost of living and the current tax structure have reduced the quality of life for everyone except the upper class, who must be in corporate headquarters or among the stockholders. Inflation simply wrecks the life-styles of the administrative staff. Their raises and benefits don't compensate for the rising costs they face. My people are pretty discouraged."

Perry Bradshaw, a twenty-four-year veteran and a frontline supervisor, voiced his feelings: "The heart has gone out of people everywhere. We've lost our special thing, our belief in ourselves. We're going nowhere but downhill, reacting to change and to the advances of others. Americans have lost their game plan for leadership. Where are the great leaders, the heroes? They're gone, that's where. Both political parties follow media polls that they conduct, not some political system that they believe in. Nobody knows what to believe anymore."

The overwhelming concern throughout this company was that change was altering America so extensively that the operation of the company was undermined. The declining morale of the country was demoralizing the workplace. When the people of a society respond to complex change by diminishing their past beliefs and present expectations without an infusion of new vision and hope, that society becomes increasingly dysfunctional. Four ways in which this negativity is being expressed in the lives of American adults in the 1990s are cynicism, powerlessness, personal isolation, and hopelessness.

Cynicism. Whatever you may think of Ronald Reagan as a politician, he tapped this pervasive feeling of disillusionment with our society. "Are you better off than you were four years ago?" he asked us in his great debate with Jimmy Carter, and we knew we weren't. Not if economic stability and progress were our measures. We knew what felt wrong even though we didn't know how to make things right. As Peter Finch exclaimed in his final movie, capturing the feelings of many Americans, "I am mad as hell, and I'm not going to take it anymore"—but take it we do as we deepen our negative attitudes and feelings.

Powerlessness. If you experience your world as being out of control for very long, you assume that events surrounding your life are uncontrollable. If you feel powerless much of the time, you give up feeling that you can shape your destiny. "Organisms, when exposed to uncontrollable events, learn that responding is futile," concludes Martin Seligman, an expert on helplessness.[5] He goes on to say that people who feel helpless have increased fear and depression and reduced motivation to exert influence. Ever since 1960 or so, we have been a people in search of a soul, feeling powerless before the complex forces of the world—even though we are still the most powerful nation on earth.

Personal Isolationism. America has always both suffered and benefited from its geographical isolation. Today's isolation is more psychological. In the 1970s and 1980s, many upwardly mobile Americans responded to their weakening grip on the world with personal isolationism: "If we can't make our dream happen in the workplace, our society, and beyond, then we'll make it happen in our personal lives." They simplified our caring, expansive dream— "Give me your tired, your poor, your huddled masses yearning to breathe free"—into individualistic issues—acquiring things, capital, and fun. It is no secret that in the past twenty years we have neglected our communities, the world, and the dream itself.

Overall, our adult American response to change is a sense of loss followed by a reduction of our values to individual interests. We feel deflated, defeated by an enemy we neither understand nor have an opportunity to combat. Buying more things for ourselves is our ultimate weapon for feeling good. Federico Fellini, the Italian film director who created *La Dolce Vita,* suggests that we are experiencing a loss of psychological cohesion: "People are losing their faith in the future. Our education, unfortunately, molded us for a life that was always tensed toward a series of achievements—school, military service, a career and, as a grand finale, the encounter with the heavenly father. But now that our tomorrows no longer appear in that optimistic perspective, we are left with a feeling of impotence and fear. People who can no longer believe in a 'better tomorrow' logically tend to behave with a desperate egotism. They are preoccupied with protecting, brutally if necessary, those little sensual appetites. To me, this is the most dangerous feature."[6] Once a people reduce their dreams to acquisitions and status symbols, their appetites become voracious. Enough is never enough.

Hopelessness. People who cling to reduced privileges within a society in great turmoil lack hope—lack a belief that the future will fulfill their lives. Without hope and a sense of the future, people lead lopsided, unrewarding lives, no matter how successful or wealthy they are. Without hope, both personal life and the social fabric disintegrate. Hope produces energy, motivation, courageous living. The absence of hope produces reminiscence and dying. At our worst, our lives yearn for the past, consume the present, and feel empty about the future. The greatest dilemma facing American adults is not a "midlife crisis" but rather a cultural failure of nerve. I remember when, as a professor of philosophy in the 1960s, I was questioning my class in the noble tradition of Socrates to lead them to doubt the current assumptions about life and a student came up to me, in tears, saying "Dr. Hudson, I have been questioning my life for a long time. What I want from you is direction and an example to follow. I just want a sense of direction." I was visibly shaken, but I got the point. People today want and need role models and mentors with future-oriented scenarios, not more doubts or endorsements about the past.

We live between eras, and we continue to trust the dying era without sufficiently exploring the new age being born. It takes courage to move away from our cultural moorings into the raging river of change and opportunity. In the past, the American dream thrived when our country faced external threats that tested our beliefs and unity. Today's external threats are legion, but without an identifiable "enemy" to ignite us. Tomorrow's dream must come from within us, born from our inner beliefs. There are few precedents to guide us into the rebirth of our dream, only the possibility that as we leap into the unknown we will have the courage to create the lives and society we so desperately want. With that leap we may find the dreams and hope we deserve.

The New Adult Challenge

I believe that we have the courage to create new lives and a new society. As we press into the twenty-first century, many of those who shortchanged the American dream are making friends with the enormous changes taking place around us. They are looking for recurrent patterns within change that provide dependability and meaning, connecting our past to our present and future. The dream is ready to be restored to its twin core values of personal worth and social caring. For the most part, this new and vigorous leadership will come from adults who are ready to do more with their lives than merely succeed and consume. Many who are now seeking leadership beyond themselves will rekindle the American dream in the twenty-first century.

The transformation of our failure of nerve depends directly on our finding new personal comfort within the forces of change and chaos. What do we have to do to let go of what's not working in our lives, while taking on what may work in the context of the world we experience today? This book suggests ways to manage the forces of organization and disorganization in our lives, using change as a primary vehicle for constructing our future—from within us to the far reaches of our society. Two central issues embedded in our personal and cultural impasse are our emotional difficulty with loss and our difficulty in imagining a future for ourselves as glorious or more glorious than our past. If Americans learn how to process and to move through the profound loss that grips them, they will begin to discover immense capabilities for shaping the future. This book describes ways to begin this in the lives and settings of America's new dominant minority—adults.

The childlike version of the American dream was anchored in the notion that the containers of life would provide lasting happiness for those who exerted effort, sought education, and stayed committed. It was an outward-in vision. The adult version available to us today is that our fulfillment is grounded in our ability to live with all types of change without stable containers. The new dream is anchored in personal empowerment and social determination. It is an inward-out vision.

A central challenge for Americans today is for the adults in our society to create new continuities for their lives within the dimensions of change itself. For too long we have mourned the premature death of our dream. The time has come for a rebirth of an adult version of the same dream. It is not too late to revise our expectations and vast resources to fit the frontiers of today's world. This is the challenge:

- *The Internal Challenge.* We are being challenged by a new frontier so personal that it requires us to explore new personal depths within ourselves. If we can break the bonds of the myths that feed our powerlessness and at the same time discover visionary capacities for making our own lives work, we will be capable of resurrecting not only ourselves but our institutions and society. We have the human readiness to do so. As we learn to manage the structuring and destructuring of life in a world of change, we will invest in human destiny again and become renewed as leaders, careerists, parents, and spiritual beings.[7]

- *The External Challenge.* We are being challenged by a new frontier so vast that it spreads from our souls to the far reaches of the planet—and beyond. We need to extend the dream that we call American into the very worldwide forces that have kept us scared and powerless for the past thirty years. Before a world government can exist, this challenge requires a global consciousness, a reverence for the one environment shared by all, the presence of new forms of capitalistic cooperativeness, new solutions to glaring economic inequities, and experimentation with international teams and alliances. American renewal requires a deep commitment to pluralism, diversity, and new opportunities for social contributions from women and men, the young and the old. The external challenge is to release an American dream capable of inspiring new hope for people, organizations, society, and nations beyond our own. Any social agenda that falls short of this vision will fall into the jaws of our chronic cynicism and navel-gazing.[8]

The social resource that I believe to be most ready for this challenge is the growing contingent of adults between the ages of thirty and seventy-five, frustrated with their lives but ready for new beginnings. They are connected to the past, immersed in careers and families, experienced in democratic process, and determined to leave the planet in better shape than they found it. Instead of being orphans in the land of future shock, they are the new dominant minority in a land that is sick of feeling sorry for itself. "Where are the Jeffersons and Lincolns of today?" asks John Gardner, founder of Common Cause and now professor at Stanford University. "The answer, I am convinced, is that they are among us. Out there in the settings with which we are all familiar are the unawakened leaders, feeling no overpowering call to lead and hardly aware of the potential within. . . . How do you send out a call to the unawakened leaders? How do you make them aware of their leadership potential? How do you make leadership feasible and tolerable for leaders? . . . It is my belief that with some imagination and social inventiveness we could tap these hidden reserves—not just for government, not just for business, but for all the diverse leadership needs of a dynamic society."[9]

Beginning in the 1990s, adults will have the clout to effect personal and social transformation. Even though they must develop a new political consciousness, they already have links with power, the prerequisite moral restlessness, and a deep passion for transforming the American dream from its childlike versions into adult scenarios addressing today's needs. The power center for reversing our prevailing cynicism and atomistic behaviors into renewed leadership for the common good lies in the personal resilience of the mature contingents who will dominate American life for at least the next quarter century. They remember when America's excellence came from its unyielding hope. They have the capacities for self-renewal and the abilities to put the enormous resources of this nation to work for inventing a new future that we can believe in.

Adult empowerment in America today requires much more than psychotherapy, self-help, adult education, and human resource development. The primary context of our disempowerment is cultural, and each of us will gain most when we commit ourselves to the transformation of our common consciousness. Without that, our efforts at psychological and institutional renewal will be little more than Band-Aids on a wounded giant. When Richard Gephardt, a Democratic member of Congress from Missouri and House majority leader, completed a tour of foreign nations in 1990, he expressed a frustration that many adults feel: "I'm embarrassed, almost ashamed when I see the sacrifices leaders from Mexico to Czechoslovakia are asking their people to make. They have so little, and are daring so much. We have so much and are asking so little of ourselves."[10]

2

Finding Fulfillment
in Cyclical Lives

All our lives long, every day and every hour we are
engaged in the process of accommodating our changed
and unchanged selves to changed and unchanged surroundings; living, in fact, is nothing else than this process of accommodation; when we fail in it a little we
are stupid, when we fail flagrantly we are mad, when
we suspend it temporarily we sleep, when we give up
the attempt altogether we die.   —*Samuel Butler, The
Way of All Flesh*[1]

Our world has changed, but conventional wisdom has not. To make
sense of adult life today, we need a fundamental change of consciousness, from linear to cyclical notions of how life works.

Linear and Cyclical Ways of Thinking

Linear means "in a straight line," implying that our lives and society are supposed to get better, year by year, generation by generation. According to this point of view, adult lives progress through
predictable sequences: learning, loving, working, living, leading,
and succeeding. In linear thinking, adult life is viewed as an orderly
development following universal principles and rules. Life is lived
for future goals and results, and is driven by perfectionism and
social constraints. *Cyclical* implies going in circles, with the repe-

tition of familiar patterns—night and day, the four seasons, birth and death. From this perspective, the purpose of life is to master the repetitive patterns in our ever-changing experience. Cyclical thinking looks for human meaning in the ongoing flow of daily experience, from world news to family events to personal concerns. It assumes that life can make sense in good times and in bad, in growth and decline, in beginnings and endings. Cyclical thinking tolerates high levels of ambiguity and finds pathways for living in dark and unseemly places, if necessary.

Ever since America began, linear thinking has dominated our consciousness, with its basic notions of progress, perfectionism, success, happiness, and planned change. A linear perspective portrays life as a series of advances from simple to complex, from lower to higher, from good to better. Linear thinking aims at results that are seen as serial improvements; life is viewed as incremental, additive, purposive, and predictable. As we orient our lives to cyclical thinking, one major shift in our thinking is from progress to process.

From Progress to Process. The promise of progress was a great motivator for middle-class Americans in the eighteenth and nineteenth centuries who sought increased security, power, and well-being in a nation insulated from the rest of the world. First we tamed the wilderness and then human culture evolved. But today's middle-class people are bogged down in that culture. They are more frustrated than fulfilled by the notion of progress, which seems like a promissory note that has been withdrawn. Because the conditions of today's world are often discordant, those who endorse a linear perspective feel that they are failing or going downhill when their lives experience a crisis or surprise. If they are unable to sustain progress and arrive at success, security, and happiness, they feel discouraged, disappointed, and upset. Many of the frustrations of adults today stem from the dysfunctions of the linear way of thinking, not from American incompetence. If we would alter the way we think instead of feeling bad and inadequate, our lives could be challenging and rewarding again. My grandfather expected my father to exceed him in educational and financial attainments. My father expected the same of me. I do not expect my six children to exceed me on these linear measures; some of them may, but my main concern is that they live fully and well, day by day.

In a world where order predominates over change, the notion of lives unfolding as linear progressions is tenable. But where change keeps order in its shadows, finding meaning in life's peaks and valleys makes more sense. The expectation of progress is that order will triumph over chaos, rather than that they will coexist. A world with frequent pockets of chaos requires a perspective that can find meaning in the bad times as well as the good. Cyclical thinking seeks order within the change process itself. Life transitions, job losses, political surprises, and accidents are windows for learning rather than barriers to progress.

What we can know and master in our kind of world is the "process" of ongoing change, not "progress" toward ultimate results. As a process, our lives are a continuous, cyclical stream of continuities and changes. Orienting our lives around the changing patterns in our daily experience instead of around our presumed destinations permits us to enjoy the journeys we are on, and to invest in learning, living, and leading.

From Acquiring Happiness to Mastering Change. Another linear notion in the American mind is the belief that happiness is a place or state of mind that we arrive at and sustain as a permanent acquisition. We think of happiness and security as items to be possessed. For example, in children's stories, the good man and woman marry and live "happily ever after." In a world where change is a dominant force, there is no such permanence, and all acquisitions—material and otherwise—sooner or later dissolve into the river of change. Happiness and security are not exceptions. We can't possess, buy, or insure them. We have no ultimate safety or security with our looks, bodies, money, marriages, children, education, career, achievements, possessions, investments, insurance, legacy, nation, or religion. What most of us have is limited protection, measured security, temporary safety. Yet the adult culture in America overwhelmingly lives as if human destiny depended on the acquisition of happiness and security. Such a culture is bound to have a high level of disillusionment and despair, even if it is the greatest nation on earth.[2]

In our topsy-turvy world we can learn to live with both happy moments and unhappy ones, without feeling derailed or impotent. Throughout our lives, we experience ever-changing proportions of blessings and curses, safety and danger, sureness and insecurity, ecstacy and misery. The challenge of the cyclical perspective is to develop human competence in both our up and our down times to facilitate a conscious mastery of the journey—wherever it takes us. When we learn that there are very few places in the human journey where we cannot find major resources for affirmation and fulfillment, we will have transcended the myth of happiness and security. There is a story about a Western man seeking enlightenment in India who, before dying in a cave, inscribed these words on the cave wall: "Oh boundless joy, there is no happiness." Feeling joy in the heights and depths of life's never-ending adventures is much more realistic and profound than expecting to arrive at a lasting state of happiness.

From Negative Aging to Positive Elderhood. The linear perspective portrayed the promise and energy of youth unfolding throughout the adult years. When the twentieth century arrived, it was heralded as "the century of the child," with hopes that the careful upbringing and education of children would sow the seeds of permanent progress. By 1900, the country was dotted with colleges and universities, all devoted to "launching" young people into reliable orbits of adult life and responsibility. While romanticizing the importance of youthful attributes, this perspective saw little of value in old age. When you got old and had to stop working, you got out of the way so that someone younger could carry on—to be old is to prepare to die.

This point of view fosters "ageism" in a society, characterizing old people as feeble, nonsexual, incapable of serious work, and lifeless. The myth of aging as steady, linear decline creates social prejudice against the old, and it keeps those in midlife and retirement reminiscing and looking backward, wanting younger bodies and dreams. Ageism robs thousands of people of enormous possibilities that they are capable of attaining as they get older. Elderly people who buy into these notions have low self-esteem, little motivation, and poor future prospects.

A cyclical perspective replaces this way of thinking with accurate information about the multiple dimensions of aging—some good news and some bad news. For example, with most of us, our interior awareness gets richer as we age while our physical abilities slowly lessen. The increasing sense of integrity is profound, while the physical losses are gradual. Sooner or later, we all experience decline and death. But the terminal phase of aging is, for most of us, a small and relatively short-term part of the total adult experience. Our ability to grow and to contribute continues throughout most of life. It's a matter of making the most of the trade-offs, which represent a continuous process throughout the adult years. The cyclical perspective finds value and meaning in every life period, including elderhood.[3]

The Linear View

The linear view portrays the human journey as a gradual unfolding of human improvement, with fairly specific pictures of when and how the events of the adult years should unfold. There are specific times throughout the life cycle that are appropriate for adult decisions and actions—when to go to school, to marry, to have children, to go through a career, to retire.

Childhood through early adulthood is preparation for life:

- You grow up in a nuclear family in one geographical location, with intact parents, a mother at home full-time, regularly scheduled family meals, planned vacations, and a life together through the high school years.
- At eighteen or thereabouts, you leave your family of origin to finish your education, enter the military, or begin a career.
- In your twenties, you find a life partner, marry, and settle down to family life and a career.

The adult years are for sustaining love and work:

- During your twenties, you have children, and you assume the primary parent role if you are a woman or a secondary parent role if you are a man.

- If you are a man, you invest in your career; if you are a woman, you invest in home and family and secondarily in work, as needed.
- If you are a man, you sustain your career, which you envision not only as a ladder leading to your fulfillment but as your principal contribution to the happiness and success of your family needs. Your primary adult identity is with your career roles.
- If you are a woman, you envision your fulfillment through your marriage, family, education of children, maintenance of the home, and volunteer work or employment, all of which are supposed to contribute to your happiness. Your primary adult identity is with your nurturance and caring roles.
- You rent, or preferably, buy a house, provide for your family, and plan for your children to obtain a better education than you did.
- You provide leadership for schools, religious organizations, and civic groups; you support your country in any way that it asks you to in times of armed conflict; you contribute to the improvement of your world.

Elderhood is the time for completion and stepping aside:

- You leave your career behind and begin a life of retirement.
- You live a life of leisure activities, with travel and the development of hobbies and possibly some part-time or volunteer work.
- You cultivate new friendships with your peers and deepen your religious affiliation.
- You dedicate yourself in new ways to your children and your grandchildren.

In the adult years, the linear plan calls for constancy, stability, and leadership—with family development, vertical career climbing, and cultural enhancement. Those who work hard and love well are supposed to succeed and be rewarded. Not only is individual life a linear progression; cultural life is supposed to be evolving as well. Science pushes back the boundaries of ignorance and, through applied research, industrial America gets "better things through chemistry." Businesses are supposed to prosper and grow; medical care will constantly improve; and the nation will evolve into a moral world power. The linear view, lived out as a dominant cultural pattern for adult life until about 1960, was deeply imbedded in the teachings of religious groups, educational institutions, voluntary associations such as the Boy Scouts and YMCAs, the Kiwanis and Rotary, corporate America, and the mass media.

There are four major characteristics of the linear way of thinking: First, it operates according to a normative and prescriptive picture of how the adult years should happen. It justifies different roles for men and for women, and for adults of different ages. It shapes personal destiny with a cultural design. This requires a socially cohesive, homogeneous culture. Second, the linear view portrays the adult years as a sequence of events within a social timetable with predictable outcomes. A linear life means a planned linkage of age- and gender-related roles at specific times in the life cycle—marrying, having children, developing careers, and retiring. Third, it assumes a simple equation that if an individual does what he or she is supposed to do to live well, then happiness and success will follow. From an individual point of view, the focus is upon the rewards of personal life, not the complex life journey through ever-changing forces, options, and commitments. Fourth, the linear view assumes that control over change is possible. As long as change enhances the linear plan, it is positive. But change that slows or subverts the plan is negative, unnerving, and perhaps demonic. Living in a world that is out of control is unthinkable.

The linear view was an amazingly successful motivator for the early centuries of our country. It worked to keep Americans attuned to building character, families, communities, businesses, and a nation. But today, not only does it not work or motivate; in our kind of world, it sustains the very dysfunctions described in Chapter One—people who are angry, disappointed, scared, reactive, and disempowered.

The Evolution of Adult Reality in the Twentieth Century

Winthrop D. Jordan observes that "The concept of adulthood . . . did not appear in America at all until after the Civil War and not really until the early twentieth century."[4] It wasn't until during and after World War II, when considerable attention focused on understanding adult behaviors and dysfunctions, that research on the adult years began in earnest. Bernice Neugarten, one of the pioneers of adult development, wrote in 1967 that "as yet we have no developmental psychology of adulthood; and psychology as a science has just begun to study the five or six decades that constitute the adult portion of the life span with something of the fascination that it has been studying the first two decades that constitute childhood and adolescence."[5] Since about 1945, the public concepts of adult reality have evolved through three stages:

1. The adult years represent a steady state of being all grown up, stable, dependable, and, most of the time, bland. For centuries, it was the understanding that when people became adults, they stopped growing and became fixed as predictable, responsible persons for the rest of their lives. Growing was over. The adult years were shaped by the personality and experiences of the child. Adults were expected to be devoted to what the father of psychoanalysis, Sigmund Freud, said were their principal activities: love and work. To some, this sounded less than exciting, hence phrases like "over the hill," "put out to pasture," and "mellowed out." While adults were expected to be consistent and responsible, they were also portrayed as predictable, boring, and sexless. Someone said that middle age is the time between foolishness and wisdom, without much character of its own. "In over two thousand years," write Bernice and Morton Hunt, "very few people have ever written about middle age by way of either praise or condemnation, for in our culture it has not been seen as a separate and special time of life. There was only youth, and when that was gone, old age."[6] This point of view was coherent with linear thinking. Adults were the work force for progress and the propagators of a better future.

2. In the 1950s and 1960s, an alternative picture of adult life emerged—adult life in general, and the midlife years in particular, are a crisis time. This perspective viewed the adult years as characterized by turbulence and crisis—turbulence in the young adult years, crisis in the thirties, a midlife upheaval at about age forty, and further convulsions in the fifties and sixties. Erik Erikson and Carl Jung set the stage for this concept in their seminal writings. A

"crisis," as they pictured it, was a crossroad in life that evoked strong emotional turmoil but could result in opportunities for new growth. "The crisis might lead one person to divorce his wife and marry his secretary, and another to quit her job and go sailing around the world. Still others might get depressed and take up drinking, or become angry and abusive. Others might seek to change careers, as Albert Schweitzer did when he retired as a concert organist and became a physician in Africa. The alleged 'crisis' often had to do with changes in the body, an awareness of the inevitability of death, feeling trapped in the decisions of early adulthod, an itch for roads not yet taken, and a sense that time is running out."[7]

Edmund Bergler's *The Revolt of the Middle-Aged Man*,[8] published in 1957, promoted this point of view, as did the writings of Elliot Jacques, Daniel Levinson, Roger Gould, Lois Tamir, and others. At a popular level, the midlife crisis was portrayed in poetry (T. S. Eliot's "The Cocktail Party"), novels (Philip Roth's *Portnoy's Complaint*), plays (Arthur Miller's *Death of a Salesman*), and films (*Shane* and *On the Waterfront*).

Although the concept of the "midlife crisis" was never universally accepted by adult researchers, it prevailed in the popular mind until about 1980 and still has widespread cultural support. Compared with the rosy picture of adults as steady-state performers, this one at least made the adult years look human, interesting, and growthful. While this perspective called into question a simplistic linear perspective, it was actually advocated by stage theorists who were modifying, not rejecting, a linear point of view.

3. The current popular view of the adult years portrays them as a Ferris wheel with up and down times that are repeated over and over again, as a cycle of continuity and change. Throughout the adult years, we experience periods of stability followed by periods of transition. When the vast research between 1970 and 1990 affected mainstream America, we learned that adults are neither fixed robots locked into a permanent state of mechanical stability nor crisis-laden "middlescents" stuck in transitions. Adults are human beings who adventure through both stable and unstable times, with many peaks and valleys, and have capacities for managing both. Cyclical thinking gained momentum and began to make sense.[9] Today, we view the adult years as a long period filled with positive life struc-

tures and troublesome transitions. As Henri Bergson wrote at the turn of the twentieth century, "To exist is to change; to change is to mature; to mature is to create oneself endlessly."[10] This is the cyclical point of view, the view of this book.

The Cyclical View

Ecclesiastes expresses the cyclical view: "To every thing there is a season, and a time to every purpose under the heaven; a time to be born, and a time to die; a time to plant, and a time to pluck up that which is planted." Cyclical concepts are patterns that are repeated but have different meanings at different times in our lives. They are not better or worse than earlier forms, merely different from them. When I was twenty-four I bought a powerful hi-fi set and listened for months to Peter Tchaikovsky's *1812 Overture*. I had a recording of a performance that incorporated a real cannon whose sound shook the entire room. Listening gave me goose bumps. Today, when I listen to the very same recording, no longer one of my favorites, I turn the volume down so that I can hear the music, not the noise. It's still the same recording, but it means something entirely different to me today.

The cyclical view portrays childhood through adolescence as a time of preparation for many adult directions, along with opportunities to try some of them out:

- You grow up in a family network, probably with both parents working; your parents might be divorced and/or remarried, creating a stepfamily; you might be living with a single parent. In any case, you probably have irregular family meals and episodic rather than daily family gatherings.
- Through schooling, travel, and special camps or training opportunities, you develop basic skills in sports, hobbies, and intellectual interests.
- Through TV and computer technology, you acquire a global picture of events, technology, and human problems.
- You develop a variety of friendship networks, peer contacts, and media orientations. You gain familiarity and comfort with pluralism, world issues, and ongoing disagreements.

- The early adult years are the time for establishing adult identities through life-styles and work styles.

Personal Identity

- In your twenties, you seek to define your identity as a person apart from the roles you are playing—student, son or daughter, aspiring careerist, lover, friend.
- You look for ways to test your boundaries, to find out who you are and who you aren't. You are eager to prove that you are not a carbon copy of your parents. You look for your music, your kind of clothes, your type of automobile, your preference in friends, your limits.
- You move in and out of institutions and events that foster your sense of self.

Achievement or Work

- In your twenties or sooner, you leave home to become responsible for yourself, more or less. You may attend a college or university, take a job, enter the military, travel, or invest time in a sport or hobby. You do something with your life that will connect you to the values that you believe in.
- You acquire and maintain communication skills and use them for networking and succeeding in your emerging career possibilities.
- By your mid to late twenties, you identify a tentative career path and obtain sufficient work experience to warrant plunging in to see how far you can go, knowing that there are other options and that you can change careers.

Intimacy

- You discover that leaving home takes a long time, because throughout much of your twenties, your basic life bonds remain the ones that you have had all of your life—with your family of origin, even if you are rebelling against them. You work hard to stay attached but separate, caring but free, included but unique.
- You look for mentors and role models other than your parents to validate your life direction and to endorse you as a person.
- Throughout most of your twenties, you spend time in young

adult networks, practicing being a peer and looking for friends who share your basic values and interests.

- You practice managing a household with an intimate partner or partners.

Play and Creativity

- You continue an active leisure life and keep your body in shape by eating carefully and exercising regularly.
- You sustain whatever lifelong sports you began earlier and make recreation a high value in your life-style.
- You find ways to be creative.
- You enjoy parties or times when you and your peers can be spontaneous and alive.

Search for Meaning

- You may take stands on personal and social issues that matter to you.
- You may remain active in the religious preference that you grew up in or in a new one.
- You may espouse a utopian expression of spirituality, seeking a higher road than your parents chose.
- You may keep this theme in low profile, for development later in life.

Compassion and Contribution

- You look for ways in which your career can contribute to the world beyond yourself.
- You may elect to volunteer or work for a cause that you believe in, anywhere in the world.
- If you come from well-to-do parents, you may choose to devote your life to contributing to the planet instead of making money a high priority.
- You may decide to postpone contribution until you have arrived at your own "success" later in life.

During midlife, you rearrange your commitments to these same values or themes:

Personal Identity

- You tend to overidentify with your major roles, such as work or parenting.
- You pursue continued training for professional and personal development throughout midlife. You may want to reenter some formal educational program to provide a setting for your own growth and development as both a person and a professional.
- You learn how to reevaluate your life commitments and values. You seek therapy, mentoring, and personal training as needed.

Intimacy

- You marry, remain single, get divorced, choose an alternative life-style, or live as a single parent; you may marry someone younger or older than yourself or someone in your own cohort group; as divorce occurs among your friends you realize that divorce, being single, and remarriage are possible realities for your life.
- Over a long term, you manage a household with a partner or partners and negotiate shared responsibilities and financial investments.
- You decide whether or not to have children. If you choose to and are able to conceive, you have children in a more-or-less planned way, probably during your early, mid, or late thirties, and negotiate household and parenting roles.

Achievement or Work

- You sustain work roles that develop dual careers, incomes, and professional identities.
- You invest primary time in work advancement, anticipate career changes and geographical moves, and look for horizontal career enrichment as well as vertical moves.

Play and Creativity

- You have a leisure life with interests in health, nutrition, exercise, art events, traveling, and sports.
- You invest primary time in your leisure life and consider it to be an important part of your life-style.

Search for Meaning

- You find your concern for integrity and spirituality increasing. You examine your beliefs about human destiny, beauty, and spirit.
- You take more time for solitude, contact with nature, and even trips alone. You contemplate the mystery of life.

Compassion and Contribution

- Your interest increases in providing leadership in community, professional, or national organizations.
- You find grandparenting to be a fulfilling role.
- You devote time to projects and causes that protect the environment and ameliorate social ills. You are more willing than ever to live your beliefs.

A cyclical view of adult life includes five major characteristics. First, it portrays life as a complex, pluralistic, multivariate flow, with ongoing cycles in nature, societies, and people. Families, corporations, and nations are all part of a larger, often chaotic flow that can be influenced and shaped but not completely controlled. People with cyclical perspectives view adult development as adaptation to change—change within themselves and within their environment. They also know how to seize new opportunities provided by change. Living with a cyclical view takes faith in the larger swim of things and trust in the daily flow. People with a cyclical view of world process view the world as an organic whole; they respect social realities, environmental conditions, and community concerns because everything affects everything else and shares the same universe. This view is both personal and planetary.[11]

Second, the cyclical picture assumes that life "develops" through cycles of change and continuity rather than in progressive, straight lines. It concentrates on understanding both what persists throughout our lives and what necessarily changes. The cyclical view portrays how the same basic themes are repeated throughout the adult years—themes such as love, achievement, and search for meaning. The life themes are rearranged as adults experience change from social forces, the aging process, and the internal dynamics of human development. The cyclical view focuses on repeatable life tasks that people perform in different ways at different times in the life cycle—coupling, work, play, care. What dictates human development throughout the life cycle is less one's "stage" in life than changing commitments to fundamental human values that we all share to one degree or another. Jane, at seventy-two, still maintains a full-time private practice as a psychologist, but she works not for money, as she used to, but for the human contact and the sense of being useful to others. Her leisure life, which used to be tennis singles, is now tennis doubles, and she belongs to a tennis club more for the recreational connections with friends than for anything else. Although widowed, Jane has many close friends. She is more active in her church than she used to be, and she feels more strongly about world peace.

Third, the cyclical picture honors both the ups and the downs of life, the blessings and the curses. Conflict and loss are part of everyday life, as are joy and ecstasy. Both are incorporated into the way we live and interact with one another. The cyclical understanding of life pictures society as forces and resources that sometimes form creative options for adult life and at other times become obstacles to be faced.

Fourth, the cyclical view portrays our human systems as modular, flexible, interactive, conflictual, and resilient, permitting continuous adaptations. It looks on all systems as cycles, so that couples' development, family systems, work systems, social systems, and the natural environment are all complex systems interacting with one another. All systems have up and down times, and beginnings and endings. Adults learn to shape and adapt to these systems in different ways at different times and places—designing scenarios and making them happen and, when they don't work, disassembling them and creating new ones. There is no cultural master plan, no human prescription for fulfillment. Cultural diversity is considered an asset rather than a liability.

Fifth, continuous learning is essential to the constant retooling of adult competence. Adults need not only knowledge and training to make the changing external world work but self-knowledge and training to make the internal world effective. As they age, adults need to unlearn old habits and learn new ways to live effectively.

Some adults seek learning in order to gain personal and professional competence; others pursue learning in order to develop undiscovered parts of themselves; still others seek mastery in the realm of consciousness and spiritual oneness.

The differences between the linear and cyclical views can be summed up as in Table 1 on the following page.

Tom, Mary, John, and Linda

One summer not long ago, Tom, Linda, John, and Mary got together for a month's vacation during which each wanted to make plans for the future. At fifty-three, Tom lived and breathed the linear life. Owner of his own company, Tom had devoted twenty-two years to growing his company into a winner. However, he had become bored and restless during the past year. The recession had eaten away at the profits, and Tom was looking for something new to do with his life. Tom was married but increasingly aware that his only personal identity was in his work, and he felt angry and upset about that.

Linda was fifty-three, a secretary, and contemplating retirement. She enjoyed living alone and had never married. During the past two months, Linda had had breast cancer surgery and treatment, which left her distressed and worried. "How should I proceed," she wondered, "retire and start some projects I've waited to do all my life, or keep working so I can stay close to my friends and benefits?"

John, who was working in human resources at Motorola, came to discuss his personal life. At forty-six, he had been divorced for five years and wanted to gain custody of his two young boys. Although his former wife was willing to try it for a year, he wasn't sure that he could manage being a single father with his job. Actually, John was ambivalent about what he wanted.

Mary was thirty-eight, married, childless, and a district manager for the publishing company McGraw-Hill. She worked very hard and was proud of her career attainments. However, the alarm in her "biological clock" was ringing. Should she have a baby? Was her marriage mature enough for parenthood? Could she and her husband live on a reduced income?

Table 1. Linear and Cyclical Views.

	Linear View	Cyclical View
The World	The world is more stable than chaotic. Order is separate from chaos, and chaos can be cordoned off by order. Social institutions sustain stability so individuals can succeed and prosper.	The world is more chaotic than stable. Order is a temporary holding pattern within our chaotic experience, and chaos cannot be avoided or cordoned off. Institutions and individuals seek to monitor change together so that acceptable levels of the quality of life can be experienced by as many people as possible.
Society	Development in personal life, family systems, work, and society is serial. Each serial point (marriage, having children, career, and so on) is something that we do in order to move on to some goal or result.	Development is continuous reprioritization and renewal of the same issues—identity, achievement, intimacy, play, search for meaning, and social compassion. These issues provoke life tasks that we do over and over again in different ways throughout the adult years.
	The larger society governs and guides individual and family plans.	Adults and their networks are responsible for life designs and social stability.
Personal Life	Life fits into a social master plan with defined roles, timing of events, and constraints. Personal life is a series of goals and objectives requiring long-term commitment, personal discipline, and postponed gratification.	Life is modular, flexible, interactive, chaotic, and resilient. Personal life is lived among many conflicting plans and social forces, requiring the abilities to tolerate ambiguity and adapt to new situations.
	The goal of life is to attain, acquire, and obtain results—a progressive quest that holds the promise of success and happiness.	Life is flow, an adventure into the unknown that holds the promise of continuous learning through the highs and lows of life.
	Adult life is a long period of stability in which personal strengths, intimacy bonds, career development, and responsibility work toward personal fulfillment and social progress. Transitions are not viewed positively.	Adult life is a process that moves from periods of stability to periods of instability and transition to new periods of stability, and so on. Adults need to know how to build life structures and how to manage life transitions.

Table 1. Linear and Cyclical Views, Cont'd.

	Linear View	*Cyclical View*
Family	The family is a traditional, nuclear one, with the wife as the primary caretaker of the home, being responsible for friendships, social life, child rearing, and schooling matters.	The family is an extended one, with an intimate couple sharing the caretaking of the home, including the maintenance of friendships, social life, child rearing, and schooling matters with continual negotiation of these issues.
Careers	The husband has a full-time career at all times. The wife is the full-time homemaker and parent and possibly has a part-time job or career.	Both the wife and the husband have careers or job options throughout the adult years, with economic interdependence.
Education	Education is youth oriented, to prepare for the grown-up years.	Education is a lifelong process for reeducation, renewal, and redirection.

By the end of their time together, Tom had designed a personal life apart from his company. He reduced his hours at work, delegated more of his duties to subordinates, and decided eventually to sell the company. He chose to spend most of his time at home, figuring out how to live his life without his career routines. Tom was excited about the possibility of creating a private life for himself, for the first time ever. He and Felicia, his wife, have spent more time together since the month's vacation than in the past five years. Although Tom doesn't know what lies ahead, he believes that he found the right direction for his life at this turning point.

Linda chose to remain with her career and work. She was able to reduce her time, however, to a four-day week and began some of her long-waiting projects on weekends. She also became a volunteer in a hospice and feels good about the way she is balancing her life. Although she has had periodic bouts of depression, she keeps close track of her health and friends, and lives each day as fully as she can.

John, it turned out, wanted a new career. He was very unhappy in his service-oriented job and figured out how he could safely manage a transition into accounting, the area of his professional master's degree. That's the way it worked out, three months later. He changed careers and felt he was "on course" again and in better spirits. Although he felt guilty about his parent role, he was able to arrange for two weekends a month with his children, and next year his older boy will live with him.

Mary discovered that her real issue was not having a baby but dealing with a marriage that never was. She decided to get into counseling with her husband to see whether the marriage could be saved. If it couldn't be, she was now ready to end it and live alone. Mary is very happy with her work, friends, and life in general. Her primary intimacy issues need reevaluation and renewal, and the baby question is still unanswered but less demanding.

All four of these people have learned how to redesign, renew, balance, and manage their complex lives for a while—competencies required when we live within a cyclical view of adult life.

The Two Cycles in Adult Life

There are two primary cycles that affect adult life—the change cycle and the life cycle. Each cycle maps out a different section of the adult territory, and together they provide a basis for the development of adult mastery and leadership in a world of change. Adults who learn the importance of these cycles in their lives will see the world of the twenty-first century as familiar and challenging.

The cycle of change represents the ongoing change process within adult life. Within this cycle, adults move through periods of life structure and periods of transition, which then repeat themselves. This is the most important cycle for contemporary adults to master, because it requires living creatively with the flow of internal and external change. The life structure transition process and specific skills for facilitating it are described in detail in Part Two.

The life cycle is the birth-to-death journey that every human being experiences. In the adult years, the life cycle represents changing patterns of a person's sense of purpose, from about age twenty on. Throughout a person's life cycle, this sense of purpose shifts with changes resulting from aging, social forces, and self-development. There are patterns to the life cycle as it proceeds throughout the adult years from twentysomething to eightysomething, and these are presented in Part Three.

II

The
Cycle of Change

LIFE STRUCTURES AND TRANSITIONS

3

The
Pattern of Change

If one's destiny is shaped from within, then one has
become more of a creator, has gained freedom. This
self-transcendence, a process of change that originates
in one's heart and expands outward, always within the
purview and direction of a knowing consciousness,
begins with a vision of freedom, an 'I want to become . . . ,' with a sense of the potentiality to become
what one is not. One gropes toward this vision in the
dark, with no guide, no map, and no guarantee. Here
one acts as subject, author, creator.

—*Allen Wheelis, How People Change*[1]

Living in the 1990s feels like being on a raft floating down a com-
manding river. We have a small mast and sail, a rudder, and some
poles. Sometimes when it's calm, our journey is fairly effortless; we
can moor the raft in an eddy near a meadow and camp for a while.
At other times, the white waters of the river test every skill we have
as we slide over rocks and rapids and swirl about in unforeseen
directions.

The image of a river captures two qualities central to our
experience of change: a sense of chaotic power beyond our control
and a sense of never-ending adventure requiring our continual vigilance and readiness. The river is not merely external to us, but
internal as well. When people feel at home on this river, cooperate

with the flow, learn to navigate, and anticipate the forthcoming ports of call, they learn something about how to manage constancy and change in their lives. The river journey of our lives flows in a cycle, with recurring patterns of events and life tasks. The adult cycle of change moves from relatively stable periods called "life structures" to unstable periods called "transitions" and on to new "life structures." This change cycle, which continues without stopping throughout our lives, can be diagrammed as shown in Map 1.

The Four Phases of Change

The cycle of changes has four phases or time periods. Each phase has an organizing principle that defines it, along with tasks or activities to make it happen. Each phase proceeds in a clockwise direction, quickly or slowly moving through the change process around the cycle. The description of each phase below begins with a quotation from the *I Ching,* the ancient Chinese "Book of Changes."

Phase 1: Alignment. "Assuming your cause is just, planning is needed to achieve success. . . . Do what is right and you will be rewarded. Move forward and you will get support. . . . As you succeed, continue with self-discipline and self-restraint. . . . You will be accepted and entrusted with leadership. You will have good fortune without seeking it. . . . There is no obstacle in your path."[2]

In phase 1, you are consciously and unconsciously inventing a life structure: You begin to structure your future when you become captivated and inspired by a vision or dream of the next chapter of your life. A dream is like a brainstorm, an imaginal picture of how you want your future to be. When you light upon the right dream, you feel energized and determined to make it happen. Your dream is how you really want to be. You are "on course."

You distill from your dream a dramatic sequence of how your future will unfold. You create (or borrow) a story line for how it will happen, keeping the story focused on the central events and life themes that you want to happen in the final act (career success, financial independence, marriage and family, caring for others, being at one with the universe). When the story line is a sequence of

**Map 1. The Cycle of Change: Ten Personal Skills That
Empower Adults Through Life Structures and Transitions.**

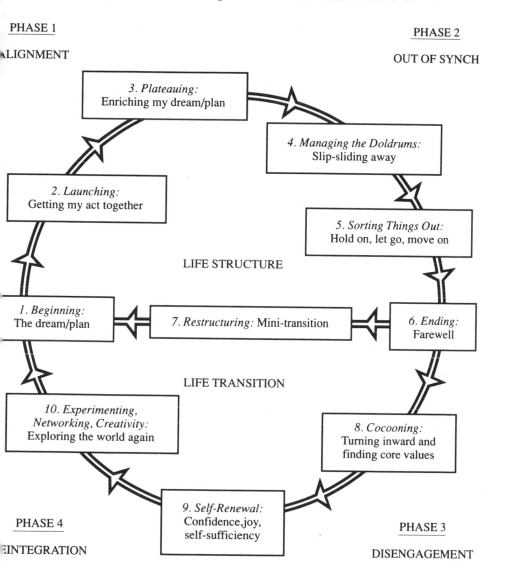

PHASE 1

ALIGNMENT

PHASE 2

OUT OF SYNCH

3. Plateauing:
Enriching my dream/plan

4. Managing the Doldrums:
Slip-sliding away

2. Launching:
Getting my act together

5. Sorting Things Out:
Hold on, let go, move on

LIFE STRUCTURE

1. Beginning:
The dream/plan

7. Restructuring: Mini-transition

6. Ending:
Farewell

LIFE TRANSITION

*10. Experimenting,
Networking, Creativity:*
Exploring the world again

8. Cocooning:
Turning inward and
finding core values

9. Self-Renewal:
Confidence, joy,
self-sufficiency

PHASE 4

REINTEGRATION

PHASE 3

DISENGAGEMENT

imagined happenings, you have a dramatic form, with you as the author, the main character and hero, the designer of the scenes, and the director. You personally endorse the drama and enter it. You are at your best. You get others to believe in your story and to play roles in your drama. You place the scenery where you want it on the stage, and create the context for your structure. The play begins! You enter stage left, and phase 1 is under way. As the scenes unfold, you weave together the dramatic development of your achievements, adventures, happiness, and success. You feel like a hero in the making!

Soon idealistic dreaming leads to realistic planning, as you launch your plan with action steps, time lines, and endless revisions. It may take many years to turn the dream into reality, and that seems all right, because this is your personal mission. During launching, you "embed" yourself in system after system, and for the most part they seem to support one another—relationships, family, career, causes, sports. You are very focused on your agenda and measured with your time.

If you stay committed to your dream/plan and keep adapting it to your life, you are likely eventually to reach a plateau, where much of your dream is realized. The plateau may be a blessing and a curse. As a blessing, it may represent your success, your victory, your ability to make the world work. As a curse, it may mean that motivation declines with the attainment of the vision. And altering the life course in a plateau is difficult; you are all wrapped up in complex systems of your commitments and can't make changes easily. You may feel that you would rather be taking up a new challenge than managing this one, which has peaked. On the other hand, you may feel that you deserve to remain in this plateau for a long time and to find ways to improve it.

Anne Bradley

Anne Bradley was ready to make something of her life. For over a year, she had been trying to forget how her employment was terminated when Touche Ross merged with Deloitte Haskins & Sells. She felt betrayed by a company that she had been devoted to for twenty-five years of her life. Three years later, she invented her own future:

"What I finally came to realize is that I've always wanted to have a business of my own—you know, a small accounting firm that specializes in working with small, family businesses. Those guys are really neglected by the Big Eight. So I've got this dream about relocating in Portland, Oregon, where I have some friends, starting my business, living in a condo on the river, and taking up white-water rafting on the side. What do you think?"

Clearly, Anne had a dream, and since she was good with details, she soon had a plan. Two years later, Anne let me hear how she was doing. "In all honesty," she said, "it's not easy starting your first business in your fifties, but I love it. I feel free and challenged again. Although I'm not as far along in my business plan as I thought I would be, I am on my way and happy to be charting my own path." There was quite a lapse of time before I received an announcement of her victory:

> To Whom it May Concern: Be it known that Anne Bradley, former subservient in a Big Eight accounting firm, has now succeeded as the owner of her own accounting firm: THE MONEY WORKS.

Phase 2: Out of Synch. "Know that all things reach their peak, then wane. Success, too, comes by degrees, moderately, reaches a peak, and does not last forever. . . . Be realistic and take a good look at yourself, not so much as an individual who stands alone, but as a person who reacts to and with others. Knowing how and where you fit into society and life is the object. . . . If the situation seems hopeless, it is because you have become accustomed to the wrong way of doing things. You are lost. The more you try, the more lost you become. . . . You are in a situation much like fighting a rear-guard action. . . . Withdraw quietly and gracefully. There isn't much choice. . . . The need for withdrawal must be so obvious there can be no doubt as to its need. When the situation looks hopeless, that is the time to stand by your convictions, true to yourself above all else. Do this and it will end well."[3]

In phase 2, you continue to manage your dramatic structure, but you feel yourself distancing from it, so you search for ways to keep it thriving. An organizing principle for this phase is "holding on and letting go" as you sort out the essential qualities of your life structure from those that need to be changed. Throughout this phase you feel your life structure "slip-sliding away." You feel less possessed by your dream and less enchanted by your attainment. You have a sensation that you are looking in on your life instead of living it. You see yourself getting mired down, diminishing your own story. Unhappy with the prospects, you look for ways to eliminate your ambivalence so that you can soar again with clarity and unconditional resolve.

You obsess over ways to reinflate your balloon; you evaluate, tinker, and reevaluate. As you brood, you become critical of yourself and others. You look for something to fix, repair, change, or blame. You look for ways to salvage your structure, to make it better than ever. You notice, however, that as your mind works harder to reclaim the alignment of your life structure, your feelings are electric with outrage. You feel angry, scared, sad, and trapped. You are stuck in a reactive mode and don't know how to get out of it.

Unanticipated events enter the drama. Other actors produce scripts, lines, and decisions that you did not write or authorize. Even though you feel somewhat jaded and distanced from your own life structure, you refuse to give up control of the story line. It's your human right! Others, however, are beginning to direct the drama, and you feel trapped in a state of affairs that you did not anticipate. You find your roles increasingly confusing, and your acts are perceived as defensive. The glorious ending that you had in mind for your success is being eclipsed by a chorus of dissonance. You are in a tailspin. Your self-esteem is diminishing. Someone absurdly suggests that you are having an "identity crisis," which you immediately deny. You refuse to let others rain on your parade, even as the clouds burst. You feel yourself holding on, yet letting go. A popular song by The Guess Who says it all: "She's come undone, she's lost the sun."[4]

In the last scene of this phase, you are making a momentous decision, as if you had reached a fork in the routes available to you. If you take the route to the right, named "Restructuring: Minitransition" (see Map 1), you can repair the structure and end up in phase 1 with the same vision and overall plan. If you take the route into a full-fledged life transition, you can exit your structure and find resources for constructing new directions. At last, a proactive choice!

The "Restructuring" route rather quickly refurbishes and rejuvenates the structure you are in, with some strategic changes— a change of geographical location, a change of employer, changes in marriage or family, a new work team, or a new product line. Unless you are overwhelmed and surprised by events that seem outside your control—such as a death in the family, an accident or illness, winning the lottery, or a business disaster—this is the route that you will probably choose. Evaluation leading to the reconstruction of a life structure usually feels preferable to exiting into a life transition. The sense of trouble in phase 2 may actually produce new determination to make the life structure better than ever. So you work hard to repair, heal, and upgrade the life structure that you have been living. (Successful adults often recycle themselves through phase 1 and phase 2—the upper half of the cycle—several times, until the life structure itself becomes permanently stale, dysfunctional, or unavailable.)

The "Life Transition" route, which usually becomes attractive only after you have exhausted your efforts to rebuild your structure, leads you to disengage from your out-of-synch structure and to enter a transition involving cocooning, renewal, and experimentation. When you take this path—or get thrown into it by events beyond your control—you feel like you are slip-sliding away, for all kinds of reasons, and none of them matters much. There doesn't have to be a worthy option. You are leaving, ending, disengaging, exiting—that's all.

The drama may turn to character analysis—an analysis of your character—and the stage may be flooded with emotional turmoil. Others may be after your roles—the script writing, the directing—and you may feel paranoid and angry. Your wonderful drama may seem tragic, or you may be greatly relieved that it is about to be over. Your exit is clear and imminent, even to you. Sooner or later, every life structure fades and becomes unworkable. Then, either it gets improved through refurbishing or you dismantle it. Even if you choose the first route and make positive adjustments in your existing life structure and continue successfully a hundred times through phases 1 and 2, the second route to complete disengagement from the structure will eventually belong to you. Sooner or later in every life structure, "out of synch" leads to a small door with big writing on it: EXIT HERE.

Why do life transitions happen? Maybe the salt has lost its flavor. Maybe you have lost your taste for salt! Your dream may have dimmed or your routines have become boring. Maybe your relationships are losing energy and commitment. Perhaps your job has been terminated, after years of loyal and successful service. Maybe your job never evolved into a career, and that is what the "departure" is about. Perhaps you have been a soldier in the Persian Gulf, and you know that your life will never be the same. Maybe you are older, and your values have changed, making the roles that you were playing in your life structure a burden. Maybe a close friend has died, or you have contracted a life-threatening disease or had an accident. Maybe you are just dreadfully unhappy, and that is the driving force.

Perhaps there is nothing intrinsically wrong with you or the structure, but you are being challenged by a new dream that calls you to leave so that you can explore a road less traveled. Maybe you received an unexpected inheritance, received a promotion that you always wanted, had a religious experience, or adopted triplets. You also may find yourself rethinking the questions that you thought you had successfully answered and discovering new questions that you hadn't asked before. As the mythologist Joseph Campbell often said, "Sometimes we get to the top of our ladder and find it's against the wrong wall."

Almost always we resist endings. Most people would rather hang on to a life structure reeking with distress than to find an honorable exit. They would rather seek to improve a dysfunctional structure that they are in than to enter a transition filled with the unknown. However, the unknown has a way of knocking on the doors of our lives from time to time, requiring our full attention. "The truth of the matter," declares Stanley Keleman, "is that making an ending forces us to start being more self-reliant, or at least offers that opportunity."[5] So you prepare to leave the structure that has defined your life for the past several years and contained your identity, your hopes, and your unfulfilled self. You feel that entering the unknown ahead is now preferable—or necessary—to drowning in the incessant echoes, pain, and traps of your inoperative life structure. One way or another, you depart, and by saying good-bye you say hello to a new journey.

Martin

At fifty-seven, Martin was a burned-out college professor looking for a future that he could believe in. While his wife, Leia, a nurse, wanted to understand what Martin was going through, she was extremely eager for him to get through his depression and on with life. With two college-age children now away from home, she had become impatient with Martin's impasse. "I work with patients at the hospital eight hours a day and then come home to my full-time patient!" she blurted with exasperation. And Martin felt rushed by Leia. "I lost interest in my work years ago," he confessed, "but what else can I do? I've never really left school. Besides, I have tenure. My dean wants me to take early retirement, but what would I do then? Rot at home instead of at school?"

Martin was feeling trapped, and while he wanted to change, he didn't know how to do it without losing what he thought was his major attainment in life—professorial tenure. It wasn't until the last day of the seminar that he was ready to rehearse an exit plan. "Maybe the dean would grant me a leave of absence," he pondered out loud. "I mean, they owe it to me, and if I could get it, I would take my family to France for the year and plan my retirement. I really would. My sister has a place in southern France that I know I could rent. It would be a wonderful change, and it might lead somewhere. I'm sick of staying stuck."

When Martin got back home, the dean granted the leave, and during his renewing year in France, Martin discovered many new dreams within him. His energy returned, and his sex life improved. As he felt his residual strength, it became easier to imagine himself leaving the college. In fact, he didn't even want to return home! He decided to resign his teaching position, remain in the same location, and become a part-time realtor. His wife and family rejoiced. In a recent letter, he admitted that "while it was a wrenching decision to leave my college and my professorial career, I feel now that a thousand tons have been lifted from me."

Jeff

At forty-four, Jeff was successful as an M.D. but unsuccessful as a husband and father. As he saw it, his profession required his primary attention, but his wife and child felt that he just didn't care enough for them. "You simply aren't available for me or for little Peter," his wife blurted out one day, "and you aren't ever going to make us your best friends. I am very sorry, Jeff, but I can't stay married to a workaholic. I want a husband who is a lover, father, and friend!"

After the divorce, Jeff continued his life as a physician but was unable to find a successful intimate relationship. For two years, he lived alone and organized his life around his work, which was easy to do. In his solitude at home, he learned new ways to reflect on his life course and to make peace with the path that he had chosen. Then he met Bertha, who worked in the marketing division of a pharmaceutical firm. Bertha was every bit as busy as he was. They both loved their brief but intense intimate times, as well as their demanding jobs. They decided to marry; afterwards, they led separate lives most of the time, with occasional excursions to interesting places. Although they knew that other couples felt that theirs was less than a complete marriage, Bertha and Jeff felt good about the balance that they had created between their work and their life together.

Renette

At midlife, Renette seemed to have much of what she wanted—a good marriage, employment in a small research firm, and two children. Yet she hated her fat body. For a long time, she got down on herself, and her depression diminished her effectiveness at work and at home. Gradually, she withdrew from all of her social connections. She quit her job, refused sex, and became a minimal mother. Filled with personal disgust, she joined a weight watcher's group, began an exercise program, and very gradually reclaimed her attractive body and self-esteem. Renette continued on the same life journey, but she had a new sense of purpose. Now she initiated activities with her husband and went on trips alone with the children.

Sam

Sam was sick and tired of his situation at PNN, an electronics firm where he was an area manager in Texas. Having grown up in Maine, Sam wanted PNN to relocate him in the Northeast and, of course, he wanted a promotion as well. But PNN had flattened the corporation, eliminating middle managers and leaving little opportunity for anyone to rise within the firm. At forty-eight, Sam felt that he had peaked, and he felt trapped. He found an hourly engineering position with AT&T in Boston and decided to switch companies, even though it meant a demotion and less salary. "When I exchanged companies and geographical locations," Sam explained, "my wife and three kids liked life a whole lot better. They liked me better, too. I actually find my current work very challenging, but my main challenge is to lead a balanced life, and I'm doing that. It feels right."

Phase 3: Disengagement. "There will be misfortune, but no serious harm. The real, natural you is resilient and strong. Be your natural self and you can do no harm. When misfortune comes, let nature take its course. The situation improves by itself, without the need for any action on your part. . . . Reexamine and rededicate yourself to your motives and values. . . . Inactivity should not disturb you, for you can use the time to contemplate who and where you are. Be yourself, but rise above selfishness to achieve a selfless serenity. . . . Do these things and you will achieve union with the universe."[6]

In phase 3, you exit the extended stage and turn inward for the continuing drama, to rely on your inner resources. Your game plan is twofold: to shed the onion skins of your former life structure and to become self-reliant. At first you have no lines, no roles, no recognition, nothing. You may even feel like a nothing, a nonbeing, an actor without a role or a play. You have left the outer world of action and have entered the inner world of soul-searching. There you gradually recognize a different stage for the metamorphosis of the self.

You grieve the loss of your structure and feel as if your own life had ended. Your sense of a future is very bleak and your energy level low. Although you began the process in phase 2, you feel very burdened with yourself now that you are in phase 3. Your lamentation and mourning have gone on much longer than you want: "The bottom has fallen out of my world," "Nothing matters now," "The meaning has gone out of my life," "I'm not there anymore." Ever so gradually, you let go of the external structure as it clings to your mind—lost dreams, lost roles, lost beauty, lost muscles, lost parents, lost careers, lost children, lost marriages, lost income, lost hope—and you live for a while in a "neutral zone" where you are, psychologically speaking, by yourself, in suspension, in limbo, and more aware of who you are not than who you are becoming.[7]

Typically, but not necessarily, you feel a hollow loneliness that doesn't go away, and you fear that you've been abandoned not only by your past but by your future as well. You wander around, looking in on your life, as if you were a ghost or spirit from a Dickens novel. The ghosts from your past confront you, and the ghosts from your future taunt you, but eventually they have less and less impact as you grow stronger and find new life within. In time, you feel not merely healed but vital and alive. It is a quiet fire, within, and it brings warmth and new confidence. Your eyes mirror the resilience that you have found. You want little but feel much, and most of all you feel in touch with the deep murmurs of your own heart. Your deep-seated values arise to shape your new human agenda, and you get ready to journey again.

The big surprise is that the attunement that you feel in your life at this time has more contentment and fulfillment than the "success" and "identity" that you wanted so desperately to hold on to in your former life structure. As your self-renewal deepens, you are overwhelmed by gratitude and joy. You are ready to launch a new adventure, much better fitted than the old one to your present life and destiny.

Disengagement is a time for "being," not "doing." In time, people who are devoted to working through loss find resources within them that they didn't realize they had. With healing and renewal, reintegration with the external world begins again. This time, new external extensions of the self will be chosen, like new clothes, to fit current dreams and values and competencies and to accommodate current social conditions and opportunities. The "dark night of the soul" fades into morning's sunrise, and the cocoon breaks open for the butterfly to begin its skyward journey.

Frank and Helen

Frank and Helen were profoundly shaken when their two children were killed in an automobile accident two years ago. It doesn't matter now just how it happened. What matters is that Frank and Helen were thrown into a total reevaluation of their lives such as they had never experienced before. They didn't want to talk much to anyone, and they felt embarrassed at their fragile emotions. On the living room piano, they made an altar of pictures of how Marie and Joe had looked in their all-too-brief years of life. At one point, Helen decided to take a trip to Vienna, alone, just to think things through. Frank said that he understood. But while she was gone, he cried more than ever.

Frank said that he wanted to "plan his life," but clearly he needed first to find some inner strength; he blamed himself for the accident, even though he hadn't even been near the automobile. He was neglecting his work to such a degree that he had received a negative job review, with a three-month notice to shape up or ship out. Frank was not able to shape up. "What should I do?" he asked. "What really matters, now?" he pondered, without an answer. When Frank recognized that he had to get a break from his work, he obtained a leave and later returned successfully. But during his leave of absence, Frank and Helen made some momentous discoveries. Helen put it this way: "I fell in love with Frank all over again. He became so human and tender." Frank said, "I learned that there is more of me than I knew. I have become more sensitive and more determined to live now, and to love now, and to put my life where my beliefs are." For months, they hibernated in their home and talked about everything that they were thinking and feeling, as they used to do before they were married. Both of them talked about how lonely the grieving period was and how dreadfully long it took and continues to take. "But in the end," Helen said, "we are more connected to what is important to our lives. In a strange way, we are the living legacy of our own children."

Phase 4: Reintegration. "Be simple, free, and uncomplicated. . . . Develop virtues based on inner strength and signify them by outward self-restraint. Be yourself; do not emulate others. . . . Solve minor problems now while the solutions are still simple. . . . Remain somewhat aloof from the world and quietly improve yourself. In this way you will make of yourself something which will endure. . . . Do not take action prematurely. You must be ready, seasoned, with mature judgment, if you are to succeed. . . . You cannot succeed without the help of others. . . . Eventually an experienced person will come to help you and success follows."[8]

In phase 4, you expand your self-renewal space to include the world around you. This is a time of rebirth, play, and experimentation. The inner self and the outer world find new ways to dance together. The organizing principles are exploration, creativity, and networking. Feelings are predominantly positive and expressive, and the world seems safe again. You slowly begin to link your renewed self with the possible scenarios for your life in the world that surrounds you. You are fresh and dreamy again. You feel creative and filled with energy, like a child: unencumbered, free, willing to try new ideas. You experiment with options, network with new kinds of friends, and play with possibilities without making many commitments. You engage in new learning projects and yearn to travel. You feel no need to rush and every reason to savor these moments of discovery. Sooner or later, you discover some path that feels right for a new life structure, and the cycle begins again. You become heady, optimistic, refreshed, ready, and prepared.

Jim

When I first met him, Jim, at forty-seven, had just been fired as the executive director of a prestigious YMCA in Chicago. Although he dressed like an executive and smoked big cigars, he talked like a man in distress. His voice was fragile, his humor raw, and it was obvious that he had been shaken to his roots. At first, he was not able to admit that he had been fired from his job. He was not prepared to face the transition he was already in.

Jim entered Y work when he graduated from Springfield College and became an executive director at age twenty-seven. In fact, the only type of job that Jim had ever had was as a CEO of one Y or another as he worked his way up from small to large operations. Jim was Mr. YMCA; he thought, breathed, and lived the Y world. When the board of directors at the Chicago YMCA decided to fire Jim, he declared war on his board and sought to reclaim his job. He was angry, depressed, and confused. He felt that his life was at stake. Within a week, he was deeply into a life transition without knowing it.

Who was Jim without his career identity—his YMCA roles, experiences, and accomplishments? To Jim, he was a nobody, and his self-esteem and confidence were on the rocks. He had no identity apart from his work role, even though others found him affectionate, thoughtful, playful, and interesting—as a person. As Jim gradually accepted the transition territory that he was traversing, he realized that he was losing everything he had spent his life gaining. Although others offered him comfort and concern, he stayed armored in his grief.

People in transition need plans that help them discover their inner resources and faith in forces beyond themselves. Jim was low in trust and had an equally low awareness of his own interiority. Nevertheless, his pride required him to demand a new job with a YMCA as a CEO, immediately. He did not realize that he was, for now, unemployable. In time, Jim made it clear that he was burned out with his executive roles and that he wanted to renew his life and discover who he was as a person apart from career roles and status; to renew his marriage, which he'd ignored for years; to renew the fathering of his three teenage children, who were school dropouts in considerable rebellion; and to change his career direction to an entrepreneurial occupation that he could run on his own.

Jim mapped out a year's "sabbatical" that would serve as a twelve-month period of soul-searching, renewal, and new beginnings. He held a big "sabbatical" party, where he announced his plans and thanked his friends for their support for his new direction. That party was like a rite of passage for Jim, distinguishing his past from his future and providing him a dignified way to publicly "let go" and "move on." During this grieving-healing period, Jim did fix-it projects around the house and even added a room for his teenage daughter. He went on daily walks with his wife, Rosemary, and their marriage grew closer together than it had ever been since their honeymoon ended. Jim maintained a daily journal to keep track of his inner thoughts, and he spent two hours a day at a health center where he swam and worked out.

Several months later, Jim left for Europe, to drift about with his oldest son, whom he knew the least of all his children. The son was responsible for the planning, while Jim practiced the art of listening and following. It worked for both of them. After six weeks together abroad, they returned, filled with stories of adventure and love for one another. This sojourn exceeded the expectations of both father and son and prepared Jim for reentry. By the end of the year, Jim had discovered new inner resources and confidence. He was clearly into "exploring the world again" and was beginning to experiment with new career ideas and friendships. He had the makings of a consulting business with nonprofit organizations, and a financial planning business for people like himself. In a message I received from him, he remarked, "I should have left years ago. I'm embarrassed to say that after all these years, I'm learning how to live, but it's true. I feel like a different person. Although my life is full of loose ends, I know I'm doing the right thing. After all these years, I am ready to build my future the old-fashioned way—upon my character."

How the Cycle of Change Works

Now reflect upon the excursion we have just taken through the cycle of changes. What are the critical issues to grasp, in order to use these concepts in your own life? To begin with, you need to be able to locate where you are in the cycle, at this moment in time, and which life tasks are central for your future empowerment. You will probably find yourself at various places in the cycle if you think about your various adult roles—spouse, parent, worker. Your marriage may be in the doldrums, while your parenting is going well in a launching phase. Meanwhile, your career or work role may be undergoing a transition. However, as a "person," beneath the roles—the inner self who talks to all the parts and tries to monitor cohesion and joy—you are at approximately one place in the circle. It is that residual self or core that guides a person, with all his or her roles and parts, on a "life course" throughout the life cycle.[9] The two basic alternatives are to be in a structure or in a transition. A life structure represents a cohesive chapter of your life; a transition is an opportunity to retool your inner self. A life structure embeds you in the human systems around you; a life transition frees you to discover more of yourself. Neither is better than the other, and both are necessary places in the flow of adult life. But as a person, you are engaged, at any given time, either in building a life structure or in redefining your life purpose through a transition process. To be a successful human being, you need excellence in mastering both, and most of us have many opportunities to do so during the course of our lives.

Adult life flows around the cycle, clockwise, slowly or quickly, like a river. A life structure happens when adults are able to align their inner strengths with resources in their surrounding environment, resulting in a plan that works. This could be the inspired artist ready to compose, paint, or sculpt. It could be a newly married couple establishing their careers and home around a shared dream. It could be a fifty-year-old ready to try a new pathway. Transitions happen when life structures are unavailable, painful, or out of alignment. A transition is a journey into your inner strengths, resulting in your renewal as a person. Some transitions represent fairly rapid restructurings of the same life structure, such as a job change, a move, or a promotion. Other transitions are slow and transformative, leading to new and different life structures, such as personal changes following the death of a spouse or child, being fired from a job, or a divorce.

Both life structures and transitions are dramatic forms. You lead your life into stories that you find believable. You inspire, imagine, create the script, convince the players, learn the lines, act out the parts, direct the drama, and defend the actions. You take care of yourself, heal, and become self-sufficient. Of course, you are guided and constrained by a multitude of factors beyond your control, but the bottom line is that you are ultimately responsible for your own life structures and transitions. Even if tragedy befalls you, you are the only one who can decide how to continue your story. As long as you can choose to live differently and extend your story chronologically, you are authoring your own story. This is the way you explain your life to yourself and others. You are a person, with a story, on a journey, weaving your way through the scenes of your life. If you do not write the script, someone else will, and you will learn about your lifeline through symbiotic relationships and roles. But if you write the script, it will be a "life design," an intentional plot to make your world work—the world of your own experience.

Ten Skills for Managing the Change Cycle

There are at least ten basic skills that represent the most important abilities you need to grow and develop as a person within the change cycle, to succeed at creating life structures and at producing significant self-renewal during life transitions. These are human competencies that assume strategic importance at specific times in your life. The ten skills are approximate notions. People require many other competencies for making their lives work, but these ten are the generic, human tasks in which adults today need basic proficiency for the weaving and unraveling of their lives.

Although each change cycle skill has a time in the cycle when it performs a critical function, all ten abilities are important at all times, because to some degree parts of our lives are simultaneously at various places in the cycle. During a life structure, there will be many times when minor transitions must be managed, and during transitions it is necessary to maintain a minimal life structure in order to take care of oneself. Each of the ten skills represents a strategic activity for a particular time and place in the cycle. Each ability has a unique time in the cycle when it has special power for keeping life proactive and moving forward; each functions like a Zeitgeist and then needs to give way to the next, keeping you on course with optimal choices for your development at different places on the river. Each change cycle skill leverages you through a particular portion of the cycle of change and prepares you for the next leg of the journey. Knowing which competencies to favor at various points of your personal cycle is the wisdom of adult life.

1. *A dream or vision* provides conviction, inspiration, and energy for constructing a life structure. A *plan* schedules the dream with available resources and possibilities.

2. *Launching* requires personal commitment, perseverence, and adaptations—and social and economic alignment.

3. *Plateauing* sustains and deepens a successful, functional life structure.

4. *Managing the doldrums* comes to terms with decline, negative emotions, and feeling trapped in an increasingly dysfunctional life structure.

5. *Sorting things out* results in a personal plan: what to keep, what to eliminate or change, what to add, and how to proceed into a revitalized life structure.

6. *Ending* a life structure with dignity and care requires an ability to say "farewell" with gratitude and clarity, leaving you free to consider your next options. There are two possibilities at this point, restructuring or a life transition.

7. *Restructuring,* which conducts a minitransition back into a refurbished life structure, can be used to move across the center of the cycle if the life structure can be improved with some specific changes. Restructuring is like minor surgery, with a strategic plan to make the life structure work better—a new location, a new job, a new home, or a new partner. The same basic values and goals prevail, but the action steps, setting, and/or players in the drama are altered.

8. *Cocooning* is the first activity of a life transition—turning inward to take stock, to find your own basic values, and to disengage emotionally and mentally from the life structure. If the life structure cannot be redeemed, or if the optimal choice is to leave it in order to find a new and different one, the first step is to exit into a life transition where this skill is required. A life transition is like major surgery, usually resulting in personal development, new life options, and even transformation.

9. *Self-renewal* follows from successful cocooning. It is the ability to be self-sustaining, producing confidence, energy, and hope. Self-renewal also involves a reevaluation of core issues and beliefs.

10. The final and tenth skill of the cycle—*experimenting,* engages you in creativity, learning, risk-taking, and networking.

When the self is ready to venture back into a life structure, it takes on this skill. As the self gains strength in its own sense of purpose, it feels alive and playful, and begins to link up with new social support and new information about life options. The self, now feeling anchored and purposive again, spends its time exploring new possibilities for a life structure. Sooner or later, a new and compelling dream takes over and a new life structure begins. Chapters Four through Six will explore the cycle of change and its ten empowerment skills in detail and with examples.

4

From Dreaming
to Restructuring

Freedom and captivity coexist. We cannot escape from
our structures; we are condemned to structuring our
worlds since this is the form of life in which we exist.
But although we are imprisoned, we are free to choose
what form our prison should take. . . . If we accept
that our constructions are structures and not reality
itself, and that each person has his own construction
of reality, then we have to live with uncertainty. But
we can choose to define that uncertainty as either prison or freedom. I prefer freedom.
—*Dorothy Rowe, The Construction of Life and Death*[1]

A life structure is not born in a vacuum. The social environment
must provide sufficient stability, resources, and freedom for the
drama of a life structure to unfold. A life structure requires a dependable financial base and social opportunities. A life structure
springs from a healthy self, brimming with creative energy, honed
skills, and inner determination. People beginning life structures
have often just completed training programs, extensive travel, or
learning experiences that prepared them for a leap into the future.

Getting Ready

People ready to create life structures experience a shifting of gears,
out of the inward orientation of destructuring into the social expan-

siveness of structuring. This is the time for moving from simple to complex, from inner to outer, from self to systems, from separation to interdependence, from short-term innovation to long-term embeddedness. Adults who are prepared for a life structure see the world as fair and friendly, ready to fulfill their life needs and goals. Structurers are single-minded—to create a future by weaving all the expanding parts of their lives together around a central purpose or mission. Starting with visionary possibilities, structurers devise plans that they launch, and if the long haul of launching is successful, a plateau is reached. Otherwise, they arrive at an ending sooner than they had intended.

The Dream/Plan

The first change cycle skill that a structurer requires is the ability to evolve a dream/plan. The dream is the driving force for the life structure, a source of passion and values. The plan is the plot for making the dream happen—the methodical details for manipulating the everyday world.

The Dream. Your dream is a vision of yourself in the near future. What is the future? Not something waiting for you but something you create through your imagination. The future is possibility waiting for form, the not-yet waiting to be programmed. Dreamers can taste their visions and feel compelled by them, as if they were self-evident truths. "We hold these truths to be self-evident," said our founding fathers, as they laid out the American dream that has guided us for more than 200 years. "I have a dream," yearned Martin Luther King more recently in Washington, D.C., as he painted a picture of equality and fairness in America. John Lennon's song "Imagine" is a dreamer's commitment to human transformation, shared by a generation now in midlife. The dream comes first. Then reality chases after the dream to make it happen. Dreams have the following qualities:

- A dream is a compelling picture of a desirable future. It is a poetic picture, not a literal statement. Once invented by the imagination, it hovers over a person as a lure toward the future.

- A good dream is simple, clear; it is easily recalled and rehearsed.
- A dream is a promise that is self-evident and convincing, an idea whose time has come. To think it is to go for it. It feels right, and it's going to happen.
- A dream is a visceral yearning, not a prediction or wish list. It taps a deep inner sense of personal destiny and provides pictures and voices for your inner sense of purpose. It is a picture of what you most deeply want your life to count for. A dream provides a total picture for how you want your life to become.
- A dream is a pull toward higher ground, an inspiration for becoming. It is not a dream to want a new car, an exotic vacation, or even a new career. A valid dream is comprehensive, anchored in the courage to be.
- A dream is a spiritual promise of a new quality of life, a deeper sense of being, a promise for human betterment that is just beyond your reach but worth reaching for and possible to approximate.
- A dream inspires and motivates; it doesn't order people around. When you live as a visionary adult, you have a dream, even if the dream doesn't translate into marching orders for every hour of the day. A dream is energy; whenever you think of it, you get a burst of personal power.
- A dream works like a rudder guiding you toward your chosen destination, keeping you "on course."
- A dream is like a haunting refrain. You know that you have one when it won't let you go and others are attracted to it within you. You know that you have a vision when it seems already to be guiding you toward its reality, and you don't have to explain it to yourself.

Much if not most of the dreaming that humans do takes place in childhood and adolescence. We encourage children and young adults to dream and to launch plans to achieve those dreams: "What do you want to do when you grow up?" In the adult years, however, when life is more complicated by many commitments and entrenched responsibilities, dreaming tends to be limited and episodic—a trip to Hawaii, moving into a new house, having an affair. Yet in truth, we never "grow up"; we just keep growing, and our human need for holistic dreaming pervades all of our life and never ends.

As far as we know, human beings are the only creatures on earth capable of envisioning a future and then setting about to make it happen. We dream and imagine; we expect and plan; we invent and create. This is how new companies get born, poems get conceived, Olympic races get won, music gets written, and inventions get made. Our greatest human power is our capacity to imagine, vision, and dream, over and over again. It is an essential part of the life-style of the self-renewing adult and the first step in empowering a satisfying life structure.

The Plan. Visioning and planning are very different. Dreams are imaginative, softheaded, motivating, and energy releasing. Planning is logical, hardheaded, factual, and realistic. Without a purposeful dream, planning is reduced to mechanical busyness. Without a realistic plan, dreams are random wishes—daydreams at best. Dreams impregnate new directions; plans help new directions develop and happen.

Few dreamers are good planners; few planners follow a dream. The two often war with each other, like hearts and heads, leaders and managers. To empower your life today, however, you need to be both a dreamer and a planner. When you plan, you take the visionary pictures of a dream and connect them to sympathetic worldly forces. A good planner protects the dream in two ways, by looking for environmental forces working against the plan and by adapting the dream to available resources.

Planning is more than a bunch of skills; it is an inner force, a felt competence, a strength within us. Planning is how our integrity gets the world to cooperate with the dream, and the dream with the world. The planner pushes forward with logical steps, like choosing reliable stepping stones to cross a stream. Through strategic thinking, the planner embroiders the dreamer's vision with the complexity of the world, weaving together technical and human resources required to bring the life structure into reality. In the life of any successful structurer, the possible dream becomes a probable plan.

A competent life planner follows four principles: First, he or she keeps the dream central to the plan. The plan is merely the instrument of the dream, never the raison d'être of a life structure. The dream stirs up awe and excitement for the journey, while the plan commits a person to an explicit course of action. A good planner implements good dreams; he or she is value driven. An incompetent planner becomes addicted to the mechanical details of management and short-term results; he gets lost in the forest.

Second, a competent life planner constructs plans that draw upon his or her own proven strengths that worked well in previous life structures. If you are a forty-five-year-old just beginning a new life structure, you need to know what has worked for you in previous life structures. A primary advantage of aging is the reservoir of experience that you accumulate; use it or lose it. People are full of "transferable skills." Competence gained from career can be used in family life, and vice versa. "When I ask middle-aged people to tell me what they do well," writes Judith Bardwick, "they say:

> I have an ability to make things happen and I enjoy that.
> I'm a good husband.
> I'm a good listener.
> I think I get along with people.
> I communicate.
> I'm very proud of my children and they love me and I love them.
> I'm a good manager.
> I organize things well.
> I have a sense of humor.
> I'm very good at helping people I care about.
> I'm a good friend.
> I find creative ways to solve problems.
> I feel good about my perspective on life.
> I'm honest and ethical.
> I can create an atmosphere of cooperation.
> I bring common sense to a situation.
> I demonstrate leadership.
> I'm aware of myself for the first time.
> I'm a good tactician.

I have good judgment.
I am a responsible person.
I have a very good relationship with my wife.
I am a very good wife and now I'm comfortable in that
    role.
I have maintained my integrity and have not sold out.
Middle age is value-added."[2]

What earlier were parenting skills may evolve as management
talent, and leisure skills of the past may shape an entrepreneurial
direction in tomorrow's life. Sales ability may now become redi-
rected as diplomatic skills, and the peak performer who liked to
"win" may evolve into a person who likes to "be." The most important human resources for the life planner are the virtues that
have worked in the past. Almost anyone who has survived forty
years of life has developed advanced personal skills that can create
new paths and opportunities.

Third, a competent life planner faces squarely his or her
limits and undeveloped abilities. By early midlife, virtually all
adults are lopsided human beings. By then, you have almost always
specialized in something—a career, parenting, profiteering, house-
keeping, serving, or a leisure life—and as your unique abilities
consume you, your undeveloped self and your deficits become more
and more obvious. As you specialize you forget basic skills in other
areas, and you further neglect your already neglected parts. By the
time you are forty or so, you are bound to feel that your life is out
of synch, merely because you have overaccentuated some of your
abilities, neglected others, and become dependent on other people
for significant segments of your life.

Carl Jung said that the real planner in the second half of life
is our "Undiscovered Self," which yearns to get born in our forties
and fifties. As we age, our neglected parts get louder voices for a say
in our (and their!) destiny. What were our so-called weaknesses may
now seek to become our strengths. They need training, education,
and opportunity. Some adults feel trapped in their own success,
where they feel bored as their specialized competence continues to
encapsulate them. The planner in us seeks to understand our weaknesses, to protect us from them or to turn them into assets.

Delores is a computer analyst wanting to become a manager. What skills does she already have? She may need training in leadership and interpersonal skills. Is she trainable and educable in those skills? How might she find out? Where would she get the training? What kinds of job openings would exist for her at salary levels that she can accept? Those are key planning questions.

George is a CEO wanting to retire and start a nursery, but he doesn't know how to stop thinking, talking, and behaving like a CEO. He panics at having to do all the chores himself, without an orchestration of helpers. What does it take to alter his management style, his personal needs, and the roles that he wants to leave behind?

Pamela is a full-time parent who now wants a career as a lawyer. Although she had a brief career as a lab technician in her twenties, she will need to enter law school and establish herself in that career. How can she draw from her wealth of experience to leverage herself ahead? How will schooling mesh with her existing life-style and commitments? Has she already worked with lawyers to be sure that this direction is part of her "dream"?

Maurice was addicted to his work, and he yearned to break his habit and begin again. When he met Marie, an investment broker fifteen years younger than he, he wondered what it would be like to be a househusband, with some volunteer activities and perhaps some children in the future. They married, and seven years later, he had quit his job and conquered his workaholism. He also was the full-time father of two small children and active in the docent programs in the local art museum and botanical gardens.

Fourth, a competent planner keeps adapting his or her dream to the changing realities of the social environment. The planner does not turn chaos into planned change, as so many say. Rather, the planner swims in the sea of change as cooperatively as possible, searching for available ways to a preferred destination. The planner constructs a relatively short-term game plan, with evaluative principles built in, so that the turbulent waters can be tested in an inductive, ad hoc way, little by little. The planner is an adapter, determined to shape a structure but not sure of every move to make. A plan is a living document, not a stone etching. Few dream/plans turn out the way they began. They take shape and get reshaped along the way. As new opportunities arise, the planner shifts gears to take advantage of them, if they serve the dream. When new obstacles appear, the planner creates new strategies to stay on course. At times, the planner may have to negotiate with the dreamer to modify the dimensions of the life structure in order to proceed. A capable planner is definite and flexible, committed and adaptable, centered and learning, loyal and clever.

Launching

The second change cycle skill for making a life structure succeed is launching, which puts the dream/plan to work. With launching, the imaginal dream and the realistic plan get projected into the systems of the world to see whether they congrue and stay in orbit. The launching process represents the months and years that it takes to bring the full life structure into reality. It is birthing time, a time for working and waiting, an expectant but busy phase in the construction of the future.

The launcher's job is to get the systems of the world to cooperate with the dream/plan and to modify the dream/plan so that it can fit the systems around it. The launcher aims at a successful completion in a plateauing orbit—a victory that can be sustained. But sometimes he or she chooses to abandon the life structure. Perhaps the mountain is too high, or resources for the climb have been expended. Perhaps the importance of the destination has changed, and the trip is called off. Although launchers aim at plateauing and winning, the good ones are prepared to abort if they have to. And if a launcher has to exit, he or she will decide either to renew the same life structure under different circumstances (restructuring) or to engage in a life transition so he or she can start all over again in new directions. The launching ability has two essential components—commitment and personal mission.

Commitment. To have a life structure, a person needs commitment, which means much more than compliance with the plan.

Commitment is persistence, dedication, interaction, and an intention to win. Commitment begins with adherence to one's own integrity. It is a steady covenant to be true to yourself and to those who share your path. Commitment is lived values. "A value is only a value if it is life-preserving and life-enhancing," writes Allan Bloom. "Commitment values the values and makes them valuable. . . . The hallmark of the *authentic self* is consulting one's oracle while facing up to what one is and what one experiences. *Decisions,* not deliberations, are the movers of deeds. One cannot know or plan the future. One must will it. There is no program."[3] True commitment is inner-driven and anchored to the dream within. Henry David Thoreau said, "A man must find his occasions in himself. . . . If one advances confidently in the direction of his dreams, and endeavors to live the life which he has imagined, he will meet with a success unexpected in common hours. . . . If a man does not keep pace with his companions, perhaps it is because he hears a different drummer. Let him step to the music which he hears, however measured or far away."[4]

While commitment is an inner decision to be definite, persistent, and determined, it is a learned behavior. Commitment requires faith, trust, hope, and patience—all inner capacities. Commitment requires risk taking, teamwork, and long-distance management—all outer capacities. Many adults in our society have not yet learned how to make their lives work; they lack the prerequisites of commitment, so they fall short of achieving a life structure. They need training in basic life skills that will help them effectively combine their intentionality with the resources of the world around them. They need training in two primary areas of true commitment: attachment and achievement. The ability to attach stems from emotional bonding and inner comfort with others and with adult roles. The ability to achieve stems from clear thinking and actions that make the external world approximate the dream. Both attachment and achievement are necessary skills for creating successful life structures. Both can be learned.

Commitment is more than inner determination; it requires worldly savvy and risk taking. Plans are merely blueprints for action. Launching requires leadership, collaboration, networking, adaptation, incorporation of new opportunities, safeguards against new threats, and timing. Successful launchers have internal gyroscopes keeping them balanced and moving toward their dreams; they also have radar, keeping them apprised of worldly conditions. Sorting out the signals, launchers make their moves.

Personal Mission. When you have a dream and a plan working together in the construction of a life structure, you have a "mission," a circumscribed purpose that defines your use of time and space for the duration of this particular life structure. People with a mission know where they want to go. A person with a mission is clear about what he or she will and won't do to serve the priorities of the plan. The boundaries for taking action are relatively crisp and definite. Life is a challenge, and the singular focus is to reach the goal line of a successful plateau. This is the all-American place to be: aimed at winning. "Winning," said A. Bartlett Giamatti in a speech when he was president of Yale University, "has a joy and discrete purity to it that cannot be replaced by anything else. Winning is important to any man's or woman's sense of satisfaction and well-being. Winning is not everything, but it is something powerful, indeed beautiful, in itself, something as necessary to the strong spirit as striving is necessary to the healthy character."

To win, you must grow your dreams in the structures of the world around you. That is not easy. Every social system has its own rules and prerogatives, and they do not easily cooperate with individual priorities. A successful launcher convinces whatever systems that he or she needs to cooperate with his or her dream/plan or adapts his or her dream/plan to the systems in order to find congruence. In that exchange, however, a trick is played: Once the dream is embedded in the world, it begins to be entrapped; it begins to die, and the external structures begin to control the person. Sustaining your personal mission means staying on the path that belongs to you, and this requires continuous evaluation of the journey. The ability to evaluate your journey is critical to staying on course. "Am I on course or off course?" the launcher asks, and if he or she is off course, corrective measures are taken. The launcher wants to win but loves the challenge of winning almost as much. He or she wants to be a peak performer with optimal performance. If the plan is not working or the dream is judged to be outdated, the healthy launcher aborts the mission and moves the structure as rapidly as possible to disengagement, where a decision is made either to take the minitransition for restructuring the life structure or to begin a life transition in search of new directions.

Plateauing

The third change cycle skill is plateauing, the art of sustaining a successful life structure. Oscar Wilde once remarked that "In this world there are only two tragedies. One is not getting what one wants, and the other is getting it."[5] Plateauing is knowing how to stay at the top of your realized dream and to keep enriching the dream/plan for as long as it makes sense to do so. People who succeed in achieving or becoming the life structure that they have been pursuing discover that making a plateau work is a new ball game. Some people like it and thrive on it. They bask in the recognition and rewards and strive to enhance their position. Others experience themselves slipping into a pensive reevaluation and a loss of motivation.

There tend to be two distinct periods of plateauing, early and late. The first few months and years of plateauing serve to sort out the long distance runners from the discomforted. The plateau pursuers lack the capacity to enjoy their own success. They don't really want to succeed; they just want to prove that they can win. For them, being there is not as exciting as getting there. Some people who arrive at a plateau feel an absence of challenge, and they move toward exiting and disengagement. They may have a fear of success that keeps them from settling into the plateau. These are often loners who move from job to job, from relationship to relationship, and from city to city, repeating their pursuit of success without achieving sustained success. They are pursuers of a plateau, not plateauers. They have not learned how to love success and to thrive on it.

The long-distance runners are positive plateauers who become their finest selves in their plateauing roles. This is their victory, and they want to invest in it. They renew their vision within the plateau so they can keep growing within the structure. They learn to mentor others, to shape policies, to serve as ambassadors for their organizations, and to leave some legacy. They have staying power. They maintain their success by pursuing new levels of attainment, influence, growth, discovery, and contribution. Or, if parenting was the core of the dream plan, they grow with their children to find more of themselves. Long-distance runners function with what Abraham Maslow called "unconscious competence," the effortless, masterful capabilities of high-performing people. They thrive on constancy, loyalty, honest criticism, curiosity, and a zest for life. Although they enjoy the security and safety of their successful life structures, they keep growing within their plateaus and do not see themselves as having arrived at the top of their climb.

Instead of climbing another mountain, long-distance runners can sit and enjoy the one they are on and find new adventures there. Instead of having to prove themselves again, they can improve who they already are. Instead of boring themselves and needing a "road not yet taken," they find new and fulfilling destinations on the road that they have already mastered. A plateau is meant to be a dynamic and ongoing celebration of a life structure, a time of considerable stability, creativity, and recognition. If the world cooperates with more order than chaos, healthy plateauers tend to their knitting.

Managing the Doldrums

Phase 2 in a life structure is feeling out of synch, as if the plateau and even the life structure were "slip-sliding away." During even the most successful plateaus, gremlins invade to disturb the peace. With the flattening of your personal mission in the plateau, there is a tendency to lose momentum, to rest on your oars, and to defend the status quo. As your motivation fades out, forces inside and outside of your life structure invade to challenge your halcyon days. Sooner or later, you begin to look in on your life structure and to question it, as if part of you were already living outside of it. You want to improve it, you think, but your questions penetrate your inner confidence. The comfort, optimism, naiveté, and unconditional determination are blunted by a growing chorus of discomfort, pessimism, and worries. Out of your own success have come forces that are now working against you, and you begin to question whether the "success and happiness" that you have achieved are lasting friends. Instead of enjoying your plateau as the success you deserve, you feel like you are treading water to avoid drowning.

"Managing the doldrums" is a change cycle that addresses a threefold sequence of regressive experiences. It begins with sensing decline ("Why isn't my life as alive and challenging as it used to be?"), which evolves to feeling trapped ("I'm mad/depressed/scared as hell, and I'm not going to take it any more") and ends up as resisting change ("Life used to work wonderfully, so I'm going to keep things the way they were"). The predictable sequence is from thinking (noticing decline) to feeling (awareness of being diminished and trapped—scared, angry, depressed) to decision-making (choosing ways to restabilize the life structure), and the job of the doldrums manager is to sort out what is working from what isn't so that a realistic and proactive plan of action—rather than a reactive one—can be followed.

Sensing Decline. There comes a time when the dream of the life structure loses its luster, even though you continue to go through the routines of pretending that the life structure is alive and well. Usually, in the plateau of a life structure, the demise begins. Restlessness, defensiveness, inflexibility, or some acting-out behaviors reveal that the plateau has led to a downward slide. You may be thoroughly bored with your plateau, but since it is the only environment that you can imagine for your life, you deny the boredom and complain, reminisce, and pretend that all is well. Pushed to the margins of your plateau, where your rewards and recognition are minimal, you yearn to make the life structure work again, but already the seeds of a transition have been sown, and you have begun to disengage from the life structure. Decliners have a sense of living in the past without a clear future. They go through their days looking in on their lives, knowing that they are living on borrowed time. They have low energy, are easily tempted by addictions, and have a high level of denial that anything is wrong. The out-of-synch process for a decliner is an inner dialogue of dissonance and conflict.

Once you "succeed" and receive the rewards of money, pres-

tige, recognition, and status—or whatever you mean by success—
you will probably want to "freeze" your life structure to keep it safe
and available forever. You assume that your marriage and family
will be happy from now on. You talk about "security," "financial
independence," "tenure," "partnership," "benefit packages," or
other ways to corral your success as a permanent acquisition. You
become protective of number one, and a bit paranoid about the
intentions of others around you. The minute you shift gears to
contain your success, you blur your original dream and mission.
Secondary gains replace your primary passion. It is not just that
your life structure has lost air out of its balloon; the various parts
of your life are conflicting with one another. Perhaps your spouse
wants you to be different from the way you are. Or you may be
working harder at your work than ever before but receiving negative
criticism for your efforts. Or perhaps the value of the dollar has
declined, and your economic position is in jeopardy.

Instead of living within a proactive dream/plan, you are now
defensive and reactive. Instead of adventuring with your structure
as a charismatic leader, you are retreating into past achievements as
a mechanical manager, and you don't know where you are going.
And, as the old adage goes, "If you don't know where you're going,
any road will get you there." Your main intent at this time is to hold
on to your gains, at all costs. Those around you who are now vital
to your life structure may think that you have sold out and abandoned your right to be in charge. The screw has turned, and your
place in the life structure may have become, in the minds of others,
a liability to their life structures. They say that you are having an
identity crisis, while you feel that a power struggle is going on
among them. The dissonance and conflict sap your energy and
confuse you. "Sensing decline" is the thinking process of an out-
of-synch person; the feeling side can be described as "feeling
trapped."

Feeling Trapped. At this point, you feel very confused. Your
emotions are like a roller coaster. Throughout the building of your
life structure, you had down times when you felt discouraged, sad,
or angry. The difference now is that your bad feelings dominate
your space and time as if they were part of your character. You feel

outraged by the surge of negative emotions. You thought that you had earned the right to a life of positive emotions, with happiness and cooperation lasting forever. You feel betrayed by your own success, undermined by people you trusted (including yourself), lost in confusion, and unable to sort things out. Sometimes you feel angry; at other times sad. Frequently you feel scared that you will lose your life structure. Drained by the complexities of this navel gazing, you now feel as if you were a caretaker of the home of someone else—someone you used to be. As the song by Harry Chapin goes, "there's no tick-tock on your electric clock, but still your life runs down."[6]

Some people accuse you of being stressed out. Others say that you have burnout or a midlife crisis. You keep waiting for the feelings of stagnation to go away, but they get worse and worse. You try to reassess your options but decide that it's better to feel bad about the decline of your life structure than to feel the loss of it altogether. As someone once said, "The only difference between a rut and a grave is the depth of the excavation." Judith Bardwick has captured the predicament of the out-of-synch person who has already succeeded in achieving a plateau: "When we are plateaued, we are not so much actively unhappy as we are just not happy. We could continue to live as we are, because usually it's not awful. But it is also not joyous. If we are truly unhappy, change is easier than when we are just not happy. When the negative is powerful, the need to change is obvious. Most of us do not make changes in our lives until the pain in the present eclipses our fear of the future."[7]

People who succeed at life structuring usually expend their energy outside of themselves, manipulating the world around them. They are seldom trained to manage this implosion of feelings within themselves. Indeed, they are seldom trained to manage their feelings at all, and this is one reason why the out-of-synch phase is so badly managed by so many adults. The decision side of "sensing decline" and "feeling trapped" is resisting change.

Resisting Change. When you sense decline and feel trapped, you resist change. Somebody is raining on your parade, trying to take your life structure away, trying to evict you! The decision here is to hold on and keep things the way they are, even if you are bored, unhappy, ineffective, and destructive. Resisters are reactive and often masochistic. In high denial, they back into their future. They tough it out and endure whatever happens as they live within a double bind: They don't know how to enjoy continuing in the life structure, but they can't or won't leave. Remember Richard Nixon's Watergate?

Robert Tannenbaum and Robert W. Hanna explain that "1. Change is loss. . . . 2. Change is uncertainty. . . . 3. Change dissolves meaning. . . . 4. Change violates scripts. . . . In sum, whenever a new situation or our own evolving growth prompts us to make a change in the construction of reality (identity, world view, philosophy of life), there is a need to hold on."[8] John Gardner says, "Human beings have always employed an enormous variety of clever devices for running away from themselves. . . . [We] can keep ourselves so busy, fill our lives with so many diversions, stuff our heads with so much knowledge, involve ourselves with so many people and cover so much ground that we never have time to probe the fearful and wonderful world within. . . . By middle life, most of us are accomplished fugitives from ourselves."[9]

The doldrums manager looks for ways either to restore confidence and commitment to the dream/plan or to end the life structure as it is now. Either you recapture the inspiration and commitment that you had for your life structure as your personal mission, or you give up the life structure and seek a new one before circumstance wrenches it away from you. The less time you are in the doldrums, the better, because they tend to become a bitter prison for the helpless and the enraged. Instead of sensing decline, you need a plan for the future. Instead of feeling trapped, you need positive feelings of empowerment. Instead of resisting change, you need to choose a future that will be fulfilling.

Sorting Things Out

The ultimate job of the doldrums manager is to help you decide what to do and who to be. You must move beyond merely repeating the past. You figure out what to hold on to and what to let go of. You conduct a thorough inventory of your life, asking only one question of each assumption, possession, relationship, activity, and structure: "Does this add meaning to my life?" If it does, you keep it; if it doesn't, you prepare for surgery of some sort. You identify necessary alterations in your life structure that you believe will improve your life. You consider the possible advantages of moving on.

Sorting things out is like a game of keepers and leavers. The keepers are the continuing aspects that work and empower the life structure—the roles, tasks, relationships, opportunities, challenges. The leavers are those items that detour you from purposive activity within your structure. Sort them out: Delegate what doesn't belong to you; eliminate parts of the structure that have led you astray; alter your roles to comply with your current inner strengths at this phase of the structuring process. Stay true to your passionate values, and rearrange your life structure accordingly.

Some of the sorting out has to do with external issues. As your life structure evolved through its plateau, it probably became more complex, with more people and systems involved, deepening your embeddedness. How do you now sustain your accomplishments without being burdened by them? How do you maintain the routines of your structure without losing your sense of mission? How do you continue indefinitely to feel visionary and committed to your life structure? How do you let others gain ownership of parts of your life structure? How do you let go of roles and functions that were profoundly rewarding to you earlier in the life structure? How do you take advantage of new opportunities when you are so wrapped up in your current situation? Ric Masten, a contemporary poet, calls it "Not Exactly a Command Performance":

> have you ever sat back
> and looked at the life you were living
> and saw that it was playing
> like a really bad B movie?
> appalled and taken back
> by the inane lines you were saying
> and the unrestrained way you were weeping
> and waving your arms about
> over acting
> but what really burns
> is the knowledge
> that someone of your reputed good taste

would sit through such silly hogwash
unable to leave till you learn
how the damn thing comes out.[10]

Sorting things out is a process of evaluating how to proceed when a life structure gets blurry and dysfunctional and your role becomes less and less clear. If you are successful at sorting, you will make four piles: things to hold on to, things to let go of, new things or skills to take on, and a game plan for when to move on to either restructuring or cocooning.

Typically, but not necessarily, a life structure lasts several years and ends when something slowly or suddenly, internally or externally, triggers an ending. A trigger upsets the tenuous balance of an out-of-synch life and provokes or requires a person to let go and move on. Some typical internal triggers of a life transition are boredom, loss, panic, stress, and a yearning for a road not taken. Some typical external triggers of a life transition are accident or sickness, loss of a job, having a baby, sudden changes in the financial market, separation or divorce, change of geographical location, becoming a grandparent, death of a family member or friend, inheriting money, empty nest, a promotion, new friendships, career change, returning to school, traveling, and retirement. Each person has life structures of varying lengths, and each sequential life structure will differ from previous ones in duration. When you disengage from a life structure, you have two choices: either take a minitransition and restructure your life or engage in a life transition that involves you in new growth and future possibilities. The prevailing preference until midlife or later is to restructure through a mini-transition. Perhaps you move to a new location to start over. Perhaps you change career positions or companies. Maybe you alter relationships in your personal life or face medical treatments that you had been postponing. In any case, you are ready to say good-bye to the doldrums and to your life structure the way it has been. Your eyes are riveted on the future.

Goodbye and Farewell

The change cycle skill to say good-bye and disengage from a life structure is an essential adult ability possessed by few. Most adults are not trained to exit or depart from their heroic space and time; they would rather stay distressed. When they do leave, they often demean themselves or attack those around them. The self-renewing adult designs exits that honor both those remaining and those leaving—a win-win strategy. Good endings are marker events—turning points that deserve rituals for celebrating the importance of life lived and life ahead.

Endings are symbolically the acceptance of death as reality, yet most of us spend our lifetimes denying the many deaths that we experience in the form of losses. It is our endings, more than our beginnings, that keep us committed to living as fully as we can. "If you can begin to see death as an invisible, but friendly, companion on your life's journey," writes Erich Lindemann, "gently reminding you not to wait till tomorrow to do what you mean to do—then you can learn to *live* your life rather than simply passing through it."[11] Perhaps Elisabeth Kubler-Ross has said this as powerfully as anyone: "It is the denial of death that is partially responsible for people living empty, purposeless lives; for when you live as if you'll live forever, it becomes too easy to postpone the things you know that you must do. You live your life in preparation for tomorrow or in remembrance of yesterday, and meanwhile, each today is lost."[12] There is no way to progress deeply into the future without taking leave of the past—making a leap of faith into an unknown future. The pain of loss becomes motivation to learn how to look ahead instead of backward. Disengagement is usually experienced as a loss, but it also is a liberation, a graduation, a commencement.

Restructuring: The Minitransition

The seventh change cycle skill, restructuring, leads back to phase 1, with a revised plan attached to a renewed dream. Restructuring is repairing and updating the same life structure, leaving it strengthened and improved. It is enacting the plans that have been made to improve the life structure and to begin again. A minitransition is a fairly rapid return to reenact the same dream with a slightly different plan. Restructuring feels like you are crossing a bridge to familiar territory. This produces a catharsis, with renewed energy, confidence, and determination. You feel on course, following your path again. You have restored a sense of purpose and mission in your life. You are on your way.

Restructuring makes sense when the structure is basically healthy, but some minor changes must be made for the structure to work effectively under current conditions. For example, you can move to a different location, change positions, or change companies but keep the career you are in, or divorce or remarry. Or you can change careers, join a religious organization, enter therapy, take an intensive seminar training program, begin dieting, or schedule time in a health spa. The minitransition or restructuring works when the dysfunctions causing distress are locatable and fixable. In effect, the old dream and life structure are rejuvenated and extended, and this actually goes on throughout the entire lives of some people who have high stability in their lives to provide continuous cohesion. During the adult years, a person may repeat the upper half of the circle several times, maintaining a life structure by reconstructing it over and over.

Restructuring is like a personal strategic plan that extends the old plan by reformulating it. The deep places of the self do not have to be searched and transformed. However, if a restructuring fails or proves futile, a person ends up, naturally, cocooning and then proceeds through the life transition route on the bottom of the cycle described in Map 1. A minitransition is a purging of the life structure, whereas a life transition is a purging of the self. One is the way of strategic planning for structural reform; the other is the way of personal transformation. One is to repair and to upgrade what is; the other is to metamorphose toward new possibilities. A minitransition is like getting an automobile repaired; a life transition is like acquiring a new car. Virtually everyone elects the way of minitransitions—over and over—until leaving the life structure itself is either a worldly necessity or less painful than remaining. At some point in the life cycle, everyone finds the path into a life transition to be necessary or preferable to the restructuring route. A competent adult needs to master both minitransitions and life transitions at different times in the life course. Neither is intrinsically better, and both are necessary and inevitable.

The route through a life transition takes much longer than

the minitransition but provides profound personal renewal and leads to a new and usually different life structure. The choice of routes is not always an option. If you experience a trigger event with sufficient emotional force and reality information as to require an immediate exit from the structure—as with the death of a spouse— cocooning will begin, and efforts to restructure will be futile. However, for a great many people and organizations, restructuring is the only acceptable format for dealing with intense change. They dread the thought of entering a full-fledged transition, which they perceive as failure, a waste of time, a loss of status, or pure terror. So they repeat the same patterns of achievement and decline from their past, often with decreasing passion and vision. Better they had gone with the river the other way, into a life transition. When you are overwhelmed by change and faced with losses beyond your ability to contain, you choose or accept the path that leads through a life transition. As you approach it, it feels like an impossibility, yet most everyone emerges from one with new life and perspective. Mircea Eliade, an outstanding teacher on myths and rituals, has written: "In no rite or myth do we find the initiatory death as something *final*, but always as the condition *sine qua non* of a transition to another mode of being, a trial indispensable to regeneration; that is, to the beginning of a new life."[13]

In 1908, the Dutch anthropologist Arnold Van Gennep published *The Rites of Passage*, describing the life events that constitute human turning points: separation from the group or society; transition or revision of the personal agenda; and incorporation back into the group with new roles and functions.[14] The next four personal skills that guide the cycle of change through a life transition—disengaging, cocooning, self-renewal, and exploring— perform the functions of separation, transition, and incorporation.

5

From Disengaging
to Cocooning

Any real change implies the break up of the world as
one has always known it, the loss of all that gave one
identity, the end of safety. And at such a moment,
unable to see and not daring to imagine what the future will now bring forth, one clings to what one
knew, or thought one knew; to what one possessed or
dreamed that one possessed. Yet it is only when man
is able, without bitterness or self pity, to surrender a
dream he has long cherished, or a privilege he has
long possessed, that he is set free—that he has set himself free—for higher dreams, for greater privileges.
—*James Baldwin, Nobody Knows My Name*[1]

In November 1980, when Jimmy and Rosalynn Carter left the White
House, they plunged into a disturbing life transition. Their lives
were at a dead end—the former president had suffered a crushing
defeat by Ronald Reagan, his peanut business was one million dol-
lars in debt, and the Iran hostage crisis remained unresolved. Rosalynn felt as dejected and rejected as Jimmy did, perhaps more. After
they returned to their home in Plains, Georgia, each wrote separate
accounts:

Jimmy: Many people have to accept the same shocking
changes in their lives as we did that winter: the involuntary

end of a career and an uncertain future; the realization that "retirement" age is approaching; the return to a home without the children we had raised there; new family relationships, for which there had been no preparation. And in our case, all this was exacerbated by the embarrassment about what was to us an incomprehensible political defeat and also by some serious financial problems that we had been reluctant to confront. . . . Although my disappointment was great, I kept it bottled up for a long time.

Rosalynn: There was no way I could understand our defeat. . . . Would we ever look back on this election and say losing was for the best? . . . Not long after we came home, Amy went off to boarding school in Atlanta, our last child to leave home. We were lonely without her. . . . There was another adjustment that we had to make. For the first time we were both at home together all day every day, and as much as we care for each other this sometimes proved difficult. . . . There was still the longer-term question of how we could make our work more meaningful.

Jimmy: We became confident that we would find significant outside activities while living in the quiet environs of our youth. We especially enjoyed the luxury of walking through the woods and fields for miles without seeing a single house. . . . What we had done was to seek out, in our chosen home community, those things that were the most meaningful to us. . . . There is no doubt that the healing period after the political defeat was also a learning process for both of us, sometimes together and at other times a slowly evolving understanding deep within us individually.

Rosalynn: One night I woke up and Jimmy was sitting straight up in bed. He always sleeps so soundly that I thought he must be sick. "What's the matter?" I asked. "I know what we can do at the library," he said. "We can develop a place to help people who want to resolve disputes. There is no place like that now." . . . He talked on enthusiastically about other areas where negotiation might help—in domestic disputes and in dealing with civil laws. A center to settle disputes. For the first time since our return to Plains I saw Jimmy really excited about possible plans for the future.

Jimmy: Since leaving the White House we have had a chance to revive a number of our old interests and pursue some new ones, a process that we hope will continue for the rest of our lives. There is no way to know how many years we will have to spend together, and we want to make the most of them. In addition to having a good time, we have taken on some challenging projects, but our tendency has been to move toward the simpler activities that we can share with each other and our friends—and enjoy now and for a long time to come.[2]

Now, over ten years later, Jimmy Carter appears all over the globe, as an ordinary man with a heart, mediating disputes from Ethiopia to Nicaragua. Although his presidency seemed to end in personal disaster, and his brothers and sisters have since died, Jimmy's current life and work now symbolize—perhaps better than the presidency did—his deep beliefs in universal human rights and world peace. The crisis of his transition became an opportunity for finding new ways to connect his personal integrity to social happenings.

Transitions Are Normal

Life transitions happen. They happen to presidents and to ordinary people. They happen to rich and poor, to men and women of all ages. They are a part of life. They represent down times during which new personal resources are created or discovered. Just as every automobile sooner or later needs a major overhaul, so do we. Life transitions are normal and inevitable parts of adult life; they clarify life issues and life direction. They are retreats into the deep recesses of our real selves. Successful transitions simplify, purify, center, and empower a person's life course. They purge the past and define the future.

Transitions often happen because of circumstances that we don't control, so we end up in some transitions not of our choosing, as with many who survived such disasters as the San Francisco earthquake, the Charleston hurricane, the Santa Barbara fire, and the Persian Gulf war. Or they happen because we get older or our values change or our jobs end. In a time of rapid change, transitions occur more frequently in our lives. Many things trigger change that we cannot control. Yet sometimes they happen just because we choose them.

Transitions follow a predictable pattern—from loss to rebirth—whether they are personal transitions or transitions within marriages, families, corporations, or nations. Adults can be trained to anticipate and facilitate them. There are specific abilities that we can cultivate for enhancing the process. However, we first must recognize and accept the positive functions of transitions. A great many people think of transitions as a penalty box, a place for losers, quitters, and weaklings—people who can't take the heat, people who have failed or become unlucky, victims who thrive on self-pity and helplessness. With this perspective, an ending sounds like the end, and proof that we are dying. "It sounds so negative," reported an out-of-synch person in considerable distress. "Why would I want to have one?" The acceptance of an ending sounds like termination, humiliation, resignation, and defeat. Many would say that it is better to do your best to make a worn out, dysfunctional life structure work and to tough it out than to face a life transition. That very attitude, erroneous as it is, keeps thousands of people locked into life structures that have died and into routines that are lifeless.

Such high denial and devaluation of transitions come at a very high price, in stress, relationship damage, financial losses, time wasted, and the reduction of future options. Refusal to process an ending creates a storage pile of barnacles from your past that clutter all your future life options. The gradual disablement of so many adults in midlife occurs because they lack the ability and courage to let go of the exhausted or toxic structures of their lives. The truth is that saying good-bye is not cowardly when it is spoken by the voice of the courage to be. Transitions, however disorienting and painful they may be at first, are usually pathways for growth and discovery. Your personal transitions are as important as your life structures in the construction of your life course, because transitions cleanse, center, and connect you to the deeper currents of your life.

The basic issue is this: Denying the value of the transition territory is a major cultural deficit, keeping us from knowing how to manage the inevitable losses of our own lives, which in turn keeps us from being free agents for living into the future.

What Is a Life Transition?

- A transition is a natural process of disorientation and reorientation that alters the perception of self and world and demands changes in assumptions and behavior.
- A transition is a process of reconstruction affecting the interiority of the self—identity and being, values and feelings and thinkings. Transformation occurs from the inside out.
- A transition requires a "temporary" social structure for support and validation; a "holding environment" providing an atmosphere of safety, acceptance and toleration; and "transition objects and persons" who facilitate the transition process.
- A life transition affects all aspects of a person's life—personal confidence, intimate bonds, family interaction, jobs and careers, social commitments, and ultimate concerns.
- Life transitions proceed gradually and sporadically. Grieving, healing, and renewal are organic and take time. There is no shortcut, no quick fix. Adult life transitions typically take one to three years.

The transition model presented here begins with disengagement from a life structure and concludes with reintegration with social forces.

   Disengagement. There are three change cycle skills that facilitate this phase, each of which is an ability for regenerating the self: ending (letting go of the life structure in its dysfunctional form), cocooning (grieving and healing), and self-renewal (tapping core values and inner resources). Self-renewal links disengagement and reintegration. It is a new grounding, a new anchoring of the self, a new experience of "being," characterized by self-sufficiency, peacefulness, purpose, and energy. Like fresh clay hitting the potter's wheel, the self-renewing self becomes centered, balanced, and formed around the residual self with its inner strength, vitality, and esteem. Although self-renewal at first feels like a gift, it quickly becomes a conscious skill for defining personal boundaries and creating a new future.

Reintegration. The renewed self seeks interaction again with external resources, primarily through three skills: experimentation, creativity, and networking, leading eventually to a new dream/plan and life structure. The reintegration phase is a hopeful, optimistic, awakening period, often involving training, travel, and new behaviors. Being and doing begin a new dance as inner joy projects itself into the world around it.

The Purpose of a Transition. The purpose of a transition is to learn a story about your life that you don't yet know so that you can stop living merely to repeat the stories that you already do know—to free your inner self from those external structures that are now dysfunctional or unavailable and to prepare for an important journey that you have not yet taken.

In my house, in which live three young boys, we have some animals that remind us of this process. Our pet snake, for example, loses its skin every few months as it grows. Although we are so amazed at the beauty of the skin that is shed that we display it for everyone to see, we don't mourn the death; we marvel at the life. The pollywogs that we catch at a local pond grow into tiny frogs in time; the fish-form stops living as the amphibian takes on the life. A few weeks ago at a picnic, the boys picked several stalks of fennel that had caterpillars in them. We placed the fennel and the caterpillars in a covered bowl, where the caterpillars made cocoons. Today they opened to release several silent, magnificent, yellow butterflies, all born within an hour of one another. Like snakes and pollywogs and butterflies, adults sometimes lose their previous orientations and retreat into what looks like oblivion in order to incubate new life orientations and life-styles that fit them better for moving into the future.

Disengagement: Ending

When talking about entering a life transition, I often use an eight-word chant that goes like this: "Hold on, let go, take on, move on" (repeat over and over). A transition is a time to *hold on* to what is working in your life, *let go* of what is not working, *take on* new learning and exploration of options, and *move on* to new commitments.[3] All four of these are normal and necessary for growth and development. As you depart from a life structure, however, letting go seems like all there is, because you are much more aware of what you are leaving than where you are going. Only later do you discover the importance of the other three abilities. The first task, and the hardest one to manage, in our culture at least, is letting go. Why? More than 300 years ago, de Tocqueville observed that Americans "are externalizers, doers, achievers." These are essential virtues for building life structures, but there are other virtues for making life work well, and particularly for making transitions succeed. They begin with letting go.

Doers like to move from one activity to another, from one mountain to another. They like achievement and results. Doers receive recognition and prestige in our culture. But an accumulation of doings will actually disempower you if you don't renew your "being" in between doings. You will achieve less and get poorer results as you try harder and harder. You can't run a car on an empty tank. A transition renews your being and prepares you for new doings. Most of all, a transition rekindles hope—a sense of a preferred future. Just as a life structure is an externalizing development of your self, a transition is an internalizing development of your self in which new meeting points are devised for connecting your past, present, and future. A transition is a turning point, from the conscious to the unconscious, toward resources and perspectives that you don't know you have. Although there are few cultural rewards or recognitions for successful transitioning, there is personal awareness at the conclusion of a life transition that you are more in charge of your life and destiny than you have ever been before.

Hugh Prather says, "When you find yourself in a battle with life, lose. There are no triumphs over truth."[4] Mary Baker Eddy often remarked, "When it ceases to bless, it ceases to be." You have to sustain congruence with all the parts of your life to sustain self-esteem, productivity, love, and joy. If you insist on lugging your bruised, Band-Aided, dysfunctional life structure into your future and pasting it onto a new scenario, you are bound to be filled with hesitation and conflict, not a new beginning. You will probably feel condemned to spend the rest of your life in the doldrums. Better that you refurbish the vessel that takes you on all your journeys throughout your entire life: your "self," that inner creature who monitors your life space, your many roles, your private moments, your fire.

Disengagement is a change cycle skill that promotes proactive exiting, a "hero's farewell" from a successful life structure. To help you disengage, you can declare a sabbatical, take a leave of absence, negotiate a withdrawal, or design a graduation or commencement. You can create a succession plan that is fair to you and to the structure so that others can take care of the life structure that you are leaving behind. You can ask for whatever blessings and benefits you feel you deserve, but exit with style, dignity, and caring.

In his book *Loss and Change*, Peter Marris takes bereavement as a model for understanding all profound change, personal and social. He states, "The fundamental crisis of bereavement arises not from the loss of others but from the loss of self—the loss of purpose, of interest, and above all, of meaning."[5] Psychologist Ellen Y. Siegelman relates the story of Beth, a talented young jeweler, who reported: "Being stuck, being depressed is awful. But it's safe. It's—well—it's like walking around in the dark in a room you hate. . . . You can tell in the dark where every table, every nicked chair is, every picture, every ashtray. You could walk it blindfolded without bumping or scraping. It may be an ugly room, a drab room, but it's *familiar*. But when you change—when you take a risk or do something that's way out of character for you—it's different. It's like being thrust in the dark into a furnished room that is unfamiliar. This is probably a more interesting room, one you may get to like because it's going to be all yours. But the furniture is strange. You don't know where anything is yet. You might bump into something knobby and hard, you might trip and fall."[6]

Exiting is often a lonely act, even if there are friends and loved ones supporting you. The ending strips you of roles, routines, and relationships that used to seem permanent and essential to your being. As you exit from the life structure within which you spun the living of your days and years, you have only two attitudes to choose from: either you feel evicted and abandoned by the best days of your life or you feel grateful that you lived fully in that life structure and now have an opportunity to journey on. In either case, you feel the loss. "Recovery from loss," writes Ann Kaiser Stearns, "is like having to get off the main highway every so many miles because the direct route is under reconstruction. The road signs reroute you through little towns you hadn't expected to visit and over bumpy roads you hadn't wanted to bounce around on. You are basically traveling in the appropriate direction. On the map, however, the course you are following has the look of shark's teeth instead of a straight line. Although you are gradually getting there, you sometimes doubt that you will ever again meet up with the finished highway."[7]

Fortunately, transitions almost always lead to renewal. As you disengage from the external life structure, you turn inward to heal. Healing is fundamentally human and normal, not medical. It involves preparing all of you for a livable future. Healing takes time, a lot of time. There is no way to rush the river of a transition, and hurrying will only sabotage the renewal and impede the success of a new life structure. Healing not only binds the wounds; it opens new doors and windows within you. You gain access to more of your personal abilities. You find strength that you didn't know was there. You discover that by letting go of unworkable parts of your external life, you are holding on to profound continuities deep within you. As you heal, you feel free to take on new possibilities for your life and to move on into a new life structure that fits you the way you are today, driven by the deeper currents of your own heart and soul.

Cocooning

When the dream dies and you depart your former life structure, you may encounter what feels like a room with no exits—an empty soul with no future. You may feel an intense loss without much awareness of any gain or hope or promise for improvement. If you are not sad and depressed, something is wrong with you!

When a life transition begins, your life loses its reference points, its anchors in your life structure. You may feel like an abandoned orphan, a betrayed person, a mistake, a lost soul. You live in unordinary space and time, suspended in a nonscript that floats heavily through days and nights. You may well have felt this way for a long time, but now the terror of your aloneness reaches full force. Your energy dissipates, and the routines and relationships in your life seem strange and distant. You feel like a nobody, a hollow vessel looking backward on the life that you have no more. As your familiar territory becomes unavailable to you, you feel lost, alienated, and alone. Cocooning feels like a death experience—all endings and no beginnings. Typically, you go through some or all of the stages of dealing with dying: denial, bargaining, anger, fear, grieving the loss, and finally finding acceptance and moving forward. Arnold R. Beisser, paralyzed by polio since age twenty-five, now says at thirty-six, "Years ago, I realized that being afraid of dying was really a cover for being afraid to live. . . . There are advantages to an ever-present awareness of death, if it makes you realize how precious life is and that each moment should be savored."[8] The loss of the life structure is finally experienced as relief so that the vital, emerging self can construct a new structure that fits its current condition and emergent future.

Living with Loss. Managing intense loss is virtually un-American. We hospitalize it, medicate it, therapize it, and attempt to eliminate it. Yet loss is a natural part of the normal development of a human system, and it persists in our human experience. Robert Greenleaf expresses this with simple elegance:

> To be on with the journey one must have an attitude toward loss and being lost, a view of oneself in which powerful symbols like *burned, dissolved, broken off*—however painful their impact is seen to be—do not appear as senseless or destructive. Rather the losses they suggest are seen as opening the way for new creative acts, for the receiving of priceless gifts. Loss, *every loss one's mind can conceive of,* creates a vacuum into which will come (if allowed) something new and fresh and beautiful, something unforeseen—and the greatest of these is *love.* The source of this attitude toward loss and being lost is *faith:* faith in the validity of one's own inward experience; faith in the wisdom of the great events of one's history, events

in which one's potential for nobility has been tested and refined; faith in doubt, in inquiry, and in the rebirth of wisdom;
faith in the possibility of achieving a measure of sainthood on
this earth from which flow concerns and responsibility and a
sense of rightness in all things. By these means mortals are
raised above the possibility of hurt. They will suffer, but they
will not be hurt because each loss grants them the opportunity
to be greater than before. Loss, by itself, is not tragic. What
is tragic is the failure to grasp the opportunity which loss
presents.[9]

Unfortunately, few of us are trained with skills that will empower
us through transitions, and even if we did, we would remain bewildered by the disorientation of personal loss. The approved cultural
solution is to turn loss over to "professionals" who are experts at
"dysfunctions" when what we need most is to heal and renew
ourselves.

Of course, there are some people whose life transitions
trigger regressive issues that express themselves through social mal-
adaptation or mental illness; these people need medical and psychological attention when loss strikes deeply. However, most adults in
life transitions do not require medication or treatments aimed at
relieving their "distress," which is actually a vehicle for normal
growth and development. Rather, they need to learn how to grieve
and to move on through the transition territory and into new life
directions. What was wrong, sick, or dysfunctional was wrapped up
in the social setting of the old life structure, and the possibility for
new strength is maximal as they make their transitions succeed. It
is competency in transition management that they need, to find new
order in their own disorientations.[10]

Just as each life structure has ongoing, minor transitions,
each developmental transition has beneath it a sufficient life structure to provide the basic continuities and necessities of life. A developmental transition is a normal process in which we shed some
or much of our previous identity as we discover new possibilities in
our undiscovered selves. It is precisely in the gradual act of shedding, bereaving, and letting go that we gradually discover our
emerging values, priorities, excitement, and dream of creating a

new life structure. Stanley Keleman captures it with these words: "When we step out of our social roles, when we disengage ourselves from our programmed fears, when we immerse ourselves in the river of self-experiencing, we are bathed, merged in the non-verbal, non-conceptual, non-visual, non-idealistic world. We are indeed in the sea of creation. We are the sea from which we create our own lives. When you find your own answers, it is you."[11]

Cocooning takes place almost entirely on the inside of the person experiencing the loss of a life structure. The loss of a burdensome life structure is the full-time gain of the healthy inner self. Activists may see cocooning as cowardly withdrawal, but it is actually the courageous regeneration of the person. In *A Study of History,* Arnold Toynbee identified a basic principle of cultural renewal as "withdrawal and return" by leaders and creative minorities; sensitive leaders disengage and withdraw temporarily from their social milieu, and then return with new convictions and powers.[12]

Arnold Van Gennep describes cocooning as a "neutral zone"—a temporary structure apart from the beaten path, a safe place for grieving and incubation, for testing the soul and renewing the self. Feelings surface, and doubts are raised. "Do I have the capacity to get through this? How do I proceed? Do I have sufficient trust and love?" People in the neutral zone lead lives that are in suspension, in parentheses, in temporary environments with transition objects. Their thoughts take the form of attentive inactivity; their lives function with simple ritualized routines; their interactions are filled with ambiguity. Cocooning is a withdrawal from external structures in the service of getting new perspective and resources for a vital return. The cocoon itself is a separation from the outside world with sufficient protection and safety to allow the inner process of recuperation its full power. The three parts of cocooning are grieving, loneliness, and healing.

Grieving. "There is the need to mourn," declare Robert Tannenbaum and Robert W. Hanna, "to work through the dying and death of attachments to elements of personal identity, to aspects of one's view of the reality outside of one's self, to ways of being to which we have clung but that are often dysfunctional for us in the present. To mourn means to face death—little deaths, to be sure, but death, nevertheless—in order to make a rebirth possible. Each of us is ultimately vulnerable, yet most of us typically blind ourselves to this truth."[13]

Cocooning begins with grieving, where the emphasis moves from "doing" to "being" tasks, activities having to do with healing. You measure yourself by your losses and by looking backward—your only reference point at this point in the cycle. You feel like a walking corpse, without life or direction, looking in on a world that is no more. Looking ahead is bleak and virtually impossible. You are in the *DIS*'s of the self:

> disengaged—having left the familiar life structure
> disenchanted—having negative emotional moods
> discouraged—experiencing a loss of motivation
> disappointed—feeling sad and dejected
> disoriented—feeling confused, lost and at bay
> disillusioned—feeling cynical about the past and doubt-
> ful about the future
> disidentified—experiencing the absence of many fa-
> miliar roles and happenings
> disgusted—feeling angry or upset
> dislocated—being lost or disrupted
> disrespected—experiencing loss of self-respect and fear
> of rejection by others[14]

During grieving, you simplify your life, stripping away the complex life-style that you were immersed in during the life structure. Grieving is a purging of all that, a move toward simplicity and quietude. As the onion skins of time-driven living fall off, you move inward toward the secret strengths of your heart and soul. Grieving is shedding the unworkable past, mourning the loss, and saying good-bye. Grieving is letting go at the heart of your interiority, expressing intense feelings of sadness and loss. Grieving is an emotional competence conducted by the self within you, when you minimize your ego functions and allow yourself to feel your feelings and the thoughts that go with them.

Because grieving involves compounded losses at many levels within us, it cannot be rushed. Grieving people do not respond to quick fixes or premature start-ups. Healing must first take place. As with the healing of a deep wound, time must pass, and new personal resources must be found. Grieving is the working out of the feelings of loss and the gradual discovery of resources for beginning again. Grieving takes us (or our organizations or families or nations when they are in cocooning) into our archaic fears and our primordial powers, where we discover new resources, insights, and energy for beginning again. As Mircea Eliade has written, "One does not *repair* a worn-out organism, it must be re-made; the patient needs to be born again; he needs, as it were, to recover the whole energy and potency that a being has at the moment of its birth."[15]

Loneliness. During cocooning, it is normal for intense feelings of loneliness to occur. Few people seek to be lonely, but it is a state that we all pass through whenever we are cast off from our life structure. Loneliness is a natural part of the human condition. Knowing how to manage loneliness is a survival skill for a life transition. Loneliness does not mean "being alone" but rather being cut off from the personal meaning that was conveyed through the beliefs, roles, relationships and reference points in the previous life structure. Loneliness is a feeling of estrangement from past and future. People in this place in the change cycle have lost their moorings and not yet found replacements. Clark Moustakas, who has written widely on loneliness in human experience, says this: "In loneliness, some compelling, essential aspect of life is suddenly challenged, threatened, altered, denied. At such times only by entering into loneliness, by steeping oneself in the experience and allowing it to take its course and to reveal itself is there hope that one's world will achieve harmony and unity. Then the person can begin again, born as a new self, with openness, spontaneity, and trust. What I experience within myself, and what I yearn for from other persons is an acceptance and valuing, a tacit agreement to let the loneliness be."[16]

Healing. Healing is where regeneration begins. The slings and arrows suffered during the adult years—and earlier—may leave festering wounds from having been neglected, betrayed, abandoned, abused, wasted, rejected, or shamed. The wounds may stem from personal attitudes as well as the actions of others—overweight, low self-esteem, addiction to chemical substances, fears. Cocooning is a time to heal these and to get them behind you. While the healing may not be complete, it can be more than sufficient for empowering the next phase of your life. We think of healing as the physical repair of a wound or the psychological recovery from a betrayal or abandonment. The body must heal: Nutrition and exercise are important aspects of the self-repairing cocooner. The mind must heal: Finding ways to make your own inner voice the primary caretaker of your life feeds the healing process. Learning to forgive those who have violated your integrity is the only way you can heal and ultimately be free of them. "Heal thyself" is the cocooner's injunction. Pay full attention to the many ways in which you need to care for yourself. Healing is the foundation for self-renewal and the rebirth of hope. When you are healed enough to look ahead, you move on along the cycle of change. And the mystery is that the healing has not merely bound the wounds; it has transformed the cocoon into a new person.

6

From Self-Renewal to New Beginnings

To keep alive and effective, you anticipate difficulties and opportunities. You adapt, changing and growing as the individuals and the world around you change, and you periodically recommit yourself to your mission. You act to preserve what is best and discard the rest. . . . Developing a mission means seeing a pattern in the things and thoughts that get you moving; assessing your resources; then formulating your feelings into words.

—*Charles Garfield, Peak Performers*[1]

When cocoons fulfill their functions, butterflies emerge. With people, renewal begins within the self. The point in the cycle of change when self-renewal is the central phenomenon of life is when you are as far removed from structural embeddedness as you can get, after you have shed onion skin after onion skin of attachment to your past way of being and doing and thinking. It is this very distance from your past life structure that permits a receptiveness to life that you didn't know you had within you. The positive result of disengagement, cocooning, and loneliness is the rebirth of the self.

Self-Renewal

Self-renewal is a time when you feel the surge of life return as a pure gift. Some call it rebirth, a miracle, an act of God. In truth,

107

it doesn't matter what you call it; acceptance is all that counts. When you accept with gratitude the new life that you feel, you are able to "hope" again; the future is a new possibility and the world a more friendly place. There are three parts to self-renewal: (1) a profound gift from the realm of solitude—an inner rebirth of self-esteem, vitality, and sufficiency; (2) a comprehensive reevaluation of personal and social beliefs and values; and (3) a recovery of hope and purpose—a new quest for a desired future.

Solitude. Self-renewal usually begins quietly. The lonely griever becomes a person with a confident solitude. "There is a place," writes Hugh Prather, "where you are not alone, where your voice sings with every voice that has ever sung, or ever will sing."[2] In contrast to loneliness, which mourns the loss, solitude is positive aloneness, a confident presence of self-sufficiency. Self-renewal begins when the grieving self gives way to the real self—a deep and caring reservoir of abilities, resources, and affirmation. The positive forces of the self now break through to remind you of the depth and breadth of your being. You are awed, amazed, and joyful with a quiet peace. The poet Wordsworth phrased it this way:

> When from our better selves we have too long
> Been parted by the hurrying world, and droop,
> Sick of its business, of its pleasures tired,
> How gracious, how benign, is Solitude.[3]

Solitude is a quiet, deep, inner experience. Albert Einstein called solitude "the teacher of personality." Through the experience of solitude, you tap your inner sensibilities and current values. Often overlooked in our culture, managing solitude is an essential human competence. The British scholar Anthony Storr portrays the value of solitude with these words: "Removing oneself voluntarily from one's habitual environment promotes self-understanding and contact with those inner depths of being which elude one in the hurly-burly of day-to-day life. . . . *The capacity to be alone thus becomes linked with self-discovery and self-realization; with becoming aware of one's deepest needs, feelings, and impulses.* . . . The capacity to be alone is a valuable resource when changes of mental attitude are required. After major alterations in circumstances, fundamental reappraisal of the significance and meaning of existence may be needed. In a culture in which interpersonal relationships are generally considered to provide the answer to every form of distress, it is sometimes difficult to persuade well-meaning helpers that solitude can be as therapeutic as emotional support."[4]

Like cocooning, self-renewal cannot be rushed. Whereas the outer events of your life can change your human prospects in an instant, the reconstruction of inner resilience and perspective takes time. In your solitude, you discover a well of life that connects to an abundance of unused resources. You learn that there is more than enough life, beauty, and strength within you for moving ahead, and this confidence generates energy, hope, and courage. Four years after Admiral Byrd returned from his winter alone in Antarctica, he wrote, "I did take away something that I had not fully possessed before: appreciation of the sheer beauty and miracle of being alive, and a humble set of values. . . . Civilization has not altered my ideas. I live more simply now, and with more peace."[5] When Franklin Delano Roosevelt was asked how he could possibly be a good president with his body partially paralyzed by polio, he responded, "It's not what you lose but what you have left and what you do with it." That is the attitude of a person who has experienced the reconstruction of the self through solitude.

Revision of Core Values. Throughout your adult years, you have opportunities to make significant revisions in the assumptions that have guided you since childhood. It is at moments like this in the change cycle that you have an opportunity to seize your script and become its author in a more self-determining way, on the basis of information and experience that you have accumulated during your adult years. The transcendent perspective of a transition is a powerful base for revising your raison d'être.

When your conscious reflections take place in the comfort of your own interiority, you can draw upon more of yourself and claim who you are and want to become. As the inner reaches of your mind are reviewed, a rare opportunity comes to recalibrate the values and beliefs guiding your life. This secret place, filled with emotional fire as well as mental awareness, can be found in solitude by the self when it has distanced from external structures and renewed itself from within. This is the time and place to acquire more of your own human imprint and to shape your next life structure accordingly. You are still who you were, only a little more so and with considerably more awareness. But it feels like a metamorphosis, a new beginning, and that is what makes it so important in the cycle. You are able to revise some of your fundamental assumptions about who you are and what is importnt for you, leading to profound redecisions for how you want to live and be in the future. Now you can confront the polarities of adult life and arrive at new ways to balance them. There are several perennial polarities, most of which are versions of a basic struggle between wanting to develop yourself as completely as possible and wanting to demonstrate your human competence in the best way you can:[6]

1. New Self Versus Former Self

What are the basic beliefs of my new self—the values, the assumptions, the purpose of my life?

What are the residual values of my former self, and how do I integrate them with my new sense of self?

How can I merge the new into the former, and the former into the new so that I have both continuity and change?

2. Connection to Others Versus Separateness from Others

To what degree am I wanting to be connected, attached, and included? How capable am I at bonding and at sustaining intimacy with others? How important are nurturance, caring, inclusion, and interdependence at this time in my life?

To what degree am I wanting to be distinct, independent, and autonomous? How capable am I of managing my separateness? How important are autonomy, assertiveness, achievement, independence, and my need to win at this time in my life?

How can I balance my self-sufficiency with my interdependence with others?

3. Young Versus Old

How might I value the "young" in me? What "young" virtues might I sustain and increase in my life at this time?

How might I value the "old" in me? What virtues of being "old" might I incorporate into my life at this time?

How can I grow old and sustain
both the wisdom of my years and my inner child?

4. Creativity Versus Destructiveness

How am I creative and life-affirming? How do I want to express my will to live at this time of my life?

How am I destructive and abusive? How will I manage the rage, violence, and unhealed wounds within me?

What changes in my life-style are needed
to diminish my life-denying forces
and to increase my affirmation and creativity?

5. Caring Beyond the Self Versus Self-Indulgence

In what ways am I complete? How might I contribute to the next generation through mentoring, benevolence, volunteerism, political involvement, professional leadership, community leadership, or leisure?

In what ways do I need to fulfill myself and reach a new level of completeness? What do I need more of to be me: money, career success, recognition, friends, love, sex, children, grandchildren?

How can I continue to grow while contributing to the world?

The activity here is to receive the life that is waiting for you, not to do anything in particular. Renewal is a receiving, an acceptance, an act of being, and a gift of a new identity. Doing is minimal. Renewal is a discovery of self-sufficiency, a realization that you are capable of many directions and in touch with many destinies. You are beginning to look out of the windows of your mind into the external world again, and you feel at home. Your future is beginning to happen; it is grounded in the depths of your experience.

People in self-renewal live simple lives. They are not needy.

They are very awake. They listen. They feel. They use few words. Their thoughts seem linked to a deep well beneath them and to the skies above, and they are ready to live the truth as they know it, and no less. They choose to be their own persons and to march to their own drums. The renewed self feels free, alive, and beginning, not living out the last days of the last chapter but starting the first days of the next chapter, emanating from the virtues of the heart and believing again in a livable future. With renewal, the self fills with gratitude, spunk, curiosity, and hope—just to live—without a life structure to maintain. The symbolic encounter with death has led to a resurrection of life, with a simple formula for how to live in harmony with the world. Self-renewal is not a new invitation to perfection or a crusading attitude; it is a feeling of adequacy or completeness, of being exactly who you are—for now. Self-renewed people feel "good enough" to be themselves. The consciousness that comes from self-renewal reflects awe and reverence for renewal everywhere, and hope opens its doors to new scenarios for living.

Exploring the World Again:
Creativity, Experimentation, Networking

When a person in a life transition develops sufficient self-esteem and confidence to poke around in the external world, reintegration begins. Internal life weaves itself into external structures. Whereas *self-renewal* represents the rediscovery of inner resources beyond healing, *exploring* represents the rebirth of the self-in-the-world. People experiencing this phase are typically curious, daring, eager, venturesome, positive, risk-taking, sexual, and not yet ready for long-term commitments.

The healthy internal forces seek compatible external opportunities for projecting confidence, competence, and a new future. The restructuring phase involves three change cycle skills that together prepare a person to structure again: creativity, experimenting, and passion. This phase is very much like late adolescence, and we need to invent terms such as *middlescence* and *elderescence* for validating this recurring experience of vitality, learning, and growing.

Creativity is the playful exploration of new ideas and possibilities. It is untethered imagining. It is a bubbling spirit that wants to try new ways of thinking and doing. It is uncensored brainstorming, the discovery and pursuit of novelty, a willingness to express yourself in unconventional ways. Out of the disorderly universe of a profound transition comes a life force in search of new symbols, forms, and stories. Renewed selves like to play, invent, and celebrate. They like to have fun. Adults at this point in the cycle are like children again, filled with energy, whether it be channeled into the arts or science or some practical field. Often they write poetry or songs, take up dancing, begin to draw or paint, join political groups, build something, expand the garden, or travel. They like to touch and be touched. According to Silvano Arieti, an authority on creativity, the creative process springs from solitude, aloneness, and inactivity. The transitional self is like a reservoir being filled in its detachment from the external world, until it overflows with daydreaming, brainstorms, risk taking, and expressiveness. "The creative process," suggests Arieti, "is a way of fulfilling the longing or search for a new object or state of experience or existence that is not easily found or attained." Creativity is a symbolic expression of new life taking form within the person in transition, and the transition itself is the process of giving birth to creativity. People at this place in the change cycle often feel a transcendence over limits that before had constrained them. Anchored in personal energy, creativity emerges as art, science, play, and quest.[7]

Experimentation is trying out new ideas and projects without making them permanent. It is risking discovery and risking failure. The Berkeley psychologist Ellen Siegelman writes, "The urge to risk reflects the urge for competence; rightly approached, it can enhance that sense of competence, which is so intimately connected with self-esteem."[8] Experimenting is looking for new ways to do things, new ways to be you. Experimenting means having fun and learning how to learn. Experimenting is the infusion of energy into future possibilities. With new social support and information, a person begins to experiment with life options. Like a new college graduate, a midlife person in transition experiments with relationships, jobs, leisure ventures, hobbies, travel, life-style, social causes, and environmental concerns. Such a person is often "creatively unstable," and experimenting with options helps to sort out the paths that will lead to a new life structure. Experimenting has energy for effervescing, wherever it may lead. This energy serves not only the reconstruction of personal lives but reaches out to touch far-reaching places. In the words of sociologist Louis A. Zurcher, Jr., the self becomes "mutable," comfortable with and oriented toward "process, change, flexibility, autonomy, tolerance, and openness"— all natural outcomes of a life transition. Mihaly Csikszentmihalyi describes this as "flow" stemming from a person's ability to exhibit joy and meaning in everything that he or she does.[9]

Networking is a major vehicle for testing out life options during the final phase of a transition. Networking links you to new resources: exploring friendships, finding new ways to do things, gathering information, and pursuing new learning. A common environment for adults emerging from a transition is new training or reentry into formal learning. When you feel anchored in yourself, you search for new friends who are also alive and curious. You seek friends who know more than you do about the territory that you want to investigate for your next life structure. Instead of looking to friends for approval and admiration, you look for mentors and role models to guide you into your preferred future. People who are beginning to evolve out of a life transition are usually hungry for new information and reeducation. They absorb new ways of thinking, and they entertain many possibilities for their future. Like young people going to college, they seek new learning, education, and information about their future options. Sometimes they return to school for advanced degrees or for certificates in professional training programs. Adult certificate and degree programs are performing an important rite of passage for midlifers managing a transition and preparing for new life structures.

An Exiting Ritual: Choosing New Priorities

During the final phase of a life transition, adults make basic redecisions about the purpose of their lives. They build the future upon the vitality within themselves. They scan the horizon for external settings that are congruent with their renewed lives. If you are at this point in the change cycle, ask yourself these questions: What are the passionate preferences of my life, now that I have retooled myself? What are my priorities? What gives me energy, direction, and boundaries? What goals and rewards am I seeking? The deliberate selection of preferred values becomes urgent at this point in the cycle, because you are on the edge of making a commitment to a new life structure.

Life structures are powered by value commitments embedded in a dream/plan—a story of how you want your life to proceed, at its best. The dream is a time capsule of life yet to be lived, hope bottled up in a simple story with empowering values ready to shape the plan and fuel the launching. At different times in the cycle of change these values have different degrees of importance. It is during the final phase of a life structure that you have the greatest freedom to choose new core values for your life. Your choice of values inspires you with a sense of purpose sufficient for shaping new life structures, such as these:

- Political determination to improve society in some way
- Artistic expression, wherever it leads you
- Love, marriage, children, friends, and a nice home
- Wealth, pure and simple, with economic independence
- A career or job that validates you, along with a healthy marriage
- A commitment to defend our nation and serve the country
- Parenting roles along with volunteer activities that support causes that you believe in
- Individuation, to become more of yourself, and more self-driven
- Living as a researcher to find a cure for the AIDS virus
- Golf, tennis, sailing, friends, and a life of leisure
- A spiritual passion for oneness, peace, and service

The move from the final days of a transition to the beginning days of a new life structure usually happens fairly quickly. Like a whack on the side of the head comes the realization of what you want and how to proceed. You feel filled, confident, ready, and focused. Your dream for the future is helping you identify the course to follow, and you feel ready to pour your life into what seems like a very friendly world. You are alive, clear, self-motivated, and unstoppable.

III

The
Life Cycle

7

Meaning and Mission
Across the Life Cycle

Our lives are a series of births and deaths: we die to one
period and must be born to another. We die to childhood and are born to adolescence; to our high-school
selves and (if we are fortunate) to our college selves; we
die to our college selves and are born into the "real"
world; to our unmarried selves and into our married.
To become a parent is birth to a new self for the mother
and father as well as for the baby. . . . I must never lose
sight of those other deaths which precede the final,
physical death, the deaths over which we have some
freedom; the death of self-will, self-indulgence, self-
deception, all those self-devices which, instead of making us more fully alive, make us less.
—*Madeleine L'Engle, The Summer of the Great-
Grandmother*[1]

Life proceeds like a series of snapshots—infancy, childhood, adolescence. But over the years the string of cycles seems more like an
ongoing movie, with pervasive themes, turning points, and changing characters. The repetitive cycles form chapters in a continuous
story, which is the human life cycle from birth to death. The artistic
productions of Alan Alda illustrate this sequencing of adult life.
MASH, Same Time Next Year, and *Four Seasons* dramatize how
people shift gears to make changes within the continuities of their
lives.

How the Life Cycle Works

Every time you go around the change cycle, you go around the same circle of change, but it seems like a new ball game. Each subsequent life structure has a somewhat (or considerable!) different value base, cast of characters, and social agenda. Each redefines your sense of purpose. Yet each sequence is an extension of what came before and has as many commonalities as differences.

Adult life is something like a large slinky, with cycles that go on and on. Each new life period is different from yet similar to the last one. The focus changes, but life goes on. With each serial life structure, there are new, temporary answers to the perennial human questions: Who am I? Where am I going? What am I up to? Who is going with me? How will I get there? The answers that seem acceptable at thirty seldom satisfy at fifty or seventy. Throughout your years, you keep reworking these basic questions, which leads you into life structures serving different purposes throughout your life cycle.

As you move through midlife and elderhood, your sense of purpose is likely to shift from ego-driven issues to more spiritual ones, from competence and attainments to consciousness and caring. You experience a gradual decline in physical prowess along with an increase in self-clarity. However, if you experience unbearable losses and lack sufficient funds and health to enjoy life, you may become self-absorbed as you view your life cycle as a downhill ride.

At different times in your life, you have different visceral sensations about what you are up to and should be pursuing—your raison d'être, priorities, expectations. These are not all prompted by aging and developmental issues alone. If you experience unanticipated social crises—accidents, winning the lottery, diseases, divorce, loss of job—your sense of life purpose will be profoundly affected. The life cycle is like a kaleidoscope turning—while there are predictable features to the changing patterns, there are also random and never-ending surprises, some pleasant, some not so pleasant. Yet when looking back on our lives, all of us can discern chapters that make up our life cycles. Each chapter is defined by a shift in priorities, values, and purpose. When these chapters are told as a "life story," adult life has duration, a flow through time from young to old, from beginning to end. The chapters of your own lifeline represent the windows in your mind through which you view your past, present, and future. The more you can be aware of this life cycle process in yourself, the more you can shape your sequencing and take responsibility for your life.

This chapter suggests there are four major ways adults can understand and influence their life cycle: knowing the key concepts of the life cycle, employing the appropriate core values at different times in the adult journey, evaluating the best use of human systems in the various periods of adult life, and viewing the life cycle through the changing perspectives of the decades of adult life.

Key Concepts of the Life Cycle

A life cycle is what takes place between birth and death in the life of a person. It spans infancy, childhood, adolescence, young adulthood, middle adulthood, and elderhood. Life cycles are understood as personal stories or histories, with both unique and universal characteristics. Our life cycle stories form a kind of personal mythology about our lives, profoundly shaped by the myths and rituals of our families, communities, work settings, and culture. There are at least eleven concepts that form an overview for understanding the adult life cycle. These notions represent generalizations found acceptable by most scholars of adult development, although there is always healthy disagreement. Nevertheless, the following are dependable concepts for understanding the pervasive characteristics of the adult life cycle today.

1. The childhood years shape, limit, and enrich the adult years. Most adults know that they are anchored in their childhood experience. The more they can learn from reevaluating their own childhood years, the better they can build fulfilling lives. The human agenda is to rework the same issues of the younger years in new environments and to add new issues as well.[2]

2. Adults adapt and grow throughout the adult years. Adults are constantly adapting to changes within themselves and their environment. Successful adaptation occurs when adults alter their perceptions of how the world works, in a constant process of learning and relearning congruent with personal experience.[3]

3. The adult years are a process of ongoing change and continuity. Each of us weaves a different but similar tapestry, taking on individual hues and designs, as we make sense out of our experience through the loom of time. Adult life is a natural unfolding of the maturation process and a series of responses to surprise events and opportunities all of which together shape a "life course" around the evolving interaction of biological, psychological, and social processes. It is more like a series of adventures than a plateau and more an ongoing journey than an arrival. Adult change is best understood as the reworking of perennial issues within different settings and age periods.[4]

4. Social status is a major determinant of adult developmental issues and directions. Educational background, income level, occupation, status recognition, organizational memberships, cultural orientation, religious participation, geographical location, sports affiliations, and other social factors have a heavy hand in shaping adult values, commitments, expectations, reflective capacities, and aging patterns.[5]

5. There are dramatic differences between the styles and priorities of men and women during the adult life cycle. Men who invest highly in their careers in the early adult years may become more nurturing and less self-absorbed during midlife. Other men are so indelibly formed by their first life structure that they spend their adult years repeating the roles and patterns of their early adult behavior, which usually includes a primary identification with career and dependency on a spouse and others for emotional nurture and care. Women who invest highly in caretaking roles (often in addition to their jobs or careers) in the early adult years may become more assertive in their middle years. During midlife, women who have not been in careers often push beyond caretaking roles into tasks involving external challenges and financial independence.

However, there are many variations in the developmental patterns of adult men and women.[6]

6. *Careers and work environments have considerable influence on adult lives.* A majority of adults, male and female, now work throughout most of the adult life cycle. Dual career marriages are now normative. Most adults spend more time in their work settings than they do at home alone, or with any other commitment. Their roles at work affect their behaviors in all the other parts of their lives. Many adults organize their lives around their work, and critics of this phenomenon call this "workaholism" or "work addiction." Others argue that the work organization is the primary social system in which today's adults learn and achieve personal empowerment. In any case, the work culture—with its stress and challenge—impacts the ordinary lives of adults. As adults age, the meaning of work changes, and most adults seek to alter their career roles. Careers and corporate structures are more fragile than they used to be, and it is normal now for adults to expect career crises and career changes throughout the life cycle. When adults retire, they often have difficulty creating life plans if their former work identity was their primary sense of self.[7]

7. *Adults in midlife and elderhood often become preoccupied with their mortal limits, death, and time left to live.* While this may sound morbid, it often functions to inspire them to live fully now and to follow their deepest values. They experience shifts in perspective, from quantity time to quality time, from grandiosity to realistic attainments, from casual friends to lifelong friends, from procrastination to action. Adults learn that their time is measured, and they pursue new ways to find greater depth in their more limited sense of destiny.[8]

8. *Adults in midlife often experience an increase in individuation and introspection.* As middle-class young adults move further into the adult years, they usually move from external injunctions and constraints to internal ones, from pleasing others to pleasing themselves; status comes more from internal rewards than from external recognition. Through introspection, self-evaluation, and

reflection, midlife adults deveiop a sense of self that provides resilience and constancy. Mature adults learn how to restructure their
lives, tending toward self-direction and individuation. Observable
signs may include a greater sense of humor, new ability to compromise and engage in teamwork, new hobbies or interests, and a
desire for solitude. [9]

   *9. During the adult years, leisure—or, more fundamentally,
play—takes on new meaning, as a vehicle for living rather than as
a vacation from working.* Adults learn much about their own lives
from reading, traveling, going to movies and plays, playing golf or
tennis, watching TV, weekending with recreation vehicles, engaging in crafts or art classes, joining an orchestra, volunteering in a
museum, or trekking in the Himalayas. [10]

   *10. A major trend in midlife is the pursuit of personal integ-
rity.* This is manifest through increased interest in deep-seated
values, wholeness, a capacity for mentoring future generations, the
mastery of life itself, and the presence of seminal wisdom. This
increased sense of personal integrity often joins with an outer sense
of being connected with life everywhere, through nature, friendships, political activities, and spiritual intuition. Integrity fosters a
personal sense of purpose, a passion for being, a mission in life.
These same qualities of adult life continue to develop in their fullest
during the elder years of adult life. [11]

   *11. From midlife on, adults frequently become more invested
in leadership roles and social contribution.* With the strengthening
of the self, many mature adults feel empowered to contribute new
leadership to their lives, families, jobs, and society. They want to
make a difference, to be role models, and to contribute to the next
generation. They want to improve some aspect of the earth, to be
good stewards of the future. The trend toward personal leadership
grows with age in many lives, and draws on a deepening well of life
experience. The importance of this theme is underlined by the increasing numbers of adults in midlife who are extending their midlife behaviors into their elder years. Through nutrition and exercise
programs, they maintain healthy bodies; through relationship nur-

turance, they sustain love and sex; through continued work and financial planning, they sustain an economic means for travel and living; and by taking on positive attitudes about being "old," they seek leadership and mentoring roles. [12]

Today's adults have available to them more knowledge about their lives and human prospects than ever before in history. Not only do we have more information on more aspects of adulthood, but we have better concepts for understanding how lives get constructed and creatively altered. How to use this profound reservoir for adult empowerment is the central concern of this section that explores the inner workings of the adult life cycle.

The Six Core Human Values

There are at least six fundamental human values that compete for your loyalty throughout the adult years to shape your sense of purpose. Each represents a basic human capacity that you can choose and organize your life activities around. These values are emotional themes that generate energy and life purpose. They are primal feelings and beliefs—visceral forces, often at an unconscious level. They are often difficult to talk about, but once they are infused into a life structure, they provide internal reference points for continuity and stability. More important, they produce motivational energy that can last for many years. The six core human values are the primal incentives of adult life—deep sources of passion and commitment. In various combinations at different times throughout the adult years, you draw upon them to design and redesign your expectations. The selection and balance of core human values makes each sequential adult life structure different from the previous ones, giving each a different sense of purpose and meaning. The six abiding core values of adult life are:

1. A sense of self: identity, self-esteem, confidence, self-reliance, autonomy, personal boundaries, self-responsible behavior. This value pursues a satisfactory answer to the question Who Am I? Clarifying your personal identity is a lifelong process, but there are particular points when it becomes central. Young adults work hard to sort out their personal mission from that of their parents and peers. During life transitions, adults clarify their sense of self and use that as a basis for a subsequent life structure. In the first half of life, this life core value typically sponsors the quest for personal ego clarification and empowerment. For many adults in the second half of life, this same core value pursues a connection of the inner self with universal meaning and mystery.[13]

2. *Achievement:* reaching goals, conducting projects, working, winning, playing in organized sports, having ambition (for recognition from others, money, and results), being purposive, getting results. Achievement represents successful goal attainment and for most adults is most dramatically displayed in their work/career roles, although it is also important in sports, military, and volunteer activities. Achievement is usually a dominant core value for young adults who make their careers central to their life structures and for women rejoining the work force again in their forties and fifties. Men tend to favor achievement as a dominant form of human expression throughout their life cycles, even after they learn the importance of the other values. Women who sustain full-time careers during their early adult lives often feel a lifelong bond to this core value. Achievement is also important for older adults who often discover a renewal of purpose through projects, work, and activities.[14]

3. *Intimacy:* loving, bonding, attaching, caring, nurturing, being intimate, making relationships work, nesting, coupling, parenting, being a friend. Intimacy forms and maintains affective bonds, and is essential for long-term "attachment" in adult life. In early adulthood, women often serve as the nurturing, emotional gate-keepers of the intimate bonds they form, making intimacy an important core value in their lives. Young men often seek women who will manage their intimacy and friendship needs for them. In midlife and elderhood, men often increase their capacities for giving and receiving intimacy, through friendships, mentoring roles, hobbies, and grandparenting.[15]

4. *Creativity and play:* being imaginative, playful, spontaneous, original, expressive, humorous, artistic, celebrative, innova-

tive, funny, joyful, and nonpurposive. Creativity and play are an expression of spontaneity and joy, which are particularly plentiful in the last half of a transition. Creativity and play are sources of positive energy, full of optimism and promise. They tap a powerful life force that seeks new forms of human expression. This is a core value that children know best. Spontaneous play and creativity are regenerative forces in our bodies and lives and important to our ongoing resilience and vitality. Few adults have enough genuine play in their lives. Many treat play as an achievement rather than as an opportunity for spontaneous and imaginative expression.[16]

5. *Search for meaning:* integrity, the experience of joy and rapture, an inner connection in oneself to order and meaning in the universe, inner peace, contemplation, a sense of transcendence, ultimate concern. Search for meaning is usually a central core value during a life transition, but can be a spiritual motivator in a life structure as well, particularly in the second half of life. Victor Frankl says that at some point in the human life cycle, each person "is questioned by life; and he can only answer to life by answering for his own life; to life he can only respond by being responsible."[17]

6. *Compassion and contribution:* caring, giving, helping, mentoring, leading, improving, reforming, supporting, being grateful, leaving the world a better place, bequeathing a legacy. Compassion leads you beyond your needs to help others or to contribute to the community. Compassion and contribution are particularly powerful core values in the life structures of people over forty. They represent an attitude as much as a result, a desire to return something of what one has received in life.[18] Sister Teresa, a hero in our time, finds her life meaning through serving others. So did Albert Schweitzer, who after spending the first half of his adult years as a master musician, spent the rest of his life as a medical missionary in Africa.

Each core value has its negative as well as positive side. Too much emphasis on "sense of self" leads to narcissism and self-absorption. Too much emphasis on "achievement" results in workaholism in which a person's life is a projection of his or her work role. Too much emphasis upon "intimacy" results in symbiosis and codependency. Too much emphasis upon "play and creativity" keeps adults infantalized. Too much emphasis upon "sense of meaning" leads to a fusion delusion with some ideal state of being. Too much "compassion and contribution" lead to neglect of a private life. What makes these values important to adults is the personal appropriation of the right ones at the right time in the right proportion or balance.

Healthy life structures are powered by two or more core values that supplement and balance one another. These values become embedded in a dream/plan, providing each life structure with a different sense of purpose and mission. The dream is a time capsule of life yet to be lived, hope bottled up in a simple story with empowering values ready to shape a plan and fuel a launching. Your choice of core values shapes your choice of human activities, friends, and life-style throughout a life structure. Then, during transitions between life structures, you choose a different arrangement of core values as you move on through the life cycle.

Human Systems

We employ our values to direct our decisions within system commitments. The systems of adult life shape our lives as much or more than our professed core values. Too often, adults think they can individually change their lives, irrespective of the human systems in which they are embedded. At a basic level, we are anchored in economic, political, and spiritual systems. More concretely, we manage our adults lives in family, occupational, and leisure systems. Monitoring our connection to these human systems is a unique challenge for each adult.

On the one hand, how much fulfillment do you get from each system of your life—marriage, family, work, leisure, friendships, social networks? To what degree is your embeddedness in each system an opportunity for you to grow in the direction of your personal goals? On the other hand, how much of you is consumed or wasted by the systems you are in? To what degree do your family and work systems impede your personal goals and diminish your freedom to be you? Our embeddedness in systems can be a wonderful fulfillment of ourselves or it can be a form of bondage. How can you create a fair balance with these two concerns?

Systems are the social or environmental containers of our lives. By *systems,* we mean orderly structures and functions that engage our commitment and time and provide us with meaning. Consider these eight basic human systems:

1. *Personal System* (the maintenance of personal space, the use of personal time, health and physical maintenance, self-care and nurturing, spirituality, lifelong learning and training)[19]
2. *Couple's System* (primary intimacy, sharing, touching, sex, social occasions, leisure activities, householding)[20]
3. *Family System* (mothering and fathering, cooking/eating, TV, chores, education for children, medical care, vacations and some leisure activities, care for parents)[21]
4. *Friendship System* (work friends, leisure friends, couple and family friends, lifelong friends, same sex friends, opposite sex friends)[22]
5. *Work and Career System* (work roles and rewards, professional persona, ongoing training, commuting, benefits, career expectations)[23]
6. *Leisure System* (play, travel, hobbies, artistic expression, gardening, sports, and games)[24]
7. *Social Systems* (for example, participation in and meaning derived from community organizations, professional organizations, religious groups, networks, social causes, political groups)[25]
8. *Environmental Systems* (human influence on climates, weather, natural disasters, oil spills, and other conditions of nature and the cosmos; experience of wonder, awe, and spirituality)[26]

Systems provide us with arenas for our own fulfillment and they program us with roles and expectations that are not always fulfilling. As you change throughout the life cycle, your connection with your human systems changes, just as when those human systems change, you change. That is how embeddedness works. It is like push-pull. At its best, it's an ongoing, lively dialogue between you and your systems, where you are experiencing your competence, finding colleagues, and gaining rewards; at its worst it's feeling trapped and diminished by impersonal systems that make seemingly random changes that affect your life far more than you expect or want.

Just as a fish cannot live without water to swim in, we cannot live without human systems. Most of the time we live within our human systems and don't grasp what they are doing to us and for us. But it is possible, particularly during adult transitions, to transcend our human systems, temporarily, in our minds, to get perspective on how our systems fit our lives and on how we can choose a preferred balance of system commitments. Throughout the life cycle, we contour our human space and time with core values within human systems.

Decade Orientations

There are approximately six different chapters in adult life that serve as reference points for most of today's educated Americans between the ages of twenty and eighty. Adulthood is a very long period of time, with few socially demarcated places along the way. In my assessment of adult lives and the literature about them, I conclude that there are no adult stages, no necessary phases that you inevitably experience, no predictable chronology that you must adapt to, no boxes that you have to fit into. What we have are relatively similar reports of different age groups reflecting the personal and social experience of today's adults. The correlation of the chapters of adult life with age is more a biological and social behavior than a psychological necessity.

The six chapters or life orientations suggested here are not normative or prescriptive. They represent personal/social descriptions of the core values that adults today report as the focus of their experience in these different decades. The purpose of Part Three is not to help you adapt to these particular perspectives but to portray convincingly that each of us does move through fundamental value shifts and system changes during the adult years. You may find altogether different focal points in your life from the ones portrayed here. Or you may find that the identifiable periods of your life occur in a different order. The most important issue is that you understand how your own sense of purpose in life is changing and developing through your values and human systems throughout your life cycle.

The following chapters portray the life cycle process by describing the decades of the adult years as six periods with different versions of the purpose of life (see Map 2 on page 134). In our current society, there is a popular tendency to describe adult experience through decade identification. People who share the same age also share marker events from youth, memories, and values. Each decade, they share the same anxiety and excitement of redefining that life period for themselves. The beginning of each new decade often triggers our taking stock of our lives as we make the transition into a new chapter of possibilities. This is why there are so many special, rituallike parties for adults hitting their thirtieth, fortieth, fiftieth, sixtieth, and seventieth birthdays. Throughout adult life, each decade symbolizes a somewhat different orientation on life purpose (see Table 2 on page 132).

The themes of each of these six sequential life periods are not restricted to one decade; they are all present throughout the adult years and often cherished at various times throughout the life cycle, as are the core human values and preferred human systems. But in certain decade periods, specific values come close to defining the life purpose of a great many adults of similar ages and developmental interests. At this time in our society, they form social identification and provide psychological and spiritual meaning.

Table 2. Decade Orientations in the Life Cycle.

Age	Sense of Purpose	Human Systems	Core Values	Life Tasks
Twentysomething	Breaking out of family of origin and staking out adult territory	Personal, couple, peers, work and career, leisure	Intimacy, achievement, creativity and play, sense of self	Experimenting; making tentative attachments, working; gaining comfort and competence with money, love and sex; establishing habits of self-responsible behavior; maintaining a leisure life
Thirtysomething	Making it: achieving success in career, coupling, family (if chosen), recognition, and acquisitions	Couple, family, work and career, leisure, social	Intimacy, achievement, sociability, creativity and play, sense of self; search for meaning, compassion, and contribution	Reaching the top of a career; creating a home; parenting (if chosen); managing financial obligations; sustaining a social life; participating in children's (or one's own continued) schooling; maintaining a leisure life; caring for parents; facing possible losses such as divorce, loss of partner, or loss of career; postponed ego development
Fortysomething	Individuation, being in charge of one's own life, developing a spiritual awareness; (some people move from individuation to interdependence, while others reverse this order)	Personal, couple, family, work and career, friendships, leisure, social, environmental	Sense of self, achievement, intimacy, play and creativity, compassion and contribution, search for meaning	Reevaluating one's life; establishing clear ego boundaries; cultivating the self; becoming one person in all roles; clarifying career and marriage; examining roads not taken; measuring decisions by time left; facing the possibilities of

Decade		Life systems	Core values	
				divorce, career change, geographical moves, and addictions
Fiftysomething	Enjoying life through interdependence, feeling most oneself in the presence of nature, co-workers, spiritual awareness	Couple, family, leisure, personal, work and career, friendships, environmental, social	Intimacy, play and creativity, search for meaning, compassion and contribution	Enjoying being with others, traveling and indulging in leisure activities; deepening intimacy; favoring passive mastery at work; enjoying postparental roles; assuming new leadership roles; displaying increased social caring; preparing for increased losses
Sixtysomething	Starting over, mentoring, shaping the next generation, developing a simple joy and acceptance of others, redefining work and life priorities	Personal, social, environmental, leisure, friendship, couple, family, work	Play and creativity, search for meaning, sense of self, compassion and contribution, intimacy, achievement	Sharing knowledge and competence with younger people; grandparenting; revising work commitments; renewing intimacy; seeking new leadership roles; creating a new beginning
Seventysomething	Coming to terms, integrity, affirmation, celebration, completion	Personal, couple, friendship, social, leisure, environmental	Search for meaning, compassion and contribution, intimacy, creativity and play	Arriving at an estimate of one's life course—full, complete, and joyous or incomplete and despairing; coming to terms with death and dying; facing physical decline; experiencing intense loss; sustaining hope and trust; blessing and appreciating others

Note: About each decade, adults reorganize their lives around a different prioritization of six core human values (sense of self, achievement or work, intimacy, creativity and play, search for meaning, and compassion and contribution) within the human systems of adult life (personal, couple, family, friendship, work and career, leisure, social, and environmental).

Map 2. The Adult Life Cycle: Six Versions of Human Purpose.

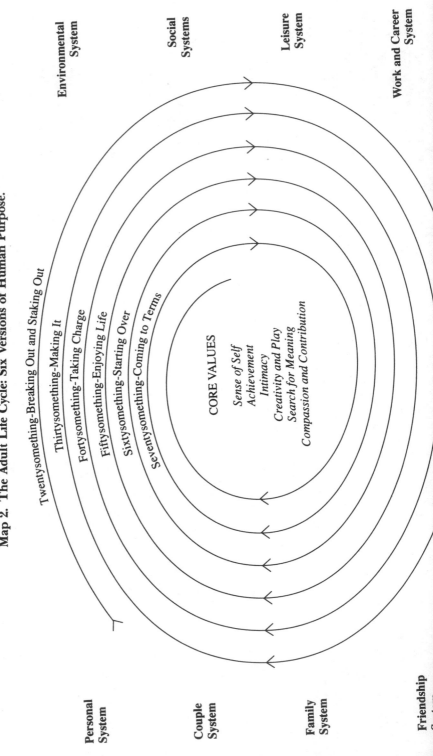

Environmental System

Social Systems

Leisure System

Work and Career System

Twentysomething-Breaking Out and Staking Out

Thirtysomething-Making It

Fortysomething-Taking Charge

Fiftysomething-Enjoying Life

Sixtysomething-Starting Over

Seventysomething-Coming to Terms

CORE VALUES

Sense of Self
Achievement
Intimacy
Creativity and Play
Search for Meaning
Compassion and Contribution

Personal System

Couple System

Family System

Friendship System

8

The Twenties and Thirties:

Breaking Out, Staking Out, and Making It

The young adult is at the height of his physical and mental vigor as he launches upon making his way and establishing his place in the world. . . . Now, more than ever, alternative ways of life must be renounced to permit the singleness of purpose required for success and to consolidate his identity; and his intimacy becomes reserved for a single person to make possible meaningful sharing with a spouse. . . . Vocational choice and marital choice are two of the most significant decisions of a lifetime. . . . The novice learns a way of life along with the knowledge and skills of the occupation. . . . The arrival of the first child transforms spouses into parents and turns a marriage into a family. . . . The parents need to be persons in their own right with lives and satisfactions of their own, firmly related in marriage and gaining satisfaction from it, rather than having their individuality and the marriage become subordinated to their being parents.
—*Theodore Lidz, The Person*[1]

During their twenties and thirties, adults leave their families of origin and design the first chapter of their adult years. Although few are prepared for the responsibilities and loneliness of adult life, most are eager to design their own lives.

Twentysomethings: Breaking Out and Staking Out

The adult years begin when adolescents break out of their family of origin and stake out the adult territory of love, work, and play. The primary goals are identity, intimacy, role mastery, and individuation. The twenties represent a period marked by audacity and grandiosity, self-doubt and emotional instability, playfulness and risk taking, intense learning and mental rigidity. For most, it is a scary, wonderful time.

The Experience of Frances Horn

During college at the University of California, I found a place in which I could be a star with an ever-widening stage. One of the campus activities was the student YWCA, a liberal group with national and international affiliations. I made my way up that ladder and became chairman of the western region and then of the National Student Council. . . . But I developed pernicious anemia and was effectively flattened for months. I missed the last semester of my senior year and could not graduate with my class.

As I lay on a couch listening to music and looking out of the window that spring, I was forced to do some reshuffling of my values, and the quiet time was not wasted. For years I had been goal-oriented; I had "busted a gut" to achieve, and to prove how capable I was. I had used will-power and a bright mind to push things through in the way I wanted them to go.

Then in May I was asked to be one of six people, three men and three women, to go from the United States to an international student meeting in India in the fall. . . . Shortly before I was to leave for Europe on the first segment of the trip around the world, one of the staff members of the student YWCA at Berkeley, who had lived for some years in China, said to me, "Frances, when you are in the Orient I think you are going to find that superficial cleverness will not be enough. The people you will meet will see through that because they know the meaning of real wisdom." I was angry and resentful at what I sensed as her critical tone, but I pretended not to be. However, her words stayed with me and came back to me as truth during the journey. In particular, I recall an instance in China when I was giving a talk which had to be translated. I became painfully aware that personality-level charm and charisma fell flat in translation, and that only solid, honest communication reached such an audience.

As I look back now at the young woman I was, I am struck by the contrasts between parts of myself which were so different, out of touch with one another, and so unconscious. I see the bright, capable, independent leader who can and does manage and manipulate groups of people to suit her goals, who needs to be first and who selects people and circumstances where she can be first. And I see the little girl, unsure of herself, unacceptable to herself, perilously dependent on the opinion of others for self-validation. I see a young woman, sophisticated and naive, worldly and unworldly, facing outward and facing inward. . . .

For me, the pattern that dogged my footsteps on the new path was the deep self-rejection behind the superficial appearance of capability. I lived with the unrecognized belief that I had been found inadequate, unsatisfactory, "less than." To compensate, I needed to be not only "more than" but *the* best, *the* first. Instead of maintaining myself consistently at a relatively balanced level, something would seem to attack my vulnerable ego and I would plunge down to minus 100. Then, instead of moving back up to a centered level, I often shot on up to plus 100, or if possible to plus 1,000, to overcome the sense of lack and of being "less than."[2]

The Up Side. When sufficiently on their own to stake out this chapter of their lives, twentysomethings try on adulthood as if it were an infinite wardrobe of possibilities. They Velcro themselves to relationships, jobs, new ideas, songs, and financial obligations. They also un-Velcro themselves whenever they feel like it and look at life as an experiment that they are not yet fully within, even though their security needs require the appearance of commitment.

The twenties are a time for experimentation, uncensored fun, and adventure. If you are healthy and lucky, the foreign territory of adult life becomes a staging ground for "the new generation." This is a time when freedom and dreams and friendships contain the culture, and love and sex are bigger than life itself. Twentysomethings proceed as though they can and will create the life they want, with or without help from the rest of the universe. They will make their dreams happen, no matter what. They don't think that the constraints of previous generations apply to them. Theirs is a new generation, a new age, with new rules and magic. Siegfried Sassoon once made a remark that speaks for this decade: "At the age of twenty-two I believed myself to be unextinguishable." This dreamy optimism sometimes expresses itself through increased empathy with others, particularly the poor, the oppressed, or people in mental or physical pain.

Although twentysomethings experiment with moral decisions, they seldom have sufficient experience to calculate the price that they may pay for the choices they make, nor do they believe that their choices are irreversible. Their arrogance allows them to try their dreams, take a chance, and try something new; but in time they discover that they have altered their life course with the choices that they have made.

When they were adolescents testing the boundaries of the adult world, twentysomethings had the protection, support, and guidance of parents and parent figures. Now there is vulnerability to twentysomethings' strong-mindedness; they want total freedom and access to the adult world, along with assurances, guidance, and approval. They are not sure how to ask for or get a safe passage into the adult roles that they are seizing. Mentors are pursued for models of the way toward success and safety. Peers are pursued for reassurance and approval. But it is difficult to trust a mentor if you haven't resolved your trust with your own parents. Compromises with brash dreams are often made to find security and jobs with adequate salaries. Twentysomethings often settle for immediate rewards and recognition, and their larger dreams get trapped within their smaller acquisitions.

After years of education, training, and preparing, it is finally launching time. But when schooling ends, a whole new ball game begins, for which they are not prepared. Up until now in their lives, their schooling experience has kept them oriented toward behaviors appropriate for their age group, but from now on, their primary orientation will be toward their work environment, with its diverse adult populations. In their private life, they must learn how to love beyond courtship—to sustain and nurture marital (or live-in) and friendship commitments. They must now master the management of time and money and a leisure life. The challenges are wonderful, but the responsibilities often seem overwhelming. Few twentysomethings feel as prepared as they want everyone to believe that they are.

Today's young adults often live together before marrying. Most adults marry in their twenties. The majority of these are now dual-career marriages, in which both the husband and the wife are full-time wage earners. This is a relatively new phenomenon in American life, and one that is transforming marital roles and family life. In today's world, both intimate partners work, participate in household chores, play, dream, seek a full adult script, and are determined to transcend their families of origin. Couples in their twenties have much in common as they join together to find successful paths into the full adult world. They share a common subculture, lofty expectations, sexual pleasure, and a hunger for affirmation. Leisure is increasingly important to twentysomethings, who find considerable meaning in play, physical prowess, health, creativity, travel, and time with friends. When successful twentysomethings hit thirty, they feel proud of their experimentation with life and view themselves as on their way.

Mature twentysomethings are open to experience, eager to adventure, and self-accepting. They take responsibility for their own lives, stay committed to continued learning, and maintain a philosophy of life—an internalized set of beliefs and values that are both unifying and directing.

The Down Side. No matter how prepared twentysomethings are to leave home or how angry they are with their parents, breaking out of a family of origin is almost always more difficult than expected. This represents the first predictable, major transition in adult life, usually filled with cocooning behaviors, self-renewal, and lots of experimentation. Family systems experts judge that this transition takes several years to work through, not merely for the young adult but for all the members of the family system. Few manage this transition knowingly or easily.

Twentysomethings are so devoted to leaving their family of origin that they seldom give sufficient thought to the qualities of the adult life that they want to arrive at. They think that those qualities, along with careers, financial security, and mates, will be bestowed upon them automatically, since they have now arrived at adulthood. It seldom occurs to them that they have to learn how to master the adult years. For about twenty years, they have been the children of their parents and monitored by school systems. Now, with the flick of a switch, they are supposed to be "on their own," "grown-up," and "responsible." Meanwhile, beneath the veneer of sleek muscular boldness lies a childlike scare. Twentysomethings and thirtysomethings spend their decades sorting out who they are from who they were. When ideas and emotions are still on loan from the family of origin, it is hard to own them. Throughout this first life structure, even though they are driven by the conflictual messages of parents, mentors, and peers, twentysomethings want to believe that they are in charge of their lives.

Some twentysomethings are early peakers who reach or surpass their personal goals during their twenties. They get thrown into social recognition for some role that they perform—a musical or acting career, sports success, possession of inherited money. The person behind the role usually doesn't have a clear identity, so the role dominates for a while. Unfortunately, people who build their life structures around their physical prowess or beauty often find that their lives peak in the twenties and thirties. After the peak, life is a downhill slide. Like one-string guitars, they have no more songs to play. Early peakers who decline behave much like old people who have only the past in which to live. Early peaking is an increasing problem among some upwardly mobile twentysomethings.

Every generation of twentysomethings is slightly different. Times change, and people change. For example, there is less difference between male and female roles among twentysomethings today than there was a generation ago. Today's men and women in their twenties share in education, careers, intimacy, and leisure interests. Both sexes ask the same questions: How much intimacy and commitment do I want and how much independence and freedom do

I need? How important are achievement, success, and money in relationship to quality time with friends, family, and causes that I believe in? How can I keep fit and maintain an active leisure life? The difference between the sexes is much more dramatic for thirtysomethings than for twentysomethings in today's world.

Our society used to have buffer zones that provided transitional environments for "youths" as they moved from adolescent rebellion to adult identities. Colleges, universities, the military, the Peace Corps, and apprenticeship roles in careers used to acculturate young people gradually into the adult years. Young people in the 1950s and 1960s could take a "psychosocial moratorium" during which they could experiment with various roles, values, and belief systems. They could travel, participate in religious or political groups, enter the work world for survival money, and live together. This "youth culture" gave American twentysomethings extended time to know who they were and how they wanted to live.

Today, it is not so easy. The undergraduate years have lost much of their general education function, and college cultures now reflect the society rather than providing incubation laboratories for maturation and socialization. The buffer for "practicing" adult personal and social behaviors has worn thin. There are few schools left that facilitate a rite of passage into adulthood. College majors do not always link with today's careers, and the anxiety over financial matters has led many to shortchange learning for training so that they can launch careers and find some security in the adult world. That is why so many twentysomethings are becoming instant adults, jumping into jobs and relationships, postponing much of their emotional and inner turmoil until later in life. The adolescent transition into the adult years—the only culturally approved transition in all adulthoood—has been shortened and shortchanged by a society lost in its own identity crisis.

The new twentysomethings have more cultural diversity than ever before, representing a variety of national, ethnic, and socioeconomic backgrounds. Today's twentysomethings face troubling social dilemmas. They enter the adult years at a time when the society struggles reactively with an AIDS epidemic, drugs, an economic recession or depression, wars, environmental scares, and widespread terrorism. Where is the welcome mat? If this is their inheritance, what are the future prospects? What can they hope for? What should they "work" for? Is it any wonder that many in the current generation of twentysomethings report that they feel abandoned and neglected by their own culture? Alienated, some get locked into survival and subculture roles before knowing who they are as adult persons. [3]

Twentysomethings tend to believe that they have all the time in the world to shape their lives. They often settle for immediate rewards and recognition, and their larger dreams get trapped within their smaller advances. They assume that their mistakes can be reversed. But in reality, some of the gates that young adults walk through close behind them and can be reopened only with great difficulty, if at all: career decisions, geographical choices, intimacy selections, parenthood, bank loans, and life-style preferences. Even those twentysomethings enraged by the apparent waning of our society will eventually learn that not to decide to do something with their lives is a decision that affects their own future options. The barely formed adult in us makes many decisions that have to be lived with for the rest of our lives or altered with considerable pain.

The three greatest dilemmas facing twentysomethings are achieving an adult identity, sustaining intimate bonds with others, and developing a distinct career. Because the acculturation forces are increasingly weak and diverse, more and more twentysomethings are failing to achieve one or more of these three developmental goals of the twenties. A lack of one or more of these can lead to intense loneliness, and anyone who works with twentysomethings knows how lonely they often are. This is an age group increasingly prone to accidents and suicide.

As they approach thirty, twentysomethings begin conducting an audit to see whether they are on course with their dream and with their peers. This zero-year transition is very common; it produces a rigorous evaluation of the decisions of the past decade, leading to new decisions to either deepen existing commitments or to alter them significantly. Dan Brown called his evaluation "Thirtynothing":

Waking up the morning of my 30th birthday with my three-year-old snoring in my ear and the cat trying to gnaw my foot through the blanket, nothing seemed different. GTE still hadn't rehooked my phone. The rent was still past due. My main source of income was still a job digging ditches and bending nails, which, glancing at the clock, I was again late for. I lay there for a while, waiting for my well-earned wisdom to kick in. Nothing came. . . .

Why, I thought lying there, is it the dawn of my 30th year and I am still in the dark? Turning 30, I figured, meant crossing the invisible line from promising phenom to wily veteran. Or at least it would be the year I quit considering myself in terms of an athlete, make a compromise with my dreams. But noooo. When shooting hoops or taking Sunday batting practice with friends, I'll still be scanning the sidelines for some old codger who will shuffle up to me and say I'm just what the Lakers or Dodgers are looking for. Hell, I'm not 30, I'm simply 10 for the third time. . . . There doesn't seem to be a lot of progress.

Cindy, my wife, didn't say anything until I was pushing the car out of the driveway. "Hey, speedster," she shouted from the front door, "bull your neck, don't sweat the small stuff, and remember, progress is highly overrated." After pop-starting the car, I took the first corner like Mario Andretti.[4]

Thirtysomethings: Making It

From the late twenties throughout their thirties, most adults spend their time "making it." They want to "arrive" fully, to feel the comfort of life beyond waiting and receive the rewards and recognition of having arrived. No longer initiates into adult life, thirtysomethings are committed to making the world work for them, which means investing in long-term issues: careers, marriages, parenting, and social leadership roles. Feeling that they have made valuable corrections in their life course on the basis of what they learned in their twenties, thirtysomethings plunge into a race for first-class citizenship in the adult world.

Mary and Derek

Mary: I was thirty-one when Cheree was born. Nothing has changed my life more than becoming a mother. I felt so close to Cheree, and

I reorganized my life around her needs. I changed many of my friends to other mothers of infants. I decided not to return to work for at least six months. Derek began to work extra hours so that we could maintain our income level, and he really liked being home on weekends, when he could have special time with Cheree.

Derek: My law firm asked me to become a partner when I was thirty-four, and I couldn't say no, even though I knew it would mean longer hours and more work. It also meant a permanent position, recognition, and higher salary.

Mary: Everything was easy with Cheree until she could walk, and then we had to rearrange the house. Although I loved to be with her, she was a full-time job. I went through several "mother's helpers," but I still felt the need to be around Cheree during those years. I was more tired than when I worked at the hospital. After talking it over with Derek, I decided to have another child to complete our family, so that by the time I reached forty the kids would be in school and I could return to work. Little Christopher was born when I was thirty-five.

Derek: By the time I was thirty-six, I was fairly well recognized for my legal specialty. I was talking frequently at conferences and regional meetings. I felt good about my attainments.

Mary: By the time I reached thirty-seven, my life was in a tailspin. My relationship with Derek had all but disappeared, and I was very angry with him. At the very time the children needed him most as a father, he increased his busyness at work and spent less time at home. I was desperately trying to return part-time to my career to supplement my parenting chores; I needed a life of my own. Our social life, which I managed, was almost entirely with parents of kids the ages of ours, and while on paper everything was coming out the way we wanted it, I was bitter and unhappy.

Derek: The guys at the office all hear the same story from their wives: "You're working too much and not coming home early enough in the evenings. I need you to be my partner with the family!" I don't know why Mary doesn't realize the predicament I'm in. In order to maintain my position in the firm, I have to be a leader, and that means long hours—and more pay. On the other hand, my closest friends are my work buddies. They're the greatest—but Mary doesn't know them much at all. When I go home these days, I feel like a stranger. Even the kids know better than I do where things are and what's going to happen. And I must admit, my sex life isn't the greatest. But we'll catch up after the kids get older. Right?[5]

The Up Side. Thirtysomethings want their piece of the rock, and they feel an urgency about reaching their goals. Forty is an approximate deadline that many young adults unconsciously set for reaching the goals that so often constitute "making it": career recognition, financial attainment, marriage and having babies, friendships, status, acquisitions, life style, leisure life, travel, and social leadership roles. There are many variations, some excluding marriage, others including marriage without children, and still others creating alternative life-styles. The pressure is the same: Make life happen to its fullest in this decade. Thirtysomething has a large agenda and a clock that is constantly ticking.

The two major issues for thirtysomethings are achievement (work, money, recognition) and intimacy (coupling, family, parenting). As children arrive, the division of labor between mother and father increases exponentially. Mothering, in particular, is a transformative experience, and women who have waited until their thirties to bear children usually are highly devoted to the mothering roles. However, those roles usually strain the mother's ability to follow her established career path. Strains also appear between the husband and wife as the two gradually evolve two virtually separate worlds of experience, joined primarily by parenting roles. Typically, he plunges deeper into career and financial responsibility as she immerses herself in building a family unit. However, fathering has gained interest among men as a primary identifier, and it is not unusual now to find men choosing to reduce their work hours or alter their careers in order to be active in parenting roles. Likewise, mothers today usually have careers to return to, and shared parenting and wage earning is common among thirtysomethings.

Thirtysomethings want to achieve authority, independence, and respect. They are basically tired of being "young" apprentices, and they want responsibility and rewards. For many, this is an exhilarating decade, filled with opportunity and challenge. These thirtysomethings get what they asked for and feel as if they are in a permanent orbit as the forties begin. Many thirtysomethings, however, find this decade to be a time when expectations and reality thrash about in a civil war of inner and outer conflict, leading to a midlife transition and a major life evaluation at the end of the thirties tunnel.

During the next ten years, America will experience an age-quake among its thirtysomethings. The baby boomers will be exiting this decade, and a small cohort with a more pessimistic outlook on life will replace them. How this will affect the profile of future thirtysomethings is difficult to say. Will the aging process work to bring the new group into line with what is written about thirtysomethings here (which is based heavily on the baby-boomer group)? Or will social and economic differences require a rewriting of this chapter?

The Down Side. The thirties may well be the most complex adult decade to manage. It is driven by a pressure-cooker agenda formed in the family of origin and modified by the experience of the twenties. This is the major adult period of expansive mastery based largely on blueprints obtained from parents, peers, mentors, or society itself. The internal drive is to reach external expectations. And the expectations are not really negotiable, because they are mostly unconscious imperatives and injunctions.

This is the decade when young adults feel driven to reach too many goals at superlative levels too fast. Not only is there a huge agenda to complete but it usually must be completed "perfectly." The thirties are years of role overload as the clock ticks toward self-imposed deadlines for realizing dreams and messages in their heads. By roughly forty, at the latest, they want to arrive at the fulfillment of their early adult dreams—success, happiness, financial security, and a life-style filled with trips, friends, children, and recognition.

Thirtysomethings want and expect permanent acquisitions in the adult world. They want to get beyond "preparing" and "waiting." They want to arrive. Men typically focus in on their jobs as their special assignment for achieving and producing financial results. Women find it difficult to balance all the life roles that they feel they should have, usually including jobs or careers, husbands or lovers, children, household design and maintenance, friendships, care of aging parents, and a social life. Houses must be bought and furnished, status symbols acquired, and financial equity stored away.

By thirty-five, you may well feel quietly terrorized by the one-dimensional prospects of your life. As you work feverishly to make your life permanently secure in the adult world, your life has evolved into a series of habitual routines. Intimacy is now in its long-haul phase, and routines have settled into well-recognized and anticipated conversations, touching, and sex. If thirtysomethings are in conventional marriages, family life is oriented around the growing needs of the kids, and this displaces the ego needs of mom and dad as they slide through their multiple roles as taxi driver, sports promoter, school monitor, disciplinarian, and food provider. For careerists, there are the daily routines of work: commuting, settling into the work space, plunging into the tasks at hand, taking a break, working some more, lunch, edging back into work, conversing through the late afternoon, commuting, and reentry into home space and time. Thirtysomethings typically work long hours with great intensity in pursuit of quality living, which they postpone because their lives are driven by high expectations for external attainments. Quantity issues overpower quality ones.

There is an undertow as well. For most thirtysomethings, life is planned, not spontaneous. It functions by masterplan and habits more than by free choice. The great decisions of life have been made, and you are waiting for the results. However, you are enmeshed in commitments from which you cannot easily extricate yourself; this is unlike your twenties, which were characterized by newly felt freedom and adventure. You are now lodged in complex intimate relationships, work and career agreements, financial commitments, and routine maintenance functions.

When you're a thirtysomething, you develop an increased ability to reflect on your life. Through introspection you begin to reevaluate your life decisions. You are still challenged to reach your goals, but you also wonder, Is this all there is? Is this what my life is all about? You supplement your routines with adventuresome weekends, visits to exotic places, intensive seminars on self-help themes, and a fanciful use of public holidays. Still, 94 percent of your time is invested in routine activities aimed at sustaining your life, leaving only 6 percent for celebrating your gains. You are goal-

rich but time-poor. Not exactly what you had in mind when you
started out.

Whereas twentysomethings are generalists determined to get
their acts together, thirtysomethings tend to specialize in specific
tasks for making it. This often leads to lopsided personalities, with
pigeonholed roles, advanced expertise, and enormous areas of undeveloped abilities. What was fun in your twenties may become an
addiction in your thirties. If you work full-time and are moving up
in your career, you may be called a workaholic, determined to
achieve at the highest level possible for all the rewards available.
After a decade or so of spending more time at work than at home,
you may feel like an outsider when you visit the kids' schools or
answer the phone at home.

If you raise children, your orientation toward parenting may
force a trade-off with your spouse: "I'll be the primary resource for
family and home even though I, too, work—and you be the primary
resource for money since you have the greater earning power," the
wife typically says. After a few years, his world revolves around his
career and hers revolves around many things, with the home, family, and her work often being the most important. He expends his
energy at work and comes home to be cared for. She expends her
energy at work and at home and expects an active partner in the
evenings and on weekends. His passivity at home is matched by her
anger at his psychological absence, and trouble often follows. The
dream that was supposed to fulfill their lives seems now to be sep-
arating them. Instead of a primary relationship, the marriage becomes an extracurricular activity.

The Midlife Transition

By your late thirties you may feel misguided by your earlier dreams,
exhausted by your frenetic activities, and trapped by your career and
marriage. You wonder whether you should examine a road not yet
taken, get into personal therapy, change careers, or consider divorce.
The closer you get to your early adult dream's deadline, which is
often sometime between thirty-five and forty-five, the less sure you
are that the ladder you have been climbing is up against the right
wall. Even if you reach your dream, you may feel disappointed that

so much of your life has been consumed in that pursuit, at the expense of other activities that now seem important to you. Carl Jung describes this transition succinctly:

> Middle life is the moment of greatest unfolding, when a man still gives himself to his work with his whole strength and his whole will. But in this very moment evening is born, and the second half of life begins. Passion now changes her face and is called duty; I want becomes the inexorable I must and the turnings of the pathway that once brought surprise and discovery become dulled by custom. The wine has fermented and begins to settle and clear. Conservative tendencies develop if all goes well; instead of looking forward one looks backward, most of the time involuntarily, and one begins to take stock, to see how one's life has developed up to this point. The real motivations are sought and real discoveries are made.[6]

Some people call the transition that often comes a little before or after age forty a "midlife transition" or a "midlife crisis" because it separates the first half of adult life from the second half. Most life transitions separate the decades or chapters of our lives, but this one serves a larger purpose. Like the fulcrum under a teeter totter, it represents the mid-point in a person's life—a major shift in perspective, values, and purpose. This transition represents a shift from external expansiveness to internal clarity. It separates your sense of endless time from limited time left, infinite options from limited choices, a denial of death from its personal certitude, expecting life to happen from accepting life as it happens, and parental or social scripts from personal ones. Sometimes these shifts are natural evolutions while at other times they are convulsive, producing disorientation and disillusionment with life as it has been lived, as for the thirty-five-year-old character Ivan in Anton Tchekov's play *Ivanov*:

> I go about with a heavy head, with a lazy soul, tired and broken, without faith, without love, without aim; I wander about among my friends like a shadow and I don't know who I am, or why I live, or what I want. Already it seems to me that

love is silly, that caresses and endearments are sugary non-
sense, that there isn't any meaning in work, that song and
impassioned words are trivial and old fashioned. And wherever I go I bring misery, blank boredom, discontent, disgust
with life.[7]

There are at least six issues that contribute to the midlife
transition:

1.   Biological changes in the body may trigger a reevaluation of
     self—crow's-feet around the eyes, a double chin, increased
     weight, thinning hair, diminished sexual energy.
2.   The gap between expectations and reality may induce a sense
     of failure and futility, particularly if the early adult dream was
     grandiose and unrealistic.
3.   Job satisfaction and career advancements may hit a plateau or ac-
     tually decline at about this time in life, fostering a reevaluation
     about work in particular and life in general. Or, career goals may
     not be met, with the result of boredom or restlessness.
4.   It is common for adults to restructure marital and family com-
     mitments at this time in life, which can trigger a deep personal
     reevaluation as well. In midlife, men tend to become less ag-
     gressive and more interested in love, relationships, and simple
     pleasures; women, on the other hand, become less comfortable
     in nurturing and submissive roles and more interested in exter-
     nal challenges, assertive roles, and their own personal develop-
     ment. These changes affect marital and family roles.
5.   Issues regarding social recognition and status may trigger new
     stock taking—a woman who is "only a housewife," or a man
     whose low-level job and moderate salary seem destined to keep
     the family in a small housing unit in the wrong part of town.
6.   There is often an increased awareness of the limits of life—
     financial constraints, reduced ambition, the amount of time
     left, and the inevitability of death.

These are some of the issues that come to a head during the midlife
transition, requiring minor or major adjustments to the life course
in order to make it acceptable. The goal of the midlife transition

is to unite life, not divide it. It connects time already lived with time left, being young with becoming old, feeling unique with feeling connected, and being in control with being nurtured by forces greater than ourselves. The central theme of the midlife transition is to get clearer than you have ever been before about who is running your life and to let it be you. William Bridges offers a useful description of a person going through a midlife transition:

> I have recently and reluctantly come to the conclusion that I am lost. Not just unsure that this is the right trail, but off any trail whatsoever. I find myself, figuratively, looking for footprints, broken twigs, any sign that someone has been over this ground ahead of me. . . . This is a time of transition for me, and I long for a little of the god's understanding. I am in that in-between state in my life, having left behind an outgrown but still perfectly serviceable past, and moving toward a future that resists all my efforts to bring it into focus. . . . What I long for this morning is some way of extricating myself from *who I have been.* I need some way to break the bonds of enchantment holding me to a self-image that needs to be cast off, now, like an outgrown shell. I assume that whatever natural process it is that causes us to burst old shells leads us to grow new ones. That's what I hope this morning, anyway. I'm not in a mood to scuttle around the floor of the universe bare. . . . One thing is sure: You have to give up on the idea of getting some one stable view of things. It's where you are in the journey that determines the view.[8]

Those adults who deny this transition continue to live "as if they were young," according to their early dream about acquisitions, security, and proving themselves. These people deny the realities and opportunities of the second half of life—particularly aging issues having to do with the decline of the body and the growth of the human spirit. At sixty, they still talk about the same concerns they prized at thirty; typically, they are wrapped up in one or two adult roles—careerist, spouse, parent, leisure activity—and untrained at introspection, self-nurture, and identification with life itself. A great many adults—particularly those who believe they are succeeding—die psychologically at the beginning of the midlife years as they lock themselves out of the incremental gains available in the second half of life. These gains are seldom a mere extension of the first half of life; rather, they come through a shifting of gears into new ways of thinking, living, and growing. Fortunately, the midlife transition is not chronologically restricted to thirty-five to forty-five year olds; it can and does occur whenever adults come to terms with the major changes in their lives—at thirty-five, forty-five, fifty-five, sixty-five, or later.

If you have been making these adaptations gradually throughout your twenties and thirties, you may not even be aware of a "midlife transition," which does not need to be a traumatic crisis. But if you have clung to a static, youthful picture of your adult years, you may experience a jolting turning point that will prompt a change of perspective, feelings, and priorities—a natural transition from thirtysomething to fortysomething for many adults today.[9]

9

The Forties and Fifties:

Taking Charge and Enjoying Life

The mass of men lead lives of quiet desperation. What is called resignation is confirmed desperation. . . . A stereotyped but unconscious despair is concealed even under what are called the games and amusements of mankind.

    I went to the woods because I wished to live deliberately, to front only the essential facts of life, and see if I could not learn what it had to teach, and not, when I came to die, discover that I had not lived. I did not wish to live what was not life, living is so dear; nor did I wish to practise resignation, unless it was quite necessary. I wanted to live deep and suck out all the marrow of life, to live so sturdily and Spartan-like as to put to rout all that was not life, to cut a broad swath and shave close, to drive life into a corner, and reduce it to its lowest terms.   *—Henry David Thoreau,*
           Walden[1]

Adult life in the forties and fifties continues most of the activities and commitments of the early adult years, but with new perspectives and concerns. Fortysomethings are often preoccupied with self-analysis and taking stock. They know they have reached the midpoint of their lives, but they are not sure how to address both the unfinished business of their twenties and thirties and the inevitable realities of getting older. Fiftysomethings have generally come to terms with midlife and have found positive ways to enjoy it. Many fiftysomethings report this decade to be one of increasing self-esteem, deepening intimacy, expanding leisure, reduced economic pressures, and improved sense of perspective on life.

Fortysomethings: Self-Reliance

As adults move into their late thirties and early forties, many of them feel driven to be in charge of their own lives. Tired of waiting in line for first-class adult citizenship, they want to control their own destiny. That is what self-reliance—the dominant pursuit of today's fortysomethings—is all about. However, others in their forties have unfinished business left over from their twenties and thirties. They want to finish that before devoting themselves fully to their own personal issues, so they choose to master interdependence, the art of achieving win-win relationships with others with whom one lives and works. The critical question is, Which is your dominant concern at this time in your life—self-reliance (to get more clarity about you and your personal agenda) or interdependence (to find new and better ways to relate to children, friends, career, spouse, and others)?

Self-reliance arrives as a decade orientation for those fortysomethings who have peaked in some major life role, such as parenting or career. Whenever you feel that you have "done your duty" to some major role in your life, you begin to look for a way to make space for your own personal agenda, much of which had to be postponed during the busy thirties. However, those who are still immersed in making it—raising kids, waiting for the final promotion, changing careers or life partners—usually shift gears from making it to interdependence, not yet prepared to take up self-reliance. Women more than men define themselves through their relationships with others, and for that reason—particularly if they have children still at home—they tend to move from interdependence to self-reliance. However, women who are following typical "male" scripts with career dominance more often shift from making it to self-reliance. Some people sequence from self-reliance to interdependence, and some the other way around.

A number of scholars on female development argue that there is a fundamental difference between the way men and women develop during the adult years. Men develop by being different, separate, autonomous, self-reliant, independent, boundaried, self-sufficient, and self-actualized. Women develop by being similar, connected, related to, caring, attached, and interdependent. Carol Gilligan described the woman's way with these words: "We know ourselves as separate only insofar as we live in connection with others and that we experience relationship only insofar as we differentiate other from self."[2] Men and women often display this difference by the midlife years, with men attached primarily to their work, where they can be self-reliant and achieving, and women with more complex attachments to families, friends, and work settings centered around nurturing, caring, and achieving roles. It is natural, then, to expect men to want to "individuate" when their careers no longer fulfill them or their intimate relationships stifle their autonomy and for women to sustain their "interdependence" until their primary commitments to children, intimate relationships, and careers have been fulfilled. However, the argument isn't so simple. These two tendencies are more male and female forces within all of us than gender distinctions per se. Some women, for example, follow the "male" line of reasoning and end up stressing self-reliance first, just as some men follow the "female" line and move from interdependence to self-reliance. With the options available to today's adults and the multiple roles that we can all have access to throughout adulthood, each person must choose the decade orientation that fits his or her own lifeline.

Marvin Banasky

For me, the forties have been a series of wake-up calls. These signals for impending change appeared gradually, yet they were inescapable. During my thirties, my life was filled with symbols of stability and success, and simultaneously the cracks in my inner security were ever widening.

My first wake-up call alerted me to a profound restlessness within me. As I reflected back on my life, I lacked an understanding of what I was about. I felt as if I had been radar-locked onto achievement goals and had channeled my high energy to attain those goals for the past twenty years. At about age forty, I realized how unprepared I had been for being a husband and a father and how confused I was with my wife and family. In my business, I felt I was succeeding at someone else's business interest, not my own.

Then my wake-up signals began to give me some direction. I began to reevaluate my entire life. In my marriage, I wanted more partnership and equal sharing from my wife. In parenting, I wanted to relate out of love rather than as the disciplinarian. In my career, I wanted to start all over in some new field. It was time for me to speak up and be myself.

The next twelve months were the most disrupting period of my life. I was not ready for all the changes that would rush at me and out of me. At about the same time that the divorce was finalized, I closed down my fourteen-year-old business. My son moved in with me, and within five months my two daughters joined me, too. I felt lacking, like a glass half empty instead of a glass half filled. Little by little, self-discovery deepened.

I am now forty-five, and I believe that I am more vital and alive now than at any other time of my life. As I look back over my odyssey, I realize that my transitions were more useful to my journey than I had wanted to believe while I was in the midst of them. Each year, I feel that I am achieving deepening satisfaction, and even though I do not know my ultimate goals, I trust I will find them—or, more likely, create them.[3]

Marilyn Mosley

At forty-one, I am a single parent, the sole provider for my household, and the director of a private high school. My three children are between the ages of fourteen and eighteen, and the eldest will be going to Bennington College this fall. My relationship with my children is evolving into one of friend and confidant, and I am very pleased about that.

My twenties and thirties were a vulnerable and confusing period for me. My expectations and my realities were in different worlds, and I felt fragmented much of the time. The thirties were traumatic for me, as I moved from Baltimore to California with three children, a troubled marriage, parental strife, and a return to school.

I am now freer to work on my own issues and to focus on my career. I am interested in making an impact on the world around me, whatever that may mean. I want to leave a legacy of a better earth-nation-state-city-home-family—whatever I can do. As I think to myself, "I have forty years of life left, and I will commit them to making a difference."

I used to think that I was immortal, that life would go on forever. I had so much to contribute and all the time in the world to do it. That has changed for me. I am more aware of the ticking of the clock. I am beginning to think smart, to create strategies for my life. It's no longer appropriate for me to be a ship afloat without a rudder. I am now interested in financial plans, health policies, wills, life insurance, and other "reality issues." After all, sixty-five is twenty-four years away. It's time to think and create for my future.

My quest for marriage has ended, but I do hope for a fulfilling relationship with a life companion. I am interested in creating a partnership with intimacy and friendship. My identity is not as tied up in my body as it used to be or in using my body as a sexual tool. I am looking for a different quality of relationship: communication, creativity, and spiritual aspirations are my primary concerns. I am not seeking to rescue a man or to be rescued.

I know I am far too busy. I keep postponing my own development and interests in order to raise my children, which I thoroughly enjoy. I am also providing my parents with emotional support. But I long to be alone, to visit my friends, and to travel. I often ask myself, "How do I shift gears and place more emphasis on my personal interests?"

I am preparing to become a fifty-year-old woman. I want to know what it will be like. At thirty, forty was ten years and a lifetime away. Aging was not a process that I was interested in knowing more about. Now I am ready to acknowledge my age and to learn from it. I am a woman and no longer a girl, and I like the woman in me. Planning for the future, with intimacy, contribution to the world, and nurturing strong family ties, is the heart of my tasks at this time in my life. Being forty brings with it a certain intensity and pensiveness. I feel that I am a woman with her own life slowly emerging.[4]

The Up Side. The forties are a time for inward reflection, reevaluation, simplification of the life course, and deepening of the human journey. The goals are to chart your own path, to be your own person, and to possess your life. The shift toward self-reliance may be part of a life transition, since the changes in behavior and values are often enormous. Commitments sometimes change dramatically, as do marriages and careers. With a keen sense of racing against time, people in midlife shift from quantity to quality activities, from external acquisitions to internal satisfactions, from pleasing others to pleasing themselves.

Adults pursuing self-reliance have two goals, one developmental and one transformational. The developmental goal aims at a completion of the first half of life: to evoke a complete human being capable of shaping his or her own destiny. In this context, self-reliance means the assumption of responsibility for your own thoughts, feelings, and decisions—to write your script and be accountable to yourself for your joy and sorrow. It means to take over the dream and to pull it into the here and now, to be lived daily. The developmental impetus is toward becoming a self-responsible person ready to live more deeply and more simply, driven from within and not by parental voices or external forces. Some of the developmental commitments of fortysomethings are:

- Renewing the self
- Evaluating and renewing the couple relationship
- Learning to parent adolescent and young adult children
- Learning to care for aging parents
- Investing in leisure time
- Obtaining training in new personal and professional skills
- Reevaluating career options and paths

Self-reliance means becoming accountable for your thoughts, feelings, relationships, and commitments. It is an inner decision to be in the world differently than before by not pretending to be who you aren't and not waiting for impossible dreams to happen. Arriving at self-reliance, fortysomethings gradually withdraw from superficial activities, invest in growth and development, and begin to live by their own intentionality. They move beyond organizing their lives around their roles in jobs, marriage, and parenting. Without reducing their external effectiveness, they seek ways to invest in themselves. More than anything, fortysomethings want a "private" life—a place within themselves they can always retreat to. In work settings, this may mean getting off the fast track of upward mobililty. At home, the postparenting years usually arrive during the forties or fifties, making it possible for new projects, education, and relationships. The result is a shift of perspective, from external compliance to internal motivation. Fortysomethings attend to their own interiority with the same intensity that has already been expended on the external world. After interviewing many middle-aged men and women, developmentalist Bernice Neugarten drew this conclusion:

> Most of this group, as anticipated, were highly introspective and highly verbal persons who evidenced considerable insight into the changes that had taken place in their careers, their families, their status, and in the ways in which they dealt with both their inner and outer worlds. . . .
>
> We are impressed, too, with reflection as a striking characteristic of the mental life of middle-aged persons: the stock-taking, the heightened introspection, and above all, the structuring and restructuring of experience—that is, the conscious processing of new information in the light of what one has already learned; and turning one's proficiency to the achievement of desired ends.
>
> These people feel that they effectively manipulate their social environments on the basis of prestige and expertise; and that they create many of their own rules and norms. There is a sense of increased control over impulse life. The successful middle-aged person often describes himself as no longer "driven," but as now the "driver"—in short, "in command."[5]

The transformational goal in pursuing self-reliance is to prepare for the second half of life, moving into the life of the "self," a spiritual aspect of mature life—to participate in universal truths through gratitude, love, and laughter. This transformation might be called "the psychological birth of the adult," because it opens the doors of the mind and heart to respect the past, to live in the present, and to anticipate the future. You feel as if for the first time you were in the presence of all the puzzle pieces that your life represents. Carl Jung, who called self-reliance "individuation," said that its aim is "completeness" with yourself, so that you live not to project yourself but to be yourself. You move from living out of your ego needs to living with your "self." Instead of striving out of your incompleteness to find life, security, and safety, you enter a receptor mode and accept the life deep within and around you. Jung describes this process with moving words:

> We are all thoroughly familiar with the sources of the problems which arise in the period of youth. . . . It is often a question of exaggerated expectations, of under-estimation of difficulties, of unjustified optimism or of a negative attitude. One could compile quite a list of the false presuppositions which give rise to the earliest, conscious problems. . . . Thoroughly unprepared we take the step into the afternoon of life; worse still, we take this step with the false presupposition that our truths and ideals will serve us as hitherto. But we cannot live the afternoon of life according to the programme of life's morning—for what was great in the morning will be of little use at evening, and what in the morning was true will at evening have become a lie. . . . Expansion of life, usefulness, efficiency, the cutting of a figure in social life, the shrewd steering of offspring into suitable marriages and good positions—are not these purposes enough? . . . Ageing people should know that their lives are not mounting and unfolding, but that an inexorable inner process forces the contraction of life.[6]

Through the conscious development of an inner self, we discover connections to universal qualities of life everywhere. This spiritual awareness transforms our sense of purpose, and we begin to pursue a higher consciousness characterized by wholeness, reflection, and trust—investing our energy in forms of life and work that will outlive us. A popular view of spiritual people is that they are weak, emasculated, and otherworldly. In the context of this book, *spiritual* means just the opposite—strong, bold, and profoundly present. Spiritual awareness creates what Robert Bly calls "the inner warrior," a person who chooses to heed the voice within and to follow it. Spirit gives birth to integrity, depth, risk-taking, and the courage to be.[7] Spirituality is empowerment of human resources that exist in their most complete form in the lives of mature adults. Anchored in trust, experienced in gratitude, this spiritual force reaches for human meaning beyond (not in place of) mere pleasure, power, and possessions. It searches for abiding values and lasting contributions. It promotes the highest level of risk-taking—human caring. It generates profound compassion.

The Down Side. Fortysomethings are typically evolving from being specialists in some external role to being generalists in themselves. It is common for fortysomethings to feel "lopsided." When they were young adults, they applied themselves and became fairly good at something—selling, managing, raising babies, teaching, playing basketball—and their friends and mentors agreed: "You're really good at that. You should get more training and move further into your specialty." So they did, and as they perfected their specialties, they found less and less time for all the other parts of their lives, so that by their forties, they are very good at a few things and remarkably undeveloped in the rest of their human capabilities. So we find fortysomethings wondering how to develop their undeveloped parts. For women who have spent their twenties and thirties as homemakers, wives, and mothers, this may mean reentering school to prepare for a career, economic self-sufficiency, and leadership responsibility. For those who have spent their twenties and thirties in full-time careers, it may mean having children and nesting. For most men, who typically overidentify with their careers, it means getting in touch with the universe within them—the land of interiority, feelings, and spirituality.

Picture, if you can, a room full of lopsided fortysomethings feeling an urgency to develop the parts of their lives that until now have been handled through symbiosis, dependency, neglect, or repression. If they have shaped their lives around their careers, they may now feel remorse about the intimacy that they neglected—the achiever who didn't get married, the absent father who wasn't emotionally available to his children, the woman who forgot to have children, the gay man or woman who stayed in the closet. If they have shaped their lives around caring and nurturing others, they may now feel a sense of failure at unreached personal goals—career paths uncharted, financial independence not secured, private life undeveloped, leisure goals lost, bodies neglected. Fortysomethings seek well-rounded lives with overall human competence. They seek balance and completion.

Fortysomethings are sometimes called middlescents when they behave like grown-up adolescents thrashing about to test their boundaries. They use anger, depression, and other emotions to break away from what isn't working in their lives. What makes middlescents different from adolescents is their extensive commitments: to marriages, children, jobs, civic roles, financial obligations. Repossessing your soul without wrecking your life is not always easy. Although being true to yourself requires a rigorous inner honesty, it seldom requires trashing all that you have been. This is a time for sorting things out, simplifying, and choosing stepping stones that lead to the future that you truly want.

Fortysomethings want to be their own persons and diminish their dependencies. How do you do this when your career has brought you to an advanced position or to a reputation as the best internist in town? How do couples with twenty years of dependency in their marital relationship transform their marriage to a model based on equity and mutuality? How does a fortysomething change his or her parenting style when the children are quite accustomed to manipulating the old style and to resisting change? How can fortysomethings change habits of deprivation, indulgence, and addiction? Do you continue to aspire to all that you can be, or should you reduce your goals and choose a simpler life? The internal dreams of fortysomethings are usually very different from the external dreams of twentysomethings. Typically, fortysomethings lower their expansive expectations while increasing their expectations for quality in their lives.

Fiftysomethings: Interdependence

Sometime before the fifties arrive, it is not uncommon for forty-somethings to tire of self-reliance. While taking charge of your own destiny is essential to your fulfillment, self-reliance leads beyond itself, to interdependence with others. Autonomy is a stepping stone, not an end point; it prepares people for relationships and leadership roles that have deeper integrity than they have had in their earlier years.

The Experience of Herant Katchadourian, M.D.

Turning fifty. The "Big Five-O." Wonderful like the dawn of a new age, brimming with promise of fulfillment? Or ominous like a tanker coming at you through the fog? Which is it? What happens at age fifty?

I approached my fiftieth birthday with great expectations. There were no major crises in my professional or personal life. But there were many loose ends on all fronts, and I firmly believed that as I turned fifty, these loose ends would get tied up; I would get closure on issues that for years had drained and distracted me like so many dripping faucets.

My expectations of turning fifty were entangled with my sense of being fully adult. Mind you, this had nothing to do with external evidence of being adult. I acted mature enough as an adolescent to pass for an adult when I turned twenty. The issue did not involve objective accomplishments or the perception of others but had to do with my own perception of what it meant to be adult. And to me that meant doing what I thought I ought to do with my life.

The day finally came when I turned fifty. For a short while there was the illusion that the long-awaited closure had been attained. But then I could hear the faucets dripping again, and I realized with some amusement that no magical transformation had taken place. I continued to change ever so slightly—sometimes for the better, sometimes for the worse—but most of the time into someone merely a little different.[8]

The Experience of Richard L. Haid

For some twenty years I have hoped that there might be another career within me where I might do something of educational and social significance. For thirty years I had been part of my father's insurance agency, which I ultimately inherited and successfully managed, located in a small city in southern Ohio.

I have always had a quest for meaning and purpose in my life, and I was not fulfilled as a businessman in recent years. Was there another career that would offer more satisfaction than what I had been doing for over thirty years? I didn't like paperwork and detail. I did like taking charge of my learning, creating something new, being in new surroundings, taking risks, and developing the potential of people and organizations.

During my fifties, all four children left for college, and my wife, Leslie, and I had an empty nest. Although she had occasionally worked part-time during her adult years, her primary devotion had been to the family and home. A new sense of intimacy developed between Leslie and me. She went back to school for a year of paralegal training, and so I did much of the cooking and cleaning and laundry. I had a sense of immediate completion from the domestic chores, and Leslie found that my doing the chores was a bit threatening.

In my business, I found it harder and harder to keep myself motivated. I was very bored with my work. Then I attended a last-half-of-life workshop at a retreat center, and when I returned home, I knew I was starting a new chapter in my life.

I became aware of my long term interest in people and their careers, and as I learned to use more of my potential, I was able to coach others to do the same. I became energized and became the first intern ever to train at a nearby outplacement firm, where I was able to help unemployed businessmen start again, as I was doing. With grief and pain, I sold my insurance agency and entered a Ph.D. program where I could design my own study in career transitions. I also started consulting and leading seminars.

People tell me that my face glows when I talk about my new career and the fascinating experiences that I am having. I now have the freedom and energy to be part of this change. My theme is What Are You Going To Do With The Rest Of Your Life? From my experience I believe that most persons have the capacity to achieve more satisfying lives than they think, especially in the second half of life. My experience as a businessman is invaluable in my new career, and my increasing maturity as a scholar is helping me move rapidly through my studies, although I like what I am learning so much that I am in no hurry to graduate. My passion is coaching persons as they take charge of their lives by renewing their learning and make career transitions.[9]

The Up Side. Fiftysomethings view life as a social process of sharing, negotiating, celebrating, accepting, and living. Interdependence promotes a decade orientation of interaction, mutual affirmation, multiple friendships, and shared enjoyment. Interdependence is an androgenous experience, occurring at a time when our masculinity and our femininity are more or less in balance and "sex" is not so much a determiner of relationships and activities. Quality-of-life issues increase, along with an openness to be in the world as it is—connected to nature, life, and the flow of things. Interdependence is like a dance with life wherever it can be found, with mutual participation, rejoicing, and sharing. The "I" of self-reliance becomes the "we" of interdependence.

Fiftysomethings typically have lowered defense mechanisms, deal with conflict directly, and have increased trust in others. Fiftysomethings do not see the present as an improvement on the past or the future as a happier time; they view the present time—now—as the only time dimension that matters. They live to live. At fifty, it is time to stop preparing and to start living.

Fiftysomethings often see their world as an extended family. For many, travel has a profound appeal as an invitation to learn more about life everywhere. This is a time when marriages can deepen and spirituality can flourish. With their children usually off to college or somewhere else, peer networks of friends take their place. The importance of work and external issues often lessens while the development of close relationships increases. Marie Dressler writes, "By the time we hit fifty, we have learned our hardest lessons. We have found out that only a few things are really important. We have learned to take life seriously, but never ourselves."[10] For the most part, fiftysomethings are preoccupied with living, not with themselves. "Perhaps middle-age is, or should be, a period of shedding shells," states Anne Morrow Lindbergh, "the shell of ambition, the shell of material accumulations and possessions and the shell of the ego."[11] Germaine Greer expands on this: "You care about yourself less and less. Your vanity and pride stop getting in your way. You begin to develop a sense of proportion. . . . You stop squandering emotion on foolish things . . . or waste time on fatuities. You can escape from the dominion of your own passions and enter into a calm wherein you can fix your eye upon a worthy objective and pursue it wholeheartedly."[12]

Fiftysomethings are less inclined than they used to be to use immature defense mechanisms. They are more inclined to say what they think, express their feelings directly, be forgiving, and suppress whatever they don't know how to deal with. They isolate what they find unacceptable in themselves and either work on it or keep it in check. Fiftysomethings usually have a capacity to integrate and to become at one with their experience. The marriages of fiftysomethings often take on a spiritual dimension, with each partner serving as a facilitator of the other's life journey. At this point in life, marriage can become a central vehicle for the life course process, facilitating his life, her life, and our life. It can be the warm glow of two best friends celebrating profound companionship, including love, sex, and growing old together. It can also be a livable truce that will be either revitalized or terminated, although there are always some who would rather endure the misery of marriage than improve or give up the attachment. There are increasing numbers of fiftysomethings who are divorced, single, widowed, or living alternative life-styles. In fact, from fifty on, adults live and love in all sorts of arrangements to give and get affection, support, and fun.

Diversity of options for living and working will continue to expand in the twenty-first century.

In the career and work world, fiftysomethings who have been in careers since their twenties are usually coasting on what Abraham Maslow called "unconscious competence." They don't have to prepare very much or think about their tasks; they know how to get their jobs done at high levels of excellence. Although motor skills have begun to slow and accuracy may not be as good as it once was, the value of fiftysomethings' experience is usually more important. They bring stability and perspective to the work force, provided that they are not bored with their work or angry with their companies. Fiftysomethings are less interested in active mastery in the workplace, where they have to be present to get results; they prefer passive mastery where they can monitor results through leadership roles, policy formation, or monetary control.[13]

A significant number of fiftysomethings might be called late bloomers. They reach their peak in their careers, sports, or hobbies later than most of their peers. This group includes a significant number of women who had to postpone their own development as they married, raised families, and got out of synch with their careers but were able to achieve well in later years. In all probability, an even larger number of late bloomers would emerge if sexism and ageism were reduced in our society and welcome mats extended. The American Association of Retired Persons is hard at work on this, and given the relatively low numbers in the young generations of adults, it is likely that older Americans will have increasing opportunities for achievement and leadership in the early part of the twenty-first century.

The Down Side. The bodies of fiftysomethings are slowing down. Mirrors are less friendly; the pear shape of old age is well under way. Nutrition and exercise are more important than ever. Sexual drive diminishes somewhat, but the most notable physiological happening is female menopause (which need not be an impasse to creative living and loving). However, you are bound to hear about friends who experience strokes, heart attacks, cancer, or diabetes. You will have acquaintances who suffer early disabilities, and each incident rings bells in your head—time is running out. Energy for most fiftysomethings, however, depends more upon motivational than body issues. Are you bored, cynical, and feeling hopeless about the future? Or are you eager to make your future the best years of your life? That is the fundamental choice, and your answer determines your destiny—to live on or to decline.

10

The Sixties and Seventies:

Starting Over and Coming to Terms

To be young is to be fresh, lively, eager, quick to learn; to be mature is to be done, complete, sedate, tired. From this point of view, only the distraught young would think positively about growing up, and most of the mature would think longingly about being young. But what if we consider a different perspective? To be young is to be unripe, unfinished, raw, awkward, unskilled, inept; to be mature is to be ready, whole, adept, wise. How valid are our glorification of youth and our shame about having lived many years?
—*Lillian E. Troll, Early and Middle Adulthood*[1]

The sixties and seventies are both extensions of the previous adult years—with a continued emphasis on work, leisure, and relationships, and they are decades in which adults come to terms with their lives, as the days dwindle down to a precious few. These are years which can be like vintage wine or like a disaster area, often depending on issues like health, status, money, self-motivation, and friendships.

Sixtysomethings: Starting Over

The new generation of sixtysomethings isn't behaving like the porch-rocking grandmas and grandpas of yesterday. They plan to continue to live, love, travel, work, and even raise a new batch of kids.

The Experience of Larry L. King

Long ago—though not as long ago as I once thought—I decided that "old age" began at 60. "Old age" was self-defining; it meant, simply, that life for all practical purposes was over and done. Those who had attained it could look forward to nothing but solitary thumb-twiddling, warm mush, and the folds of the shroud. This harsh edict was handed down when I was a cocksure 20 and, seemingly, light years away from its personal consequences.

This year I turned 60, an accomplishment causing many reassessments. It is much clearer than formerly that 60-year-olds are vigorous entries in life's race. . . . Age begins sneaking up on us in soft, quiet shoes long before we are aware of its shadow. Even when it begins rattling our door, we are reluctant to bid it come in. We call it "maturity" so long as the mirror or our medical charts permit, the American culture teaching that youth is all and that youth must be served. When was the last time you saw a television grandmother, or even a matron, perched on the hood of a new automobile or *old* cowhands celebrating the end of the workday and the arrival of beer time?

Athletic events, beauty pageants, talent contests, soap operas: All accentuate youth and identify it with glamour. . . . The fear of being excluded from life's "mainstream"—as our culture perceives it—probably accounts for those traumas attending entry into each new personal decade. . . . Fifty was the age that made me snarl and throw things. I was throwing them at a television commercial telling me that those in my "age group of 50 to 80" could now buy a certain product without having to submit our ancient bones to the risk of embarrassing physical examinations. . . .

I realize that I am more fortunate than most as I face the aging process. My health is far better than I deserve, considering my body's prior rough treatments, and would be even better if I could whip a long addiction to cigarettes. As a free-lance writer, I have no job subject to mandatory retirement regulations but can work so long as I have the will and faculties to perform. Thanks to luck in the marketplace, I am unlikely to face financial deprivations in my final years. Three of my offspring are adults long past old-parent-progeny conflicts, so that we may comfortably share our time together. I have the additional benefit of a young second family—a good wife with her own successful career, and children 10 and 7 who benefit not only from their mother's intelligence and stability but also, one hopes, from an older and more experienced father taking care not to repeat the youthful mistakes he made in raising his first family.

These factors give me reasons to face each new day not with despair but with hope and with purpose. I do not mean I am always as sunny as Mary Poppins; indeed, there are days when I wake tired and grumpy and exhibit old vestiges of my alcoholic personality unless I remind myself—or my wife reminds me—that the evidence of my daily life simply does not support periodic bouts of sullen self-pity. Nine times out of ten, my morose mornings are tied to troubles with a writing project and disappear after a few good hours at the typewriter.

I will not pretend that I *like* the notion of growing old or the prospect of increasingly accommodating to old age. I remember, and now better appreciate, the pain of my father in having to make personal surrenders: no longer driving a car or climbing trees for pruning purposes or smoking cigarettes, all of which he continued into his 80th year. I do, however, *accept* the notion of impending old age in realistic terms. It requires no genius to recognize that one is not as supple or as tireless as formerly; that one expends more energies to accomplish the same amount of work and requires longer to recover. One knows that at age 60 a heart attack and other sneak debilitations are possible, and thus postpones mowing the grass on the hottest summer day or seeks help in carrying a heavy item of furniture up two flights of stairs. . . . The aging man discovers that it is prudent to keep his life insurance paid up and his legal papers current, that he will wake earlier than when younger, that his bones may creak a bit more en route to his morning shower, that chili or peanut butter do not taste as good as they once did, that 26-year-old blondes are not as interested in him as they once might have been. . . .

Thankfully, there are compensatory rewards. Our memories grow richer, and what once appeared to be random events assume logical patterns with causes and consequences—a realization most helpful to one in my business and, I would think, at least interesting and comforting to those who are not. One is likely to become more happily ruthless in avoiding what once seemed to be obligatory social waltzes. This has less to do with choosing the hermit's life than with reserving more of one's time for what one truly *wants* to do—whether it is reading a book or going to a ballgame or simply avoiding the torture of neckties and tedious dinner-party chitchat. There is a freeing liberation in discovering our true priorities and then shoving aside hindrances to those priorities without fearing harm to one's career or being marked off some hostess's "A" list. My priorities these days are work and family and a bit of time to leisurely observe, analyze, and take stock.

There is a sense of urgency about accomplishing work one feels compelled to do—yes, a sense of limited time—but there is no frenzy in it, no hanging cloud raining dark thoughts of approaching infirmities or death. One simply knows what one wants to *do* with the remaining good years and plans the doing as efficiently as circumstances permit. . . . I am gratified that life has taught even a slow learner that it is far better to hang in there, mixing it up, than to quit on one's corner stool in the early or middle rounds.[2]

The Up Side. The current generation of sixtysomethings includes Jackie Onassis, Dick Clark, Jules Feiffer, Liz Claiborne, Bob Newhart, Andre Previn, Ed Asner, and Arnold Palmer. They are all active, productive people making the most of the years ahead of them. First lady Barbara Bush maintains a busier schedule than most of us, to say nothing of her sixtysomething husband. In 1990, there were more than sixty million sixtysomethings in the United States, most in good health and many in sound financial condition. Poverty is at the lowest level in this century for sixtysomethings, and financial planning along with Social Security has made the economic prospects excellent for building quality lives.[3]

The American society is increasingly open to having sixty-somethings live, learn, work, travel, whatever. Now that retirement is an elective rather than a requirement, people are having to ask themselves "What do I want to do with the rest of my life?"—because they probably can do it. Many will go on working, begin new careers, or enter entrepreneurial ventures. Some will go back to school to learn something that their curiosity seeks to understand or their consciousness wants to explore. Others will join the leisure life and invest in their friendships. Still others will concentrate on travel and adventure, while some will retreat to private settings to enjoy nesting. People in this decade can decide several times how they want their lives to be; they are not stuck with their first choice. The sixties are a vital chapter in the adult journey—another opportunity to rearrange priorities.

A basic rumbling in the lives of many sixtysomethings is the wish to "mentor": guide, model, shape, transform, help, serve. They want to extend their talent to the next generation, to contribute what they can to the future. It is quite normal for mentoring to begin in your forties or fifties, but it often becomes the central theme in the lives of many sixtysomethings who want to invest in supporting, challenging, and providing vision to others. A mentor is someone who not only is competent at "doing" something but is competent at "being" human as well—a mensch, a complete person.[4] Some mentors have something to teach and look for learners seeking their knowledge and wisdom. Some mentors are senior careerists who model the way for younger workers, conveying the mystique of high performance and joy. They may "sponsor" specific younger men and women to ensure they get the "stuff" that can be learned from being around experienced masters. Some mentors tell stories about how the world works to feed the consciousness of those who listen, to provide memories and dreams. Other mentors seek avenues such as the Peace Corps or the social-service agencies of religious groups where they can contribute some of their expertise to those who want it. Grandparenting is a mentoring role available and fulfilling to many sixtysomethings as well as to many in their fifties and seventies. Older fathers, such as Larry L. King, are

increasingly common, and their style of parenting is very likely to
follow the mentoring process. Leadership is the form that
mentoring most often takes—leadership at work, leadership in the
community, leadership in leisure life. The urge to mentor may well
have begun when sixtysomethings were in their forties or fifties, but
now they view their lives as at their peak, and they want to make
a difference in the world around them.

The Down Side. Sixtysomethings often face a new beginning
different from previous ones. When people think of their sixties,
they often think of retirement. Many sixtysomethings choose or
have to accept retirement from long-term employment during this
decade. Although many people of sufficient means increasingly
view retirement as a new beginning for untried dreams, it is often
accompanied by profound feelings of loss. It can be a major transition in adult life, particularly for those who have built their lives
around their work. Some people do not know who they are apart
from their work roles, schedules, status, and contacts. Careerists
often overdevelop their dependency on work and underdevelop their
identification with friends, leisure, hobbies, and internal goals.
When these people retire, they tend to reminisce while having difficulty facing the future. Others seem to reverse their life-style when
they retire, pulling up stakes and heading for retirement communities, golf courses, or fishing holes—breaking the ties that they
have had with family, friends and their local community. Sometimes this shift into a sunbelt-outdoor-leisure life-style works like
a liberation long overdue, while at other times it leads to an ambiguous life in limbo, without a sense of purpose.

Although it is increasingly easier for sixtysomethings to continue their work, new conditions of employment may represent a
demotion in roles, status and pay. Also, people accepting Social
Security benefits have severe restrictions on wage earnings. Most
retired people prefer to work part-time if they can find work that
doesn't conflict with the retirement life-style and goals. A number
of new retirees turn to self-employment and run their own businesses, franchises, or craft centers. Perhaps the largest number of
retirees seek work through volunteer roles in their community, al-

though the cost of living is leading many volunteers to seek salaried positions. For many, income is the major problem of retirement.

When I'm working with clients who are struggling with retirement issues, I recommend "protirement," which means to throw yourself ahead into a new blend of work and other activities. Protirement is a positive plan for a new chapter in life, emphasizing possible options and personal renewal. It might include a new career, but more often it has to do with an unfinished life agenda that successful people have put off long enough. Protirement is a great time for shifting gears into a new life chapter that enriches and fulfills. Why not?

Friends are very important to most sixtysomethings. Many men discover new ways to be friends with others and enjoy their relationships; other men, who never learned to sustain friendships, retreat from social contact, expecting their spouses to remain their social monitors. Women are more typically accustomed to having many kinds of friends, and these relationships often flourish during the retirement years: convenience friends, geographical friends, historical friends, leisure friends, special-interest friends, cross-generational friends, mentor friends.

Sixtysomethings know that they are not at the end of the beginning; they are at the beginning of the end. The sixties may well be the final decade of good health and capabilities for travel, projects, and unfulfilled dreams. The drum is beating. The bodies of sixtysomethings work a little less well, which may be good enough for high levels of life satisfaction, but may not. Problems with seeing, hearing, bladder control, and loss of short-term memory may show their ugly heads during our sixties, unless we inherited superlative genes and immune systems and have kept our bodies in excellent condition. Everything slows down, and for every organ and function, the rule is: If you don't use it, you'll lose it! For the most part, sixtysomethings are active in leisure activities and attentive to new information on nutrition and health care. Still, aging progresses incrementally and inevitably, and the sixtysomething who can adapt effectively to whatever happens is most likely to have a positive feeling of life development. The freedom to be yourself as a sixtysomething is balanced by the daily awareness that your time is running out.

Seventysomethings: Coming to Terms with Integrity

"Integrity: wholeness, soundness, from *integer,* untouched whole, entire. 1. the quality or state of being complete; wholeness; entireness; unbroken state. 2. the entire, unimpaired state or quality of anything; perfect condition; soundness. 3. the quality or state of being of sound moral principle; uprightness, honesty, and sincerity" (*Webster's New Unabridged Dictionary*).

The Experience of Robert E. Lee

Vast reaches lie out there to be touched, explored, interpreted, reinterpreted. The world has acquired more new information in the years of my lifetime than all mankind has assembled throughout the millennia since the first Ice Age. And we're only starting.

I'm not a young man. So? Should I disqualify myself because I have fewer hours to see and breathe and think than my daughter has? Or my son? My wife's father, well past eighty, was working in his backyard the week before his heart stopped. Pointing to a row of fruit trees he had just planted, he said: "In twenty years, these will yield more than we can possibly eat!" He was right. Those trees now give magnificent pears and peaches and apples. Though he's not here to savor the taste, others do. Or perhaps he's enjoying vicariously through the tingle of a latter-day tongue. Can anyone say that planting those trees wasn't a thousand times more useful than dwelling on his age and infirmities? Emerson says everything has its compensations. Salty-saccharine Lord Tennyson swears, "Though much is taken, much abides. It is not too late to seek a newer world!" . . . I caught a glimpse of myself in the mirror a few days ago. I don't do it often, because I don't believe what I see. I feel about twenty-two—and I think there's more truth in my feelings than in my reflections.[5]

The Experience of Sarah McClendon

I never think of myself as an old lady, although I am seventy-eight years old. I keep looking at older people and thinking that they are "old," not I. . . . How does one face the realization that he or she is growing old? It does not require courage as much as it requires adjustments. Since I thrive on work, my greatest problem is coming to terms with the fact that I cannot work as much or as hard as I formerly did. . . . So I think we need to invent jobs for the elderly or suggest ways for them to work either for fun or profit—or both. The great need is to have society using their talents so that nothing of value goes to waste.

I would start such a program by registering all the elderly in the United States under the guidance of the government. In this way we would know where they lived, how to get in touch with them, what they could contribute, what their physical limitations were, and what they would like to do. Along with this we could have a register of needs for talented elderly volunteers. They could check with this register to seek jobs and opportunities for productive living in late life.

Given what I've said, I believe that it is tremendously important for the elderly to organize for political power and clout. We need to sign petitions to pass new laws, to improve existing legislation, and to check on current regulations in the health field. We need to keep watch on congressmen and other public officials and must make our desires known.

The elderly could and should serve as mentors and guides to oncoming generations. We should guide young people to think always about how to improve life in this country, both political and private. We must ask them to reflect upon the heartbreaking scene of the homeless elderly sleeping on grates near government buildings; we must alert them to the discrimination against women which is prevalent in our society and which hits so hard on elderly women; and we must make them aware of the fact that increasing homelessness results largely from the inflation of home mortgages, caused by governmental policy.

During my life I saw poverty on the farm near my home, the biggest oil boom in history with its attendant rags-to-riches stories, much progress in health care, and considerable improvements in communications. I have seen the nation go in cycles only to return, it seems, to the place where we started. What I perceive is the need for improvement, and this is what us talented oldsters must help bring about.[6]

The Experience of Malcolm Muggeridge

The hardest thing of all to explain is that death's nearness in some mysterious way makes what is being left behind—I mean our earth itself, its shapes and smells and colors and creatures, all that one has known and loved and lived with—the more entrancing; as the end of a bright June day somehow encapsulates all the beauty of the daylight hours now drawing to a close; or as the last notes of a Beethoven symphony manage to convey the splendor of the whole piece. Checking out of St. Theresa's second-class hotel, as the revolving doors take one into the street outside, one casts a backward look at the old place, overcome with affection for it, almost to the point of tears.

So, like a prisoner awaiting his release, like a schoolboy when the end of term is near, like a migrant bird ready to fly south, like a patient in hospital anxiously scanning the doctor's face to see whether a discharge may be expected, I long to be gone. Extricating myself from the flesh I have too long inhabited, hearing the key turn in the lock of Time so that the great doors of Eternity swing open, disengaging my tired mind from its interminable conundrums, and my tired ego from its wearisome insistencies. Such is the prospect of death.[7]

The Up Side. Although personal integrity is something that adults strive to obtain throughout their lives, it becomes the preoccupation of seventysomethings. At this point in the life cycle, integrity refers to the state of being complete and whole with all that is. Seventysomethings live in the space and time of "elderhood," which is the territory of sages—the wise ones whose experience and memories encompass more living than all who are younger. "One of the possible payoffs of living a long and varied life," states seventy-five-year-old Robert Tannenbaum, "is that one gains a certain amount of wisdom. I think that depends on how open the individual is to new inputs. It seems to me that the kind of perspective that one gets from having lived through a wide spectrum of experiences—prosperity and depression; war and peace; a full range of personal crises that not only involve one's self, but people close to one—provides a backdrop against which to understand deeply and meaningfully any given problem that confronts one in the here-and-now."[8] The virtue of "wisdom" in elderhood is captured in the words of one of America's leading developmentalists, Erik Erikson:

> A meaningful old age, then . . . serves the need for that integrated heritage which gives indispensable perspective to the life cycle. Strength here takes the form of that detached yet active concern with life bounded by death, which we call *wisdom* in its many connotations from ripened "wits" to accumulated knowledge, mature judgment, and inclusive understanding. Not that each man can evolve wisdom for himself. For most, a living *tradition* provides the essence of it. But the end of the cycle also evokes "ultimate concerns" for what change may have to transcend the limitations of his identity and his often tragic or bitterly tragic comic engagement in his one and only life cycle within the sequence of generations . . . a civilization can be measured by the meaning which it gives to the full cycle of life, for such meaning, or the lack of it, cannot fail to reach into the beginnings of the next generation and push into the changes of others to meet ultimate questions with some clarity and strength.
>
> To whatever abyss ultimate concerns may lead individual men, man as a psychosocial creature will face, toward the end of his life, a new edition of an identity crisis which we may state in the words, "I am what survives me."[9]

These are the elders who often look back on their life experience and reflect on it, reaffirm it, and then look ahead, to offer advice and blessing for a world that they may never experience. They share one thing: being closer to the end of life than to the beginning or the middle. There is no one breed of elder in this stage of life. There is great diversity of conditions, life-styles, and prospects. Some seventysomethings are thriving and continuing life as

usual—no big deal. Others are in special places of creativity and
contribution—something special is happening. Many are suffering
from physical pain, degeneration, or diseases—the terminal phase
is beginning; and for others, it is ending. Coping with physical
problems and developing a point of view about death are preoccu-
pations of this life period, but many elder adults who can sustain
health, relationships, visions of the future, and financial resources
continue to live full and active lives devoted to extending their
beliefs and purpose into their eighties and nineties. What contrib-
utes to successful aging and living at this period of life?—sustaining
enthusiasm instead of apathy; accepting personal responsibility for
your own life instead of blaming yourself or others for problems;
a close proximity between what you want and what you get; a
positive self-concept; and a predominance of positive emotions over
negative ones.

In the film *Gigi*, Maurice Chevalier sang "I'm Glad I'm Not
Young Anymore," suggesting that older people transcend many of
the anxieties and social pressures of youth and the middle-aged.
Elders, he sings, can be more free to say, to be, and to do *exactly*
what they believe in. Seventysomethings who feel fulfilled by their
past, active in their present, and reaching for new goals in their
future are the mentors that younger adults want to learn from and
emulate. Seventysomethings who extend middle age by being purposive and self-sufficient also extend a blessing to those younger
than they who harbor mostly negative images of "old." Our society
needs creative contact with its sages. To grow old well, young people need to learn from and revere those who have aged and developed wisely.

The Down Side. Much of our society still sees seventysomethings as "old," "worthless," "dying" creatures. Seventysomethings
project "old" characteristics that we do not want to face in ourselves—characteristics of body posture, facial features, gait, general
body contour, response time, ability to hear and see, and skin resil-
iency. Many of us do not want to look at people in this age group
because we do not know how to see their sagacity behind their
physical presence. Many elderly do not know how to see this in
themselves.[10]

Ageism shapes the destinies of many seventy-year-olds (and even fifty- and sixty-year-olds) far more than their inner plans do. Who will employ them at salaries commensurate with their proven competencies? Will federal laws permit them to accept those salaries, or will they be denied Social Security and other available benefits? What leadership roles are available for them to mentor and model the way? Seventysomethings want to make their remaining days count for something. But when they search for ways to do this, they often discover that the mainstream is not interested in what elders have to say, even though they carry, within their memories, several generations of human experience. An African motto says "When an old person dies, a library burns down."

Seventysomethings are not so much afraid of death as they are afraid of becoming dependent on others and on life-support systems. They fear that they will lose their faculties before they die or lose their savings and become dependent on people and institutions about whom they have no choice. They mourn not merely their own passing but the future events that they are sure to miss. They don't want to miss out on how the scenes of their lives, and particularly their family and friends, will evolve over the years.

Dying is not the same as aging. It is the final life transition. Dying is a psychological awareness that arrives early in life, and dying happens to some people long before they are old. Death is not reserved for the old, but it is for them an inevitable presence. As much as we laud the George Burnses, Bob Hopes, and other positive examples of old age, many if not most seventysomethings and eightysomethings have been struggling with steady decline, pain, and fear. "A limited future and a frozen past," states Simone de Beauvoir, "such is the situation that the elderly have to face up to."[11] Death does not just happen to many of us; dying is a gradual process of degeneration, decline, and resignation. While the dying person may display courage, humor, and even insight, as Kubler-Ross and so many report, there is no point in avoiding the fact that as physical and psychological problems compound themselves, the dying process is ugly and dehumanizing.

The crisis of death is that the body that until now has been the chief vehicle of life expression must cease functioning. It no longer can be a vehicle for the "self" who dwells within it, wondering what will become of it when the body ceases to function. There is no sure answer to this. But older adults have seen the face of death in every life transition they have traversed. They have lived with the unknown, the sense of helplessness, the futility of loneliness, the lack of a future. And each time, they arrived at new strength, fresh vision, and hope. Perhaps our transition experiences throughout our lives are rehearsals for our dying—our greatest resources for living with our ultimate unknown, over which we have no control. Arnold R. Beisser, M.D., who has been severely paralyzed by polio for more than forty years and spends much of his time connected to life-support machines, at the age of sixty-six had this to say about living and dying:

> It seems like I am not going to be able to hold out much longer, and when my life becomes too physically burdensome, I really don't want to. But years ago, I realized that being afraid of dying was really a cover for being afraid to live. Digging in to try to avoid dying, being preoccupied with that, keeps one from living. . . . We may need to think of life in terms of its meaning, rather than its elemental biology. . . . In a way, that to me is the issue: At what point does life lose its meaning? When one is no longer able to either contribute or to take from life, what then? . . . I don't know what happens after death; no one has come back to tell us for sure, so everyone is free to choose his beliefs. I do, however, believe how I live this moment is important. I'd better live it as though it were forever because, in a sense, it is. It may determine whether I move the world one millimicron in the direction that I want it to go.[12]

11

Getting
from Here to There

*Six Principles
of Life-Cycle Change*

And one man in his time plays many parts,
His acts being seven ages. At first the infant,
Mewling and puking in the nurse's arms.
Then the whining schoolboy, with his satchel
And shining morning face, creeping like snail
Unwillingly to school. And then the lover,
Sighing like furnace, with a woeful ballad
Made to his mistress' eyebrow. Then a soldier,
Full of strange oaths and bearded like the bard,
Jealous in honor, sudden and quick in quarrel,
Seeking the bubble reputation
Even in the cannon's mouth. And then the justice,
In fair round belly with good capon lined,
With eyes severe and beard of formal cut,
Full of wise saws and modern instances,
And so he plays his part. The sixth age shifts
Into the lean and slippered Pantaloon
With spectacles on nose and pouch on side,
His youthful hose, well saved, a world too wide
For his shrunk shank, and his big manly voice,
Turning around toward childish treble, pipes
And whistles in his sound. Last scene of all
That ends this strange eventful history,

Is second childishness and mere oblivion,
Sans teeth, sans eyes, sans taste, sans everything.
—*William Shakespeare, As You Like It (Act 2,
Scene 7)*

There are at least six principles that adults adopt—unconsciously
or consciously, in varying combinations and proportions—to weave
a story line throughout their lives and thereby make sense out of
their life cycle. These principles guide our thinking as we shift our
commitments during the life course. We draw upon these principles
to try to make sense out of our continuous and discontinuous biological, psychological, and sociological conditions—how our
inner and outer lives fit together meaningfully, even as our bodies,
minds, and settings keep changing. All six principles contain some
information combined with some rationalization.

The Internal Gyroscope

The most powerful principle that guides our thoughts and feelings
throughout the adult years comes from the decisions made as a child
about how the world works. As adults, we often "see" the world
through mental assumptions and emotional responses formed very
early and modified continuously throughout the life cycle. We proceed through life with an internal gyroscope in our heads, monitoring our lives. "Is the world safe and available to me or dangerous
and unavailable? Am I supposed to live by strict rules or figure
things out as I grow up? Do I trust myself and others? Am I comfortable with my feelings? When things go wrong, what do I do and
say? What is my favorite 'bad' feeling?" When we are young, the
gyroscope is programmed by our parents and society; when we are
fully adult, we learn to program our own gyroscope. To what degree is your childhood consciousness directing your adult behaviors, and what can you do about it? According to such authorities
as Sigmund Freud, Carl Jung, and Donald Winnicott, adults are
driven by primitive thought processes serving their basic impulses.
When you are young or not yet grown-up, the internal gyroscope
functions as if a committee held meetings in your head fairly fre-

quently to decide what you will do and think and feel. This committee, made up of parents, siblings, and early mentors, forms a long-lasting internal dialogue that decides what you should and shouldn't do, think, and feel—and assigns blame when you go astray. It is primarily concerned with keeping your life within the boundaries of what worked, in terms of emotional responses, thoughts, and decisions, in the early years. The early thought patterns of a child are more mythological than logical and lack information about how the adult world works. You understand your life course through the various voices of persons who have influenced your life. Much of the time, the primitive internal gyroscope is unconscious, but as you mature, you are more and more aware of it. As you become familiar with these voices, which at first are parents' voices and later those of teachers, mentors, and peers, you become an active participant in the dialogue. Unless you learn to reprogram it, the committee in your head will be the central monitor of personal development until your death.

When you decide to program your own life, you assume control of your gyroscope to direct your own life to the best of your ability. More than a conscience, your internal gyroscope monitors your thoughts; it oversees your feelings and influences your decision making. It is a powerful shaper of how you proceed from twentysomething through seventysomething. Adults have the capacity to replace much of their early programming with more accurate and caring information and attitudes. The mythic structure is always there, but self-conscious adults can dominate the gyroscope's functions. Learning from your own life transitions is the most natural way to reshape your mythic consciousness and reframe it around the positive features of your real self. Psychotherapy is one approach for increasing adult consciousness and power over the mental and emotional distortions of the childhood years. Group psychotherapy is often very effective at accelerating individual work. Any life experience that gets you to reflect on your freely flowing thoughts and feelings provides a basis for self-transcendence and liberation from the committee in your head so that you can direct your own life course according to your values, current information, and future goals.[1]

Future Blindness

Another unconscious principle is the inability to imagine how we will think, feel, and choose to live in the future. Particularly when we are young, we project our youthful assumptions, believing that we have sufficient knowledge and power to make the future happen. We believe that our current perspective will suffice to guide us throughout our years; we haven't yet learned that our life orientation changes every decade or so. We have great difficulty anticipating future consequences and necessary changes. So we move ahead while looking backward. Who can imagine how they will change their perspective on life as they age and gain experience? Who can anticipate the impact on their life that natural and social catastrophes will impose? How can people in their twenties have a positive picture of being in their fifties? They are most likely to believe that when they get to be fifty, they'll be very different from the fifty-year-olds of today. They'll defy aging, statistics, evidence, and all the rest—that is future blindness. How can a fifty-year-old have a realistic picture of being seventy? At fifty, most people aren't prepared to see that much value in seventy.

Future blindness serves positive as well as negative functions. It provides a justification for heroic acts that later in life we would probably not undertake with the same degree of certitude and abandon—decisions such as choosing a mate, marrying young, having children, not having children, choosing a career at age twenty-one, changing careers at thirty-seven, moving from New York to San Francisco, having an affair, traveling around the world alone, or choosing to divorce. It makes us willing to forgo consequences for intentionality and action and to indulge in risk taking and bold decisions. It helps people "just do it," "wing it," and "get on with life." But even at its best, future blindness is a form of positive denial about the future. It keeps people motivated to break out of the way they were but without a rational outline of future options and their likely consequences. It is more of an adolescent principle than an adult one, yet it is often useful to young and middlescent adults.

Generation Identity

Your identification with those who were born at the same time you were and grew up in the same world may contain residual values that shape the continuities you seek in your adult experience. Cohorts share the same marker events in their memories—the Depression, World War II, the postwar boom, the death of the Kennedys and Martin Luther King, Vietnam, Richard Nixon or the Middle East conflicts. People born in the same decade often share common cultural reference points—from political events to popular music to favorite movie stars to economic conditions to messages about how life really works. Critical historical events that occur during your childhood may shape your values and those of your peers throughout the life cycle (see Table 3).

Those who were young during the Depression of the 1930s see the world as having limited goods, so they tend to live like survivors. They also are strong believers that the American way is the best way and that we can all work together through any hardship to help our country fulfill its mission. Those of the post–World War II generation find the world to be full of abundance; expansion and growth are normal expectations of this generation of optimism, rock music, parties, and good times. This postwar generation has been called the "baby boomers" because of its enormous size—seventy-five million people, the largest single generation America has ever experienced. Its first splash as a trend-setting wave came in the 1960s with its music, life-style changes, and activism. This was the age of marches, causes, and very high expectations. By 1970, the American experience of the Vietnam War along with rising inflation and international conflicts led this generation toward security, money, and conventional happiness.

Now in midlife, the members of this generation are leading the wave of adult redefinition with their own historical values. Growing up with the new medium of television as their window to life, they believed that they were connected to the world as their land of opportunity. In their teens and twenties, they may have championed free love, drugs, and freedom. Many were involved in social causes. Most are familiar with psychotherapy, group intensives, and

Table 3. Historical Values.

	1900–1929	1930–1959	1960–1970	1970–1991
Communications	Face-to-face, newspaper, radio, phonograph	Movies, telephone, radio, newspaper, hifi	Television, movies, radio, newspaper, stereos, cassette tapes	Computer, fax, videos, TV, movies, vcrs, newspaper, cassette tapes, stereos, radio
Marker events	World War I, Depression	Depression, World War II, H-bomb, postwar boom	Social upheavals, deaths of JFK, RFK and King, Vietnam, the pill	Nixon, hostages, Carter, Reagan, deficit, ongoing global crises, Persian Gulf war
Culture	Good guys, bad guys, pro-American	Nationalistic, work-oriented, values, conservative, naive	More leisure, travel, human potential, sex, drugs, divorce	Environmental disasters, more rich, more poor, fewer middle-class, recession
Heroes	Sergeant York, Woodrow Wilson	FDR, John Wayne	Neil Armstrong, Martin Luther King, JFK	Sister Teresa, Mikhail Gorbachev, celebrities
Mood	Idealistic, optimistic	Optimistic, realistic	From optimism to pessimism	Cynicism, overwhelmed
Worst disease	Tuberculosis	Polio	Herpes	AIDS
Generation labels	Flappers, new wealthy	Survivers, boomers	Activists, New Age	Yuppies, punks, dinks, busters
Favorite music and dance	Charleston, tango	Jazz, big bands, fox trot, Bing Crosby, Kate Smith	Beatles, rock, twist, disco, Paul Simon, Elton John, Judy Collins	Madonna, Prince, the Jacksons, heavy metal, rap music

spirituality. But as they move up the career ladders, they discover fewer and fewer openings and challenges. So they look to other areas for accomplishment—to life-style issues, family life, entrepreneurial projects, social leadership, and leisure pursuits. All this is reinforced by the gradual blurring of gender roles as women move into challenging careers and men share in parenting and household roles.

As they move into midlife, they ask, "What are our best options for making life soar as we move through our forties and fifties?" "How can we blend parenting and social concerns to make our environment better?" "What do we need to know about the years ahead of us?" While they are fascinated with materialism and money, they are also moved by spirituality and continual transformation. They are the first generation to view old age in a positive way, as they experience the newly old as active, healthy, and affluent. They experiment with new options and believe that they can find answers to the problems that they encounter.[2] The big question is whether the boomers will follow their generational values into their midlife and elderhood years. Will they use their enormous influence to provide new leadership for social renewal?

People who came of age in the 1970s behave differently from the boomers—they are more conservative and worried that the world is running out of steam. Their central concerns are jobs, security, money, and survival issues such as safe sex. Whereas earlier cohorts seemed sure of some kind of future and "progress," this is the first American generation in the twentieth century to be unsure that the land of opportunity exists for them. What they see is a downhill slide into a world in which they won't be able to afford a house or to surpass their parents. This generation has begun to play a tune that subsequent young adults are likely to enlarge upon: orphans of the society, born too late to enjoy the benefits, and destined to struggle throughout their lives with declining natural and social resources, with ever-changing careers, runaway inflation, and a nation without leaders.[3]

Generation identity has considerable impact on how we see our lives and world, which leads to how we age and develop as human beings. To a considerable degree, every generation reinvents the meanings given to *aging* and *development*. Even so, as the early marker events wash away with time, their ability to provide continuity to our lives lessens. With the speed of complex change, generations are getting shorter, and with the need to keep abreast of new technology and other developments, generation identity may weaken and the emerging identification come to be with change itself. A distinct disadvantage of generation identity is that rigid adherence to the values of the past makes adaptation to change difficult. Generational values are merely marker events, part of your long-term memory bank. While they are predictably influential, every transition that you experience will transform much of your memory bank into current beliefs and purpose.

Trade-Offs

There is a principle of trade-offs that functions throughout the life cycle. Trade-offs are exchanges between something old that is outmoded or dysfunctional and something new that works better. As we age or watch our social conditions change, some aspects of our lives seem to get better while others get worse. Our bodies slow down, so we switch from playing baseball to managing the team, or from running the mile to playing chess. Our earning power may decrease, so we budget more carefully. Our kids leave home, so we develop new friends and projects. We lose our total devotion to our jobs, but we gain balanced lives with more leisure. We trade off a negative for a positive and feel good about the process. Instead of merely getting older, we get older and smarter.

Trade-offs are exchanges between minuses and pluses, decrements and increments, losses and gains. You trade off one attitude, value, commitment, attachment for some other, preferred one. Perhaps you find you've declined as a basketball player, but as a coach you are experienced and competent. Or maybe your love of work shifts from aggressive achievement to enjoying the friendships in the work setting. If you experience aging as gradual but inevitable physical decline and development as the evolution of a profoundly deepening and empowering consciousness, you will justify the loss by accepting a gain. Not a bad deal.

Other trade-offs have to do with changing external opportunities and threats. A friend of mine who smashed her knee in a skiing accident a few years ago has never walked without crutches or canes since. She could have spent the rest of her life feeling sorry for herself, but instead she seized the moment to begin a career at home as an author, and she has produced three novels and a blazing trail—on her typewriter.

There is no list of right and wrong trade-offs for adult life. Each person must decide what to diminish and what to add. Habits? Some adults make a conscious decision to eliminate booze from their lives and to take up nutritious food and sensible exercise instead. Relationships? Some midlifers choose to be single: they trade off one kind of relationship for another, which leads to other trade-offs later in life. Some couples choose not to have children in order to do other things with their lives. That is a trade-off; you gain experience in one direction and lose it in another. Careers? Career people in midlife often struggle with the decision of whether to stay on in their corporate positions or become entrepreneurs on their own. Retirement? Many seventy-year-olds feel fairly complete with their lives, while others are beginning new business ventures or political careers. What is important in a trade-off is to know on the one hand whether it reduces a concern you've been having and, on the other hand, whether it adds meaning to your life.

Trade-offs encourage choices that serve both our developmental needs and our aging realities. They also promote adaptation to change, a basic principle for successful adult development. A disadvantage of trade-offs is they tend to be short-term adjustments, not long-term principles. They are not sufficient in themselves to construct a long-term plan or a life structure. They are more reactive than proactive.[4]

Events Beyond Our Control

The principle of events beyond our control is an external principle for understanding the changes in our lives. Sometimes it is described as being in the right place at the right time or the wrong place at the wrong time. Some doors get opened or closed for us. Some doors we never get to. We experience many social and natural events, such as earthquakes, fires, accidents, wars, diseases, stress, addictions, loss of job, an inheritance, divorce, or meeting an interesting person on an airplane. The more unstable our society becomes the more influence this principle will have in our lives.

The timing of events in our lives triggers an immediate altering of our assumed stability, usually followed by changes that can have long-lasting consequences. We alter our plans and our life course. Whenever any internal or external factor upsets business as usual in a person's life, a transition of some sort is likely to ensue, leading to new assumptions, coping strategies, value shifts, and next steps. Life proceeds differently. What effect will the Persian Gulf war have on the five hundred thousand members of the American armed forces who were there? Or when a spouse dies, his or her mate is often thrown into a profound identity crisis compounded by grief. It is not unusual for the reconstruction of life to take several years.

Intruding events can also be positive, such as winning the lottery, but even then they shake up our lives in ways that we can't anticipate. With every sudden unbalancing of your life, you tend to initiate changes in your life that you are not trained for or ready to manage. When I had polio as a child, I thought that I was in the wrong place at the wrong time. The pain and paralysis were overwhelming, and there was no real medical treatment available. But after more than a year in a hospital and recuperation setting, which served as a "transition environment" away from my family of origin where I could learn new ways to think and to plan my life, I emerged with profound personal dreams and determination to follow them, which I did. Looking backward from today's vantage point, I see my experience with polio as a major turning point in my life, motivating me to design my own future at an early age.[5]

The advantage of this principle is that it promotes an understanding of adult life as a complex interaction of factors, many of which can't be controlled or even anticipated. This principle requires an appreciation of human systems, environments, forces, and nations. It also helps us to deal with death, a predictable event that often arrives as a giant surprise. Although we are not in charge of a great many of the critical events that affect our lives, we are responsible for the decisions we make in the light of those events.[6]

Visioning

Visioning the future is another principle for making sense out of the life cycle—to imagine a desirable future releases your energy and commitment to work toward your goals. Development, as opposed to aging, occurs when you are "goal-oriented" and living into a future that you believe in and can make happen. Without a positive sense of a livable future, you will either idealize your past and back into your future or resign yourself to decline and darkness.

With the speed at which our lives are affected by change today, the past is less reliable than it used to be as a resource for models and information. We need models which work well in a world of change, discontinuity, and chaos. Twenty-first-century living will be on a fast-moving wave linking the present to the future. We must all be futurists, creating imaginative scenarios and sorting out options. With the principle of visioning we are led to invent the future by imagining, planning, designing, and enacting it. We anticipate possibilities and then we rehearse the scenarios and make them happen. We create purpose and let our deep human values guide our lives.

Visioning takes visioners. Behind every dream there is a dreamer. Visions do not pop out of nowhere; they burst out of the minds of men and women who have profound memories and understand the critical issues of today. Visioning requires a holy alliance among the three tenses of human time: past, present, and future.

Past: The present can't exist by itself; it is the product of a collective memory, social evolution, and a set of beliefs about the world. When you become an adult, you are a collective memory. You mind has been programmed by those around you, by the past experience of others. You can transcend the past, but you can never repudiate it, nor can you ever afford to stop learning from it. The past is your infinite memory or data base, a resource for everything that evolves from you. If you are ever around someone who has lost his or her memory, you will discover that without a memory, there is also an absence of a living present and a hopeful future. Memory is a necessary repository for your being human. Healthy, wise adults seek to understand their past and how it informs the present, for better and for worse.

From midlife on, many adults lose their dreams and lock themselves into their memories. As they see it, their best days are behind them. Their lives have peaked, so they reminisce, reflect, and view their current lives as diminished extensions of their memories. They can't imagine heroic possibilities as they grow old. Their stories of the past will evolve from historical vignettes to heroic and magical tales embellished by the desire for lasting self-importance. People who plan their future on the basis of their past are able to extend their lives, but only as shadows of who they were. They keep repeating the old ways of thinking and doing, and feeling more foreign in a world of rapid change. They have reduced themselves to a repetition compulsion. On the other hand, adults who maintain a vision of their future along with their valued memories never peak, because they keep finding worthy new adventures when old ones end. Some features of our lives rise and fall, but our sense of purpose continously finds importance and linkages in each of the time frames. Rooted in the past, the visioner has a history and a memory, but is preparing for the future.

Present: Life is lived in the present, the here and now of our space and time. The present is the moment of consciousness, your present awareness, based on your immediate sensations, your reflective capacities, and your ability to make decisions. It is in the present that you may feel that "time drags" and that you have "time on your hands," while others sigh because "there isn't enough time" to do everything that they want to do. The present is where the future and past meet one another, as tomorrows become yesterdays. Those who confine their lives to their memories or their expectations choose to reject the joy and completeness that they already have, in the here and now. It is in the present that we evaluate the past and construct the future—in our minds. The visioner is mindful of the past but anchored in the present—awake, alert, and informed.

Future: The future is a projection of the present and the past, a mental activity that anticipates desired events and occasions. The imagination that yearns and hopes for new meaning and joy is inevitably anchored in who you are and have been. The future is also the emergence of novelty. It is hope, promise, and new possibilities. It is not mere repetition of the past, and not mere projection of the present. When we imagine the future, we project our notions of past and present into the not yet, but we add new features. We build into our visions our human yearnings for completeness and fulfillment. We dream of a future that, for us, at this time in our lives, can be better than our past has been. Human dreams have a transcendent quality, and that is why all who dream have a positive sense of a future. They trust the total time process, and not merely the present moment. Visioning a future is an act of creativity, invention, and ecstasy. Without a future vision, we shut ourselves down and begin to die, individually and collectively. Those who do vision generate the energy and motivation to construct plans for making the future happen in the present—the center of all human time—and celebrate the awe and wonder of it all.[7]

As our lives are always in motion between birth and death, our minds are forever trying to make sense out of the journey. Each person's life cycle is a long flow of time and space in which the principles reviewed in this chapter—along with others—are used to understand life's continuities and changes. Most of us use several of these principles as we seek to map out our future and understand our past. They all have advantages and disadvantages, and none is sufficient for understanding or empowering the human venture. Just as a goldfish cannot understand the significance of the bowl of water that contains its existence, we cannot get a final perspective on our life cycle. We see through a glass darkly. We all have a very brief slice of time to be on earth. Our lives are wrapped in limiting cognitive structures through which we maintain distorted visions of who we are and who we might become. Such is the human condition. We are mortals, not gods. Yet the principles that we choose to explain our lives are absolutely crucial to our destiny, for they shape our thoughts, feelings, and actions. They link us to the world as we see it and define our boundaries. They express our beliefs and define our hopes. They are all we have to measure our lives. Through them we have an opportunity to honor our past, celebrate our present, and design our future.

IV

Adults
and Global Change

12

Valuing
the Global Context

Think about the life record of humanity as one "animal." Like an individual person, developing from infancy to adulthood, humanity gradually widened its world, increased its power and its control. It originally lived, like all animals, in its natural ecological niche. And then something special happened; it moved farther and farther from its home and began to create an artificial world, the world of civilizations.

It began to take control of all life, and its actions had overwhelming consequences. It created, then had to adapt to, medical wonders, the synthesis of pesticides, the existence of nuclear weapons. As humanity grew, its ability to dominate challenged its ability to adapt. And in the twentieth century its size and power, at least for a time, have overwhelmed it. If we can teach this understanding of our history and capabilities, both students and adults might begin to channel the development of humanity in new directions. . . .

A new conservatism—true conservatism— would be dedicated to organizing a human society that can persist for millennia without degrading the life-support systems of its only home; that can avoid large-scale conflict; and that, we hope, can enjoy not only freedom from want but the political freedom that is

199

necessary if the minds of all are to cooperate in maintaining society. . . .

For the first time humanity has the knowledge to destroy itself quickly, and for the first time humanity also has the knowledge to take its own evolution into its hands and change now, change the way people comprehend and think. . . . Can we learn to become conscious of the problems that face us collectively? Can humanity win through to a new conservatism and a better world? We think so.

—*Robert Ornstein and Paul Ehrlich, New World New Mind*[1]

Adults who manage change knowingly in their own lives are usually able and willing to face the cycles of change beyond them. Instead of shrinking the American dream into private issues, they are prepared to expand the dream into broader issues of life.

Making Friends with Society Again

The healthy self is a fluid, interacting participant in the wider world.[2] "For the 1990s," writes John Vasconcellos of the California State Assembly, "we owe it to ourselves to seek to unlock the secrets of healthy human development. It is time to plumb the reaches and mysteries of inner space and discover effective strategies that could serve to improve our communities, our personal lives, and the lives of those around us."[3]

The imperative is to believe again in ourselves *and* our social systems, to make them both as life-sustaining as we can. The goal is to see ourselves and our world as one organism, requiring cooperation and compromise so that the whole earth wins. The poet Rilke says "Earth, isn't this what you want: an invisible re-arising in us? . . . What is your urgent command, if not transformation?"[4] How can we, as a society, develop the required learning and leadership for empowering the systems of our lives—our families, the neighborhoods where we live, our places of work, the air we breathe, the hospitals we use, the governments we endorse—and beyond?

Living With Chaos

The ripples of change we feel in our lives today increasingly originate with the tidal waves of global chaos. Living with chaos is a metaphor for our time, which requires adventurers akin to artists, scientists, and athletes seeking new levels of performance. The founders of our country had this very spirit, as they pushed into the wilderness of a new land to create pockets of order for their lives. Throughout the whole westward movement across the United States, living with chaos was required, and those pioneers were drawn to it, not repulsed. Except for the global scale and omnipresence of chaos, it is not a new phenomenon. Americans with a memory will recall the ways that their ancestors lived creatively with chaos; most of history has been strongly influenced by turbulence, surprises, and the unknown.

Often in the evening, my wife and I take our family to the nearby Pacific Ocean, where our three boys "boogie board" on the waves. Riding the waves on a boogie board or surfboard is the closest picture in my mind of what living with chaos is like. Join me on a brief ride:

> We approach the beach watching the waves like hunters studying the paths of a well known prey. The swell arrives from the north, building slowly, lining up in long, even rows. . . . Many of the breaks are unmanageable and more than once I am pushed back by a cascading waterfall of angry ocean. As the big wave approaches I am pulsing with a combination of fear and elation. There is time only to act and turn, and paddle with it. Suddenly I am aware of movement, a motion that is ever accelerating, and I am up. I am moving at an angle down the face of the wave and without thinking I know I've had a perfect take-off. Exhilaration.
>
> Suddenly everything stops and I see myself on a steep face of green, wet, silky water. In the next frame the wave folds over me and I am in the mid-point of a long tunnel. . . . My

movement is in all directions, and at the same time, not at all. The light is at the end of the tunnel and that is the direction of the flow.[5]

What can we learn from this? Riding a wave brings together an alliance of internal and external forces that produces its own rules, direction, and results. It can be creative or destructive. Creative riding requires balance, centering, cooperation, trust, timing and harmony, physical stamina, and courage. All of your attention must be devoted to the present moment, to merge with the crushing forces in order to ensure your survival and feel the joy. You cooperate with the forces at hand and look for life direction within them. Jack London captured this sensation with these memorable words:

> I shall never forget the first big wave I caught out there in the deep water. I saw it coming, turned my back on it and paddled for dear life. . . . They are a mile long, these bullmouthed monsters, and they weigh a thousand tons, and they charge in to shore faster than a man can run. . . . The whole method of surf-riding and surf-fighting, I learned, is one of nonresistance. Dodge the blow that is struck at you. Dive through the wave that is trying to slap you in the face. Sink down, feet first, deep under the surface, and let the big smoker that is trying to smash you go by far overhead. Never be rigid. Relax. Yield yourself to the waters that are ripping and tearing at you. . . . If the board is going fast enough, the wave accelerates it, and the board begins its quarter-of-a-mile slide.[6]

Living with chaos requires kinetic life-styles. You invent new, tentative organizing principles to make your life work for a while. You find your world filled with this and that, moving in various directions for various reasons, and you create a clearing. You produce the order you need for now with loose ends within the process of change: a temporary pattern that permits you to maneuver, think, and make decisions—in short, to live. Your focus is in the here and now, on the edge of tomorrow.

Living with chaos is collaging your way through time and space. You arrange and rearrange your colors and shapes as you move along. You pick and choose, search and find, wander and get lost, cut and paste—assembling and disassembling yourself and the universe around you. You are alive and you matter. You are a person and a social force.

The Human Dimensions of Chaos

We are just beginning to learn how to live with chaos—the absence of the familiar order we knew and the presence of alternative orders that we have yet to discern. What change has been to the twentieth-century chaos will be to the twenty-first. It is already happening. Change is not only accelerating in pace; it is affecting more and more aspects of global life in unanticipated ways. Change has become so extensive that we experience the world as discontinuous and unpredictable. We tend to think of chaos as a monster about to pull the rug out from under our lives. But for the most part, chaos is benign and neutral, structured and full of potential. It is—for now, at least—beyond our perception and control, and that is hard for yesterday's leaders, who were driven by their own needs for order and control, to accept. The world we experience is increasingly flexible, malleable, mobile, discontinuous, and not contained by some grand design—all characteristics of ways in which we will organize our lives from now on.[7]

The mythic consciousness of our time arises from this universal experience of chaos. Throughout the entire world, heroes search inner space, outer space, and electronic space for form and flow, focus and meaning, joy and bliss, direction and possibility. Even though our governments seem incapable of creating a world federation of nations, a world order is floating on the waters of turbulence, promoting a global populism and providing a universal prototype for life to proceed, even as wars and inflation promote the opposite. Chaos is a planetary force, representing an infinity of opportunities and threats that are within our reach but beyond our control. The whole world lives in this context, for better or worse. This is a mental picture that fits our time and frames the human prospect for the twenty-first century. It will take grown-up men and women to turn our experience of chaos into livable history far beyond today's nations and factions, rich and poor. There are at least five human dimensions of chaos within which American adults have an opportunity to develop learning projects and provide new forms of leadership for the next century.

   The Environment Is a Primary Reference Point for Everyone. Chaos has become a universal, operative concept for understanding our relationships with the total environment—not merely for some people or nations or corporations. Living with chaos means honoring our whole environment, becoming global citizens before there is a political structure to join. Our lives and life-styles affect and are affected by ecological conditions and human decisions everywhere on earth. The only thing to remain "foreign" is our own inability to be responsive to the interconnectedness of life everywhere. Having a future from now on requires worldwide cooperation on the use and abuse of natural and human resources.

   Like the many astronauts who have flown above the earth, we choose the whole earth as our home and find ways to live with its glory and misery. "Space travel has given us a new appreciation for the earth," confessed Apollo 15's James B. Irwin. "We realize that the earth is special. We've seen it from afar, we've seen it from the distance of the moon. We realize that the earth is the only natural home for man that we know of, and that we had better protect it." Mike Collins of Apollo 11 put it differently: "The earth is one unit. You don't have the feeling that it's a fragmented place, that it's divided up into countries. You can't see any people, you can't hear any noise. It just seems like a very small, fragile, serene little sphere. It makes you wish that it really were as serene as it appears. It makes you wonder what any of us might do to make it a happier and more peaceful place."[8]

   How can we live with a primary loyalty to the whole earth without being disloyal to country, state, corporate life, and family? How can we foster a healthy environment everywhere and protect it from permanent damage anywhere? What learning programs are necessary for this theme to prevail throughout the institutions of our society, including corporations and governments?

   Chaos Can Be Irrational and Destructive. Chaos harbors demons, the irrational, and the unknown. In a world of chaos, there is no guarantee of safe passage through life. There are possibilities for human distortion, misuse, and harm. Chaos is a flooding process of actualities and possibilities, not a moral principle. Chaos opens the gates to adventures into the higher reaches of the mind and culture; it also feeds human meanness and selfishness. We are all witnesses to global levels of self-interest, human neglect, and violence. Think of the issues that compromise human dignity on a global level: substance abuse, nuclear leaks, teenage suicides, oil spills, corporate cheating, murders, terrorism, white-collar crime, wars, hostages, moralistic arrogance, and endless compromises with decency and fairness. These are present realities, no matter how much we rail against them. We have watched them enter our living rooms from every corner of the world—Vietnam, Grenada, Beijing, Panama, Jonestown, Cambodia, Chile, Iraq, South Africa, Eastern Europe. Ours is an unsure world, with high possibilities and murky subversion. All human beings fall prey to the misuse of their own finitude by overestimating the importance of their lives and possessions in relation to those of others. In a world of chaos, the gates are open to irrational thinking and destructive behavior on a global scale, particularly through corporate and governmental greed.

It will take grown-ups in a grown-up society to accept this message and to live affirming lives anyway. So far, twentieth-century Americans have not wanted to hear it; they have wanted perversity and pain to disappear through cultural progress and psychological enlightenment. Those expectations are off the mark. To face the downside of chaos takes years of experience and an acceptance of both our personal finitude and demonic qualities in ourselves. Mature adults should be able to face the downside of their own behavior and learn ways to contain it, insofar as possible. Although we cannot eradicate human arrogance and the will to destroy, adults who recognize these qualities in themselves can and will create countervailing forces to minimize their damage, and that is a leadership task in a chaotic world.

Chaos Promotes a Universal Culture. Even while demonic forces thrash about to extinguish the human prospect, intensive change has ironically created positive, universal resources for all people. For years, we have been living in a global village without realizing its revolutionary impact on adult life itself. Chaos is no longer future shock; it is global transformation.

Almost all cities in the world today have electricity, television, telephones, computers, newspapers, and radios. They have buses, trains, airplanes, and taxis. They have hotels, meeting rooms, conference centers, and restaurants. Today, the entire world is furnished with the same basic tools for creating order within chaos. We are slowly learning to generate a "user-friendly" international system that transcends national-corporate boundaries and permits permeation from many angles and sources. These common reference points serve governments and businesspeople; they also serve the smallest universal units capable of managing order and chaos: adult human beings.

Complex change is so pervasive that it cannot be contained. Our Pandora's box of technological advances, destructive capabilities, information overload, and environmental consequences has been opened, and no one can get it closed again. Chaos extends beyond the reach of corporations, nations, presidents. As bits and pieces of information and power are increasingly available to virtually everyone, more people and agencies throughout the world have access to more and more information and power that can be used fairly rapidly. News agencies, IBM clones, software, automatic weapons, clothing, desktop publishing, explosives, ideas, VCRs, and faxes make it more and more difficult for closed societies to exist because they need to stay abreast of global change in order to stay alive, economically and otherwise. The world has been deregulated by the universal practices of commerce and governments, and a consumer-manipulated order is found almost everywhere.

Today, technological change, the value of money, and the information explosion are not directly controlled by any one government or company or even by groups of governments and companies. There is a basic global order almost everywhere, with multiple sources of support but with no one ultimately in charge. Ironically, within that seeming order lie the problems of information overload, overwhelming destructive power, unpredictable events, unheralded greed, and haphazard decision making.

Living with Chaos Requires Worldwide Cooperation. Cooperative ventures such as alliances and shared responsibilities among governments, corporations, communities, and groups become the broad context for getting things accomplished. We learn to cooperate with others and with natural forces and to trust the river while looking out for alligators. In a recent study of U.S. industrial performance, a distinguished panel of experts made five recommendations for getting America moving again in the manufacturing world. Beyond the first recommendation, to improve the nation's schooling, they all had to do with transcending individualism and turf building. They promoted sharing and cooperating with others: creating employee collaboration in technological development at every level; understanding manufacturing as including planning, designing, marketing, selling, and servicing—in a global market; implementing cooperation among work teams, between companies, with research consortia, and with governments, particularly in developing a shared national goal for manufacturing strategies; and expanding our outlook beyond our own boundaries through a new set of international sensitivities. The study concluded that "Americans need to understand that the world they live in has changed. The effortless economic superiority that the U.S. enjoyed in the aftermath of World War II has gone. . . . What Americans must do is determined decreasingly by what they wish to do and increasingly by the best practices of others."[9]

Futurist Willis Harman believes that the work organizations of the world are setting the patterns for the new age we are entering: "Leaders in world business are the first true planetary citizens. They have worldwide capability and responsibility; their domains transcend national boundaries. Their decisions affect not just economies, but societies; not just the direct concerns of business, but world problems of poverty, environment, and security. Up to now there has been no adequate guiding ethic. Although these executives and their organizations comprise a worldwide economic network, binding the planet together in a common fate, there has been within that network no tradition of and no institutionalization of a philosophy capable of wisely guiding its shaping force."[10]

That global ethic is now evolving, ever so slowly, from grassroots consciousness to social morality to governmental policies and laws. Adults familiar with change in their own lives can provide learning and leadership beyond themselves by working to strengthen the bonds that now unite the planet. "Never doubt that a small group of thoughtful, committed citizens can change the world," said anthropologist Margaret Mead. "Indeed, it's the only thing that ever has." The creation of a world government while it is still possible is a planetary necessity if human cooperation is going to exceed global destruction. How could we do otherwise?

Adults Are the Primary Carriers of Culture and Consciousness. The basic unit for sustaining cultural continuities and monitoring complex change is a fully functioning person—emotionally alive and value-sensitive, rationally aware and clear, information-processing, value-driven and compassionate, adaptable and process-oriented, and uniquely capable of inventing temporary order out of inchoate experience. During a single life at this time in history, several generations now pass. For the indefinite future, adults will be the primary carriers of culture and consciousness.

As we surge along in the swirling river of our own experience, we keep organizing the resources that work for us, improving what we can, dealing with what isn't working well, and reorganizing when better options appear. It is a sloppy, unpredictable, informal process. We take on, we hold on, we let go, we move on. We attach and we detach. We make the change cycle a social process in our culture, guided by the values within us and the flow around us.

The scenarios for the future reside primarily in human lives that arch over the temporal swirl like bridges over troubled waters. In today's world, adults and their networks function as kinetic libraries, museums, churches, and schools. They represent memory, action, and vision; past, present, and future. The central continuity of cultural time and space is taking place within people and their temporary "holding environments" of personal relationships, work settings, and networks. It is not enough to have corporate or governmental visions for the future; our visions must be anchored in the lives and intimate connections of our people. As the pace of change quickens, mature adults will be particularly crucial for providing memory and future forecasting to help the large organizations of the world make intelligent, human decisions within a global context.

13

The Self-Renewing Adult, the Self-Renewing Society

To be able to transform random events into flow, one must develop skills that stretch capacities, that make one become more than what one is. Flow drives individuals to creativity and outstanding achievement. The necessity to develop increasingly refined skills to sustain enjoyment is what lies behind the evolution of culture. It motivates both individuals and cultures to change into more complex entities. The rewards of creating order in experience provide the energy that propels evolution—they pave the way for those dimly imagined descendents of ours, more complex and wise than we are, who will soon take our place.
—*Mihaly Csikszentmihalyi, Flow: The Psychology of Optimal Experience*[1]

Today's adults conduct their lives in the many dimensions of chaos. That is our global setting, our given space and time. When Dag Hammarskjold was secretary general of the United Nations, he noted, "We are not permitted to choose the frame of our destiny. But what we put into it is ours. He who wills adventure will experience it—according to the measure of his courage."[2] Our destiny is to journey on the river of change, and this calls for a capacity to adventure well—at all times, in all seasons. Self-renewing adults are trained for the journey they are on. Adventure is what they seek and want.

Like good athletes, we can prepare to live fully in the world that we have—no matter what. We can learn to sustain passion, joy, and purpose throughout our years. We can find fulfillment in a world different from the one we were accustomed to. We can, when we have to, grieve our losses and find new pathways for our lives. Even when we endure transitions and losses, we can draw upon resources for finding meaning in our down times. Although we may fall short on some occasions and get surprised on others, the more consistently we monitor a self-renewing process within our personal lives, the more we will ride the waves beneath us and guide our rafts down the rivers that we are on. Wherever we are in the cycle of change or in the life cycle, there are ways to promote a self-renewing process, with focused energy, clarity of purpose, and honest relationships.

The object of living is to live, not merely to exist or grow old. It is to live well, not merely to succeed or get rich. What is most crucial is that adults know how to sustain themselves in all situations throughout their lives: to draw upon the crucial human skills for mastering ongoing change in their lives, even when they feel their lives are falling apart; to anchor their expectations in accurate information about their lives and times; to invent pathways for families, work organizations, and communities, even as the world churns up roadblocks and obstacles.

Ten Qualities of Self-Renewing Adults

As we race into the twenty-first century, we will feel more of the earth's turbulence in our daily routines. It is in our daily lives that self-renewal is most needed. That is where our basic human competence is displayed and measured. Self-renewal means staying at our best—body, mind, and spirit—throughout life's long years, day by day. There are at least ten basic qualities shared by self-renewing adults.

They Are Value Driven. Self-renewing people are committed to values and purpose. They know what they prefer. Their primary anchors are within themselves. For them, renewal is not mere responsiveness to change; it is the repeated revival of the central concerns of their lives within the changing contexts in which they find themselves. Something is always at stake, something matters, and time gets organized around those critical priorities. They are determined to make a difference. They are inspired to live their beliefs. Their commitment to life includes a more or less articulate philosophical framework within which their life experience can be interpreted and kept in perspective. They know whether they are on or off course.

Self-renewing people possess personal authority. They don't fake authority that they don't possess, nor do they refuse to use the legitimate authority that they have. Their lives are firm and resilient—not limp and not authoritarian. They are definite but flexible, committed but learning. They risk and dare to fail because they believe in themselves and conduct their lives on the edge of their own growth. They trust their inner voice. The scholar Charlotte Buhler, who studied the biographies of a great many adults, concluded that having a "goal" is the most important prerequisite to feeling fulfilled during the adult years: "To live a goal-directed life means to have the desire, or even the feeling of obligation, to see one's life culminating in certain results. . . . People who live this way always seem to know where they are going and to hold only themselves responsible for their fate."[3]

They Are Connected to the World Around Them. Self-renewing people stay connected to the world around them. They seek out friends who can and will talk about whatever needs to be talked about—the whole of life experience, up and down and all around. They listen and empathize with life everywhere. They care and communicate. They stay in contact with their children and/or parents, and take initiatives in sustaining relationships. They may not be joiners, but they feel that the world is there for them to enjoy, to grab on to, and to learn from. Most self-renewing people are not loners; they are profoundly connected to others and able to access the resources of their broad environment. They network information, contacts, and resources. They take advantage of art and beauty around them, visiting public gardens or libraries, traveling, and attending preferred social events. They support causes and take stands. The world belongs to them, and they belong to the world.

They Require Solitude and Quiet. Self-renewing people require times of solitude and quiet. Anthony Storr puts it simply: "Removing oneself voluntarily from one's habitual environment promotes self-understanding and contact with those inner depths of being which elude one in the hurly-burly of day-to-day life."[4] Self-renewing people know how to refill their cups before they get emptied. They plan time for introspection as well as for interaction and decision making. They have private lives that they nurture and love. They have regularly scheduled times when they withdraw from routines to spend time alone. They retreat to some "secret garden" where renewal is predictable, simple, spontaneous, wonder-full. In solitude, they look, listen, meditate, and nurture themselves. They honor their inner life and outer boundaries. For such people, solitude is a reservoir for finding more of themselves. Dag Hammarskjöld saw solitude as the source point for his personal activism: "The more faithfully you listen to the voice within you, the better you will hear what is sounding outside. Only he who listens can speak."[5]

They Pace Themselves. Our current practice is to indulge in rigorous work and maintenance schedules throughout each week, punctuated by renewal on weekends and a vacation every now and then. Occasional breaks are not enough to sustain the self-renewal process. They wash away quickly into our dominant routines. Renewal must be built into the ordinary, ongoing rhythms of our life-styles and work styles.

Self-renewing people pace themselves. They schedule episodic breaks from their routine time, such as travel, holidays, vacations, retreats, seminars, theatre, sports activities, sabbaticals. If they misjudge and face the doldrums or a transition, they pace themselves through that space and time as well. They are not trying to sustain optimal performance at everything they do; rather, they seek to be fully present and available for all the occasions of their life course. They are more interested in quality time than in busy schedules, more concerned with effective lives than with efficient actions, more committed to integrity and style than to short-term results and applause. They do not constantly give themselves away, nor do they aspire to roles that do not fit them. They measure their resilience or energy reserves to be sure that they do not deplete themselves; they seek renewal in small or large doses as needed for the long-distance journey of their lives.

They Have Contact with Nature. Self-renewing people often find nature to be a dependable source of renewal. Throughout history, the wind, rain, sun, stars, mountains, rivers, earth, seas, and seasons have been seminal resources for the renewal of humankind. It may be hearing a wave hit the beach, seeing a leaf turning yellow in the fall, feeling a snowflake drift onto your cheek, or smelling a forest coming to life in the spring. For Anne Morrow Lindbergh in her midlife years, it was an oyster shell that helped her understand how to proceed:

> Yes, I believe the oyster shell is a good one to express the middle years of marriage. It suggests the struggle of life itself. The oyster has fought to have that place on the rock to which it has fitted itself perfectly and to which it clings tenaciously.
>
> Perhaps middle age is, or should be, a period of shedding shells; the shell of ambition, the shell of material accumulations and possessions, the shell of the ego. Perhaps one can shed at this stage in life as one sheds in beach-living; one's pride, one's false ambitions, one's mask, one's armor. Was that armor not put on to protect one from the competitive world? If one ceases to compete, does one need it? Perhaps one can at last in middle age, if not earlier, be completely oneself. And what a liberation that would be![6]

Much of adult life is spent away from natural forces—in buildings and settings that insulate us from powerful renewal readily available to us. Yet there are few among us who could not spend a half hour each day in some natural environment—to look and smell and listen.

They Are Creative and Playful. Self-renewing people are usually creative and playful. They are active, not passive. Rather than sitting on the sidelines to watch the world go by, they pursue ways to express themselves. Although they watch television, they are not couch potatoes. They like to exercise, explore, and experiment. They indulge in humor and are able to laugh at themselves. They become renewed when they read books, see art they like, hear their kind of music, or experience theatre events of their choosing. They stay alive by taking in life and expressing it as well.

They Are Adaptive to Change. Self-renewing people are adaptive to change, so they keep pursuing their best options. They look for habits to give up and better ones to begin. They pay attention to what they are doing, how they are feeling, and whether they should change. They are caringly evaluative about their lives. Part of them is always looking in on the other parts and caring for the whole. They make decisions with enthusiasm and congruence and can say no as clearly as yes. Self-renewing people are competent at entering, sustaining, and letting go of emotional attachments. They feel life, and they feel loss. They seek intimacy and sustain friendships; when necessary, they start afresh. They can love and live closely with another person and can refine that love as it matures over time. They know how to adapt to new perspectives, goals, and ways of thinking. Their minds are perpetually learning new ways to distinguish what is essential from what is inessential, the enduring from the temporary. Self-renewing adults are critical thinkers who sustain the abilities to gather information, evaluate, solicit opinions of others, and make both firm decisions and firmer redecisions.

Sam, a lawyer now in his fifties, has made several changes in his adult life. As a young lawyer in his twenties, he lived on the treadmill of "billable hours" for a large legal firm in Los Angeles. By his early thirties, his compulsive work habits and chronic complaining had all but destroyed his marriage, which included two small children. He felt that his life was draining his energy in too many directions but he didn't know what to do about it. Sam's driving passion was to train young boys as Olympic swimmers. An avid crawl-stroke competitor, he filled his law office with trophies from his younger days. But he felt that he could not afford to live on the salary of a swimming instructor. As the years passed, he became an effective lawyer, both with legal matters and with client relationships. With his highly developed "people skills," he had helped build up his legal firm, where he had become a partner. By the time Sam turned fifty, he was training Olympic swimmers at a boys' club on weekends and involved with the Olympic movement throughout California. When Sam looked back on his life, he felt some remorse about his divorce, but he felt great about the way he had achieved balance and integrity in his life.

They Learn from Down Times. Self-renewing people learn from their disappointments, necessary losses, and down times. Like the lives of most people, their lives are sometimes full of funk and disorientation. They do not live lives without stress, failures, mistakes, loss, and tragedy. Their lives are not sweet or perfect. They know that they have unresolved conflicts, limited perspectives, and impulses that sometimes overpower them. They do not deny the dilemmas of their lives or their own inevitable demise. But they know how they lived through down times earlier in their lives, and they feel confident that they can live and learn through the days ahead. They do not avoid disagreements and conflict; they know that conflict around important issues leads to deeper clarity and renewed relationships. They have a high tolerance for ambiguity and disorientation. They have learned from their own life transitions, and they have sympathy for the losses of life. They know that self-renewal is often found at the end of a grieving process. They trust the process of self-renewal. They accept the loose ends and unfinished business of their lives as part of their own future agenda.

They Are Always in Training. Self-renewing people never stop learning. When the world presents a problem, they first assume that they can master it through new training. Learning is an attitude toward facing the unknown. Self-renewing adults don't feel locked into who they were so much as alive to the people they're becoming. Learning helps them feel their pulse, measure their paths, and integrate their lives. Learning unveils more of their human competence and opens doors to new possibilities. Over the years, they experience a deepening of self-mastery and world mastery as perpetual learners. Because they remain on the cutting edge, self-renewing people often become leaders.

They Are Future-Oriented. Self-renewing people are future-oriented. They do not dishonor the past or the present, but they focus their lives on the "not yet" and the "what if?" They live conscious lives today, with intentionality for tomorrow. They formulate scenarios of the future and rehearse them until they are leading anticipatory lives, vitally connecting their current conditions to desired futures. They create the future in the very act of rehearsing it.

Kay Whitmore, chairman of Eastman Kodak Company, is steering his company through unchartered waters as Kodak faces a new era of photography, which may not use conventional cameras and films. Now fifty-eight, Whitmore has been with the company for thirty-four years. You might think he would be a stern defender of the old ways of doing things, but he is just the opposite. His challenge is to sustain the current market position of Kodak while pioneering in new electronic technologies that may eventually displace chemical-processed photography. "We're going to have to continually drive ourselves, push ourselves, encourage ourselves to keep at and ahead of our competition," Whitmore declares. "What people perceive as the relatively comfortable days of old are gone, and they're not going to come back."[7]

Life Cycle Mastery Skills

What are the skills that self-renewing adults need throughout their lives for finding fulfillment within today's world? What range of abilities should adults obtain to make their lives full and joyful—at their best most of the time? What would an ideal list of competencies for preparing adults to have mastery over their changing lives and environments look like? Early in this book we identified ten change cycle mastery skills. In addition to those there are life-cycle mastery skills that empower adult life in all its manifestations throughout its long duration. Adults need competencies in all areas and roles of their lives—skills as human generalists. To have life-cycle mastery is to sustain constancy of self throughout myriad roles and settings.[8] Adults need to monitor their own feelings, thinkings, and doings. Most adults have abiding intimate relationships and children; it is no longer satisfactory to enter into marriage or parenting without extensive training and skill development. We train extensively for career areas, often resulting in people whose specialized behavior at work is more highly developed than their basic human skills. Tom Peters talks a great deal about "high-performance organizations" that thrive on continuous skill training, but those skills are primarily work-performance oriented, not basic skills for human empowerment.

Throughout the panorama of their experience, self-renewing adults pursue human competence as consistently as they can. Adults who live creatively with global chaos are more than human doers; they are also human beings who have a singular integrity pervading all of their actions weaving together the occasions of their lives. Here is one list of comprehensive skills for sustaining integrity and self-renewal throughout the adult years:

Personal Mastery

Feelings

>Maintains high levels of self-confidence and self-esteem
>Imagines, wonders, and envisions
>Listens intently and objectively to others
>Empathizes with and validates others
>Expresses feelings appropriately
>Displays gratitude and appreciation

Thinkings

>Distinguishes between trivial and significant problems
>Distinguishes between situational and patterned distress
>Recognizes, accepts, and possesses legitimate personal authority
>Gives and receives criticism
>Observes and understands the conduct of self and others
>Reflects upon sense of self and its personal life course

Doings

>Discerns and clarifies personal values in self and others
>Perceives problems and evolves strategies for their solution

Collaborates effectively and acts fairly as a team player
Celebrates, has fun, and pursues affirmations and rituals
Plans and feels responsible for making the future happen
Lives own beliefs and concerns

Intimacy and Relationship Skills

Sustains intimate bonds, with an intimate partner and/or
   with others
Has parenting skills and provides an environment of love
   and learning for a family
Within family life, models basic skills of caring, cooperation,
   and conflict management
Seeks and maintains friendships that are mutually rewarding

Communication Skills

Speaks clearly and effectively in one-on-one and public meetings
Presents ideas and makes them convincing
Creates consensus through win-win strategies
Confronts and says no when necessary
Reads with both speed and comprehension
Writes factual and conceptual material clearly and persuasively
Is familiar with relevant hardware and software
Translates raw data into useful information
Accesses and networks necessary information

Team Player Skills

Fosters trust and cooperation
Motivates others toward common goals
Organizes agendas, runs meetings, and manages time
Brainstorms and problem-solves
Negotiates and compromises
Manages conflict and pursues consensus
Validates and rewards peoples' efforts
Networks—finds and establishes new resources and possibilities
Gets along with and respects diversity in men and women,
   and people from other cultures
Delegates and shares work easily; can be a follower or a leader
Adjusts to and is curious about new conditions

Change Master Skills

Questions the status quo
Is challenged by the unknown
Is able to look at things from new perspectives
Takes risks
Is willing to make mistakes and learn from them
Is driven by personal integrity
Inspires others to be at their best
Is future-oriented and cautiously optimistic
Looks for new resources and opportunities in the change
    process
Pursues useful alliances and networks that enhance cooper-
    ation and results
Rehearses scenarios thoroughly before making decisions
Assumes responsibility for successes and failures

Becoming Learners

As we become a nation of, by, and for adults, we must redesign our learning resources to empower adults throughout their lives. Then we will become a society of adult learners expanding and refining their human capabilities. For today's adults, *illiteracy* refers not to the inability to read but to the failure to learn how to learn throughout the life cycle. Three central questions are these: How can adults get the ongoing training that they need in the life-cycle mastery skills just described? Where are the adult learning centers for providing training in these skills? Who can teach these competencies?

Unfortunately, the life cycle mastery skills are not widely taught in higher education programs in our culture, nor are they recognized prerequisites for marriages, families, occupations, or leadership. Although some of the skills are taught in corporate training programs, adult education courses, seminars and workshops, retreat programs, and professional graduate schools, our society today needs institutions whose *primary* function is to educate adults to the limits of their learning abilities. Carl Jung once asked, "Are there perhaps colleges for forty-year-olds which prepare them for their coming life and its demands as the ordinary colleges introduce our young people to a knowledge of the world and of life? No, there are none. Thoroughly unprepared we take the step into the afternoon of life.[9] At this time in our cultural history, our society would benefit greatly from creating colleges or learning centers specifically for adult learning and empowerment. These would be hands-on learning programs where adults could experience, reflect on, and act on their acquired competencies.

Our most profound need for lifelong learning is to make adult life work at every level—intrapersonal, interpersonal, family, career and work, leisure, spiritual, and leadership roles. "Adult education" is learning in order to live fully and well—to develop personal power and social effectiveness. Training involves emotional, cognitive, and decisional components throughout the life cycle. Adult learning improves the physical person, inner self, and performance through the social connections of life—marriage, family, job, friendships, society. Adults are not preparing for life; they are learning how to live better and deeper. They want to understand the world in which they are living and the world within themselves. They want competence, empowerment, and newness. They want effectiveness, influence, and results. They want lucidity, consciousness, and linkage with the universe. They look for hands-on learning environments that will guide them in these directions.[10] Their main campus is the range of their own experience, and they look everywhere for learning resources. Although they want to be expert at something, they want most to be good at being themselves—to know who they are and how to live. They are less interested in knowledge than in mastery, that elusive ability to possess unconscious competence within one's life and work. They are personally drawn to simple, deep truths and to the unities of human experience.

Adult learners are reflective, and not merely experiential. They think, evaluate, and look for patterns. They seek accurate information and maintain critical acumen in the service of making distinctions and informed decisions. As they age, their reservoirs get deeper, with more reference points and resources. They pay attention to their favorite words, dreams, and stories—the windows of the mind that help them to see depth and beauty in their experience. They reflect as well on the world about them, forming judgments about what is taking place and what actions are called for. Attuned to emerging technologies that spray information across the globe, adult learners remain anchored in their fundamental personal resources of reading, reflecting, speaking, and writing.

Adult learning takes two forms during the life cycle—developmental and transformative. Developmental learning aims at improving human effectiveness in personal life, careers, and beyond. It focuses on evolving new competence and skills. Transformative learning aims at evoking a new consciousness and self-understanding. It promotes the unities of human experience through imaginative thinking, self-expression, and actions.

Developmental Learning. In the first half of life, adults mostly pursue developmental education to feel at home in the world. Twentysomethings, thirtysomethings, and fortysomethings seek learning that will increase proficiency in their jobs, lives, and relationships. They learn in order to get their lives into self-sustaining orbits—to complete graduate school, to progress in jobs, to prove themselves, to qualify for advancement, to gain status, to change careers, to specialize in new skills, to become managers or leaders—to make it. These learning programs are focused, practical, useful, and promote the future attainments of students. Early adult learning is competency-based and seeks to master specific fields of study, professional practice, and adult performance of roles. Although young adults may be involved in transformative learning, their ego and survival needs usually guide them to make developmental learning their priority. The central theme of adult learning for the first half of life is to gain knowledge and skills for leading secure, successful, joyous lives. Learning is for getting ahead, obtaining certification or licensure, and ensuring successful passage through careers and human systems. Although some of this learning is gained in classroom courses, much of it requires experiential settings with frontline experts or mentors as teachers.

Transformative Learning. Although the learning projects of fiftysomethings, sixtysomethings, and seventysomethings continue the pursuit of new skills, the overall life focus is not on practicality, effectiveness, or proficiency. The development of the self in midlife sets us forth on a pilgrimage for a new consciousness—to design life, to shape culture, to seek the future.

In the second half of life, adults feel the need for new ways of seeing and touching the world. The world is not there merely to master but becomes the container of a human adventure into internal as well as external sensibilities. Mature adults seek transformative learning because they view life as a privilege, as a pure opportunity to engage the world as fully as possible. This learning generates new ways to think and feel, aimed at exploring and redefining the deeper currents of human experience. In the first half of life the driving images come from history and society, to explain how to gain mastery over life in the world. In the second half of life nature becomes an equal source of driving images, suggesting a source of harmony and beauty that transcends history. The unities of life seem more available, friendly, and illuminating, and learning takes the form of a spiritual journey. The key to this learning is the integration of the inner self with its outer experience, such as environmental integrity, person-role consistency, person-system congruence, and person-transcendence discovery. This is part of the unfinished business of our culture. How do we, as a society, provide this level of adult learning? Who are the teachers, where are the learning environments, and which institutions bear primary responsibility for this kind of education?

The learning patterns of mature adults seldom mesh with the traditional divisions of knowledge or the typical course offerings of universities. These students do not seek learning in order to achieve or to make knowledge relevant. The development of passive mastery and the importance of artistic, leisure, and spiritual environments for learning are important considerations for the second half of life. Learning is much more diffuse and often more esoteric than in the first half of life, when practicality and proficiency are so important. Learning now is both intensely personal and universal, engaging a person's fullest commitment. The learning process is conceptually abstract but personally concrete. For example, mature adults might seek learning by creating an object of art, writing biography or autobiography, producing a background document to justify the importance of a governmental task force, embarking on a vision quest, researching ways to enhance peace over violence, or elevating a hobby into a career or a job into a calling. These are not frivolous fluff for elderly creatures beyond the pale; these are conduits and vehicles for empowering the deepest currents of our civilization.

Sometimes adult learning seeks specialized, advanced knowledge in a particular field—as with reentry workers or professionals seeking to finish their highest degree during midlife—but the older we get, the more learning has to do with generalized, integrated knowledge of life itself. Older adults seeking formal learning may not want to "major" in a field, "specialize" in a profession, or conduct "research" on a narrow topic; they may want to explore their own thoughts and expand their consciousness. They may want to express their thoughts through art or dance. They may want to study the unities of the universe, the connections among ideas, the thoughts that unite the environment and humankind. They may seek to develop conceptual models and theories. Where are the learning environments where they can do this? What kind of professors or mentors would and could guide them? What learning resources would they need?

Mature adults are themselves the primary mentors of the society—potential sages capable of passing on values and purpose and democratic process to adults much younger than they. How can they find settings where they can be guides and teachers? Who will employ them for the wisdom and mastery they possess? How can our society engage the vast educational resources of mature adults and help them "stand and deliver"? Mortimer J. Adler, chairman of the board of editors of the *Encyclopaedia Britannica*, concludes that "a culture can endure and thrive only to the extent that it is possessed by individuals, some of whom may add to it, but all of whom should be vehicles of passing it on to the next generation."[11]

Becoming Leaders

Adult learning is directly linked to the development and renewal of adult leadership. Perry Pascarella, executive editor of *Industry Week,* makes this point in his book *The New Achievers:*

> Leadership in the workplace will increasingly become dedicated to people development—not molding people to fit the

organization, but enabling each individual to fulfill himself or herself. . . . A quiet revolution is taking place . . . in the business corporation. . . . Although we have been hearing more and more about corporate efforts in human resource development in recent years, we may miss the essential truth about what is happening: Individuals are awakening to the possibility of personal growth and finding opportunities to attain it. The team building we hear about is secondary to the development of the individual. . . . Management is heading toward a new state of mind—a new perception of its own role and that of the organization. It is slowly moving from seeking power to empowering others, from controlling people to enabling them to be creative. . . . As managers make a fundamental shift in values, a radical re-orientation to a greater worldview will enable the corporation to treat its human resources as *resources*.[12]

Peter Senge of MIT's Sloan School of Management portrays tomorrow's leaders as the facilitators of social learning: "Leaders are designers, teachers, and stewards. These roles require new skills: the ability to build shared vision, to bring to the surface and challenge prevailing mental models, and to foster more systemic patterns of thinking. In short, leaders in learning organizations are responsible for *building organizations* where people are continually expanding their capabilities to shape their future—that is, leaders are responsible for learning.[13] Derek Sheane pushes this same point beyond institutional settings to include all adult networks. He describes the characteristics of a creative minority in Ulster, Ireland, illustrating how adults can lead and exert influence:

- They have overcome the "authority" problem. They can tolerate the anxiety of confronting their own power system—they will have freed themselves from slavish submission to outmoded reward and punishment systems in their own institutions.
- They are very aware people: At some critical point in their lives, they have gone through the pain

barrier. They know what their mission is and what their values are.

- Although they acknowledge the need for a core structure and constitution in society, they have learned to make life up as they go along. They no longer feel threatened by a lack of structure and "disorder." They lead untidy lives.

- They have developed an open, and nondefensive, style of discussion and conversation. They can be forthright and feel comfortable with a very frank discussion. They welcome and use feedback about their behavior.

- They are aware of their own needs and motivations and know the difference between their personal needs and the needs of the situation. When they intervene, they do not work their personal agenda. They don't let ambition mock their contribution.

- They have understanding of mature leadership and help. They are concerned with helping people help themselves. They do not just give a starving man a fish. They also teach him to fish for himself. They keep their egos under control and avoid creating undue dependence in the group they lead or the people they are helping.

- They have a clear understanding of the total institutional crisis. They will be able to perceive the totality of problems. For example, they will take an interest and be able to see the interconnectedness of political, economic, and social problems.

- They are change agents in society. They are action oriented, and when they intervene they know why they intervene. They are purposeful. [14]

For the foreseeable future, formal and informal adult networks will produce vanguard leadership for all sectors of our society and beyond—inside and outside of existing governments, institutions, and careers. "This, then, is the ultimate objective of social futurism," concludes Alvin Toffler, "not merely the transcendence of technocracy and the substitution of more humane, more far-sighted, more democratic planning, but the subjection of the process of evolution itself to conscious human guidance."[15]

In my work with adults throughout the country, I have found a readiness among many graying Americans to move out of their doldrums into a new period of leadership and risk taking. Adults are finding the organizations in our society to be less stable than the adults who work in them. It used to be the other way around. Now, they often feel endangered by the structures that they thought would provide them security—governments, corporations, and even families. The smaller realms of their lives—personal life, friends, and immediate outreach—seem safer and healthier than the larger ones. We are a nation of workable parts and dysfunctional wholes. A way to proceed is to evolve a social system more congruent with the human dimensions of chaos. That is the general directive for today's leaders—to create organizations that are themselves self-renewing, that have both structures for continuity and processes for constant learning and change.

Warming up the old politics of the right and the left appeals to few. As a people, we need and deserve a new version of the old dream. We may have lost our way in the complexity of things, but we haven't lost our heritage. Many adults know the fundamental values of our society and history. They are restless for new leadership, and they are ready to provide it. I predict that the next twenty years will be characterized by new sources of social energy and caring, much of which will come from mature adults, who now constitute the numerical crest of our population. The American failure of nerve of the 1970s and 1980s will be tested by a concerned, entrepreneurial social force led by successful, established Americans who believe that they can get their act together again in a new way. While they have no blueprint at this time, they have energy, financial resources, social influence, and concern. In the past, we have expected young people or social movements to foster sweeping change. This time, it will be different. Like the main character in the movie *Stand and Deliver,* mature people are beginning to reclaim their heritage and insist that this country get moving again.

This time, our dream will express itself as affirmation and consensus more than as protest and dissent.[16]

The type of leadership arising from today's adults is very likely to be what Robert K. Greenleaf calls "servant leadership"— leadership to address social needs out of stewardship and concerns, not out of charisma or power drives.[17] People who arise as leaders in midlife are driven most often by a deep desire to benefit the next generation. Their leadership emerges from their gratitude for their own attainments and opportunities and a wish to give something back. Compassionate leaders who arise from genuine concern for life around them have legitimate power and greatness. I believe that there are thousands of adults now ready to become such leaders.

Our top priority is finding leaders capable of shaping the human dimensions of chaos. They must first know how to manage their own lives effectively and joyously, in good times and bad. With all that has been written about leadership, there is a dearth of material on viewing the effective management of adult life itself as a basis for creating a workable society today. As chaos etches its way into our lives, the life structure–transition process will become the critical model for managing social continuities and changes as well. Lifelong learning will be a fundamental issue in the development and maintenance of our leaders. The leaders of tomorrow will arise from the ranks of those who have learned how to befriend the forces of chaos in their own lives today.

Epilogue:

A New Profession of Adult Mentors

What kind of professional will it take to help adults find continuous learning and empowerment? When adults want help for making redecisions in their lives, with whom do they consult? What professionals are equipped to coach people and organizations through normal transitions and into new life structures? This is the current professional dilemma for those currently in the business of adult renewal: First, the academic field of adult development has no applied wing, no professional training programs or professional degrees. There are only specialized fields, such as career counseling, human resource development, organizational development, and outplacement counseling.

Second, most helping professionals who work with adult clients—psychologists, psychiatrists, human resource professionals, organization development consultants, career counselors, marriage and family therapists, adult educators, and so on—are not experts on adult life, systems, and cycles. Although they may have taken a course or two on adult development, few of these professionals have a conceptual grasp of adult development and human systems, nor are they trained in practical strategies for enabling adults throughout the adult years. Their expertise is in their specialty areas, not in the lives of their client populations.

Third, when normal adults need help, they typically are looking for short-term empowerment of their lives around situational concerns. They need generalists who can help them rearrange their complex lives and plan a more coherent future, rather than specialists trained as helpers in specific aspects of adult life: career counselors (who assess and facilitate career planning), clinical psychologists (who assess and treat people with mental health problems), marriage and family therapists (who assess and treat couples and families), social workers (who work with culturally deprived and abused populations), human resource directors (who assess personnel selection and provide ongoing training and development for employees), health professionals (who work on medical issues, usually from a specialty perspective).

In today's professional milieu, if you are an adult and consult professionals in one of the above professions to help you "design a self-renewing life plan for the next five years," the professionals will probably pull you into their specialty area, reframe your need with their orientation, and give you what they are trained to provide, not what you asked for and want. How could they be expected to do otherwise? While there are many sources of specialized help that adults can obtain from existing professionals, there is currently no profession that serves the comprehensive developmental, transformational, and system needs of normal adults throughout the life span.

Fortunately, a great many professionals today are providing these services, often with considerable effectiveness, although it is not inherent in their professional training or orientations to do so. It would be most desirable at this time to provide new training for professionals in existing helping professions so that they can enable adult clients to make more sense out of their lives, using developmental and human system skills. It is also essential, I believe, that a new profession emerge that has as its singular purpose the facilitation of adult development and transformation. I propose a model that would train professional "adult mentors" with these abilities:

I.   Adult mastery skill training: To provide "generalist" training for adults in the change cycle and life-cycle mastery skills, to enable adults to generate learning, culture, and leadership. The adult mentor would be trained to facilitate normal adult development and to advocate optimal choices. The mentor would not function as a clinician.

II.   Life/career planning: To facilitate viable future plans with adults and with systems of adults. This includes personal planning, career planning, family system planning, health and physical activity planning, leisure planning, financial planning, retirement planning, and counseling the dying.

III. Coaching: To coach and guide adults through life transitions and life structures that are not working satisfactorily:
   A.   To recognize valid emotional issues that impede or fuel future planning.
   B.   To work through cognitive processes appropriate for future living.
   C.   To model ways to make new decisions for future living.
   D.   To provide "holding environments" until new beginnings can happen.
   E.   To foster healthy human systems through planning, system design, and leadership training.

IV.   Leadership training: To train adults as self-renewing leaders of their work organizations, their families, their communities, their professions.

V.   Networking and referrals: To refer clients to community, national, and international resources for making their lives work, from networking resources and fraternal organizations to corporate resources, government programs, and social movements.

The characteristics of the new professional "adult mentor" would include:

- Expertise, above all, in adult developmental psychology and human systems management. These are the central fields that provide the theoretical insights for the profession.
- A thorough grounding in skills for processing the depth issues of human beings, and a depth knowledge of oneself.
- A theoretical and applied knowledge of family systems, career systems, and leisure systems, along with training in various kinds of interventions in system difficulties.

- Understanding of lifelong learning and the educational resources available for facilitating the various types of learning sought by adults throughout the life cycle.
- A working knowledge of health and exercise planning, life planning, financial planning, and retirement planning.
- A thorough grounding in group work. Through group process, people can receive support and feedback that result in profound changes in relatively brief time frames.
- Knowledge of how to train adults in leadership skills for managing their lives and reaching high levels of impact within their spheres of influence.

If a profession for promoting optimal development and transformation for adults and adult settings can be established, and if existing professionals can receive training in its concepts and skills, professional resources will be available for mentoring adults throughout the country for personal and social fulfillment.

Notes

Preface

1. John W. Gardner, *Self-Renewal,* rev. ed. (New York: Norton, 1981), xxi.
2. The personal case reports in Part Three are used by permission of those who wrote the material cited, and their actual names are used. However, the names, locations, and certain details of the case histories reported in the rest of this book have been deliberately changed to maintain confidentiality.
3. Robert J. Lifton, *The Broken Connection* (New York: Simon & Schuster, 1979), 88–89.
4. See three books that reveal this dilemma directly: Robert H. Binstock and Ethel Shanas, eds., *Handbook of Aging and the Social Sciences* (New York: Van Nostrand Reinhold, 1976); Caleb F. Finch and Leonard Hayflict, eds., *Handbook of the Biology of Aging* (New York: Van Nostrand Reinhold, 1977); and James E. Birren and K. Warner Schaie, eds., *Handbook of the Psychology of Aging* (New York: Van Nostrand Reinhold, 1977).

Note: An alphabetical listing of these references by author is available for $7.60 from the Hudson Institute of Santa Barbara, 3463 State Street, Suite 520, Santa Barbara, California 93105 (805) 682-3883.

5.   See Carl G. Jung, *Modern Man in Search of a Soul,* trans. W.
      S. Dell and Carry F. Baynes (1933; reprint, New York: Har-
      court Brace & World, 1983); and *The Basic Writings of C. G.
      Jung,* ed. Violet S. de Laszlo (New York: Bollinger Founda-
      tion, 1959).

6.   Charlotte Buhler and Fred Massarik, eds., *The Course of Hu-
      man Life* (New York: Springer, 1968); David C. Gutmann,
      "Individual Adaptation in the Middle Years: Developmental
      Issues in the Masculine Mid-Life Crisis," *Journal of Geriatric
      Psychiatry* 9, no. 1 (1976), 41–59; David C. Gutmann, "The
      Post-Parental Years: Clinical Problems and Developmental
      Possibilities," in *Mid-Life: Developmental and Clinical Is-
      sues,* eds. William H. Norman and Thomas J. Scaramella
      (New York: Brunner/Mazel, 1980); Daniel J. Levinson, "A
      Conception of Adult Development," *American Psychologist*
      41, no. 1 (1986): 3–4; Daniel J. Levinson, *The Seasons of a
      Man's Life* (New York: Knopf, 1978); Joseph Campbell, *The
      Power of Myth* (New York: Doubleday, 1988); Joseph Camp-
      bell, *The Inner Reaches of Outer Space* (New York: Van Der
      Marck, 1985); Robert Bly, *Iron John: A Book About Men*
      (Reading, Mass: Addison-Wesley, 1990).

7.   Erik H. Erikson, *Identity and the Life Cycle* (New York: In-
      ternational Universities Press, 1959); *Childhood and Society,*
      2d ed. (New York: Norton, 1963); *Identity: Youth and Crisis*
      (New York, Norton, 1968); Erik H. Erikson, Joan M. Erikson,
      and Helen Q. Kivnick, *Vital Involvement in Old Age* (New
      York: Norton, 1986).

8.   Roger Gould, *Transformations* (New York: Simon & Schus-
      ter, 1978); Roger Gould, "The Phases of Adult Life: A Study
      in Developmental Psychology," *American Journal of Psychi-
      atry* 129 (1972): 521–31; George E. Vaillant, *Adaptation to Life*
      (New York: Aronson, 1977).

9.   Robert Kegan, *The Evolving Self: Problem and Process in
      Human Development* (Cambridge, Mass.: Harvard University
      Press, 1982).

10.   Gail Sheehy, *Passages* (New York: Dutton, 1976).

11.   Marjorie Fiske and David A. Chiriboga, *Change and Conti-
      nuity in Adult Life* (San Francisco: Jossey-Bass, 1990); Marjo-

rie Fiske, "Changing Hierarchies of Commitment," in *Themes of Work and Love in Adulthood,* ed., Neil J. Smelser and Erik H. Erikson (Cambridge, Mass.: Harvard University Press, 1980); Marjorie Fiske, "Tasks and Crises of the Second Half of Life: The Interrelationship of Commitment, Coping, and Adaptation," in *Handbook of Mental Health and Aging,* ed. James E. Birren and R. Bruce Sloane (Englewood Cliffs, N.J.: Prentice-Hall, 1980); Marjorie Fiske Lowenthal, Majda Thurnher, David Chiriboga, and Associates, *Four Stages of Life: A Comparative Study of Women and Men Facing Transitions* (San Francisco; Jossey-Bass, 1975).

12. Matilda W. Riley, "Aging, Social Change, and the Power of Ideas," *Daedalus* 107 (1978): 39–52; Matilda W. Riley, Ronald P. Abeles, and Michael S. Teitelbaum, eds., *Aging from Birth to Death,* vol. 1, *Interdisciplinary Perspectives* (Boulder, Colo.: Westview Press, 1981); vol. 2, *Sociotemporal Perspectives* (Boulder, Colo.: Westview Press, 1982); Klaus Riegel, "Adult Life Crises: A Dialectical Interpretation of Development," in *Life-Span Developmental Psychology: Normative Life Crises,* ed. Nancy Datan and Leon H. Ginsberg (Orlando, Fla.: Academic Press, 1975); Klaus Riegel, "The Dialectics of Human Development," *American Psychologist,* October 1976, 689–699; Klaus Riegel and John A. Meacham, eds., *The Developing Individual in a Changing World,* vols. 1 and 2 (Chicago: Mouton, 1976); Urie Bronfenbrenner, *The Ecology of Human Development: Experiments by Nature and Design* (Cambridge, Mass.: Harvard University Press, 1979); Gerard Egan and Michael A. Cowan, *People in Systems: A Model for Development in the Human-Service Professions and Education* (Belmont, Calif.: Wadsworth, 1979); Gerard Egan, *The Skilled Helper,* 4th ed. (Monterey, Calif.: Brooks/Cole, 1990).

Chapter One

1. Angus Campbell, *The Sense of Well-Being in America* (New York: McGraw-Hill, 1981), 9.

2. These figures are taken from the United States Census Bureau, 1988–1990.

3. John Wilcox, "In Practice," *Training and Development Journal*, March 1989, 14.

4. Daniel J. Boorstin, *The Image or What Happened to the American Dream* (New York: Atheneum, 1962).

5. Martin E. P. Seligman, *Helplessness: On Depression, Development and Death* (San Francisco: Freeman, 1975), 74. See also Donald L. Kanter and Philip H. Mirvis, *The Cynical Americans: Living and Working in an Age of Discontent and Disillusion* (San Francisco: Jossey-Bass, 1989).

6. *Time* 104, no. 15 (1974): 7–11.

7. See, for example, Martin E. P. Seligman, *Learned Optimism* (New York: Random House, 1990); Mihaly Csikszentmihalyi, *Flow: The Psychology of Optimal Experience—Steps Toward Enhancing the Quality of Life* (New York: Harper & Row, 1990); Robert Bly, *Iron John: A Book About Men* (Reading, Mass.: Addison-Wesley, 1990); Brian P. Hall, *The Genesis Effect: Personal and Organizational Transformations* (Mahwah, N.J.: Paulist Press, 1986); Douglas H. Heath, *Fulfilling Lives: Paths to Maturity and Success* (San Francisco: Jossey-Bass, 1991); Ram Dass, *The Only Dance There Is* (New York: Doubleday, 1974).

8. See, for example, Peter F. Drucker, *The New Realities* (New York: Harper & Row, 1989); Charles Handy, *The Age of Unreason* (Cambridge, Mass.: Harvard Business School Press, 1989; Stanley M. Davis, *Future Perfect* (Reading, Mass.: Addison-Wesley, 1987); Richard Beckhard and Reuben T. Harris, *Organizational Transitions; Managing Complex Change*, 2d ed. (Reading, Mass.: Addison-Wesley, 1987); Warren Bennis et al., eds., *The Planning of Change*, 4th ed. (New York: Holt, Rinehart & Winston, 1976); Joseph F. Coates and Jennifer Jarratt, eds., *What Futurists Believe* (Mount Airy, Md.: Lomond, 1989); Robert Tannenbaum, Newton Margulies, Fred Massarik, and Associates, *Human Systems Development: New Perspectives on People and Organizations* (San Francisco: Jossey-Bass, 1985); Joseph L. Badaracco, Jr., and Richard R. Ellsworth, *Leadership and the Quest for Integrity* (Cambridge, Mass.: Harvard Business School Press, 1989); Max DePree, *Leadership Is an Art* (New

York, Doubleday, 1989); Robert Theobald, *The Rapids of Change: Social Entrepreneurship in Turbulent Times* (Indianapolis, Ind.: Knowledge Systems, 1987).

9. John W. Gardner, *On Leadership* (New York: Free Press, 1990), 181–182.

10. Quoted in David Broder's syndicated column, *Santa Barbara News Press,* 8 March 1990, A-12.

Chapter Two

1. Samuel Butler, *The Way of All Flesh,* quoted by Ellen Y. Siegelman, *Personal Risk: Mastering Change in Love and Work* (New York: Harper & Row, 1983), 27.

2. Roger Gould calls this "the myth of absolute safety," which is normal in childhood but for healthy adult development needs to be gradually replaced with the acceptance of the world as it is—with limits, dangers, risks, and death. See Roger Gould, *Transformations* (New York: Simon & Schuster, 1978). Judith Viorst makes a similar case in *Necessary Losses* (New York: Simon & Schuster, 1986).

3. John W. Rowe and Robert L. Kahn, "Human Aging: Usual and Successful," *Science,* 10 July 1987. Rowe and Kahn argue that if the concept of "successful" aging is included in the research on aging, it will portray a more accurate spectrum of older people, from successful to ordinary to diseased to impaired. Similar comments are found throughout the literature on adult development, such as this one from Else Frenkel-Brunswik, "Adjustments and Reorientation in the Course of the Life Span," in *Middle Age and Aging,* ed. Bernice L. Neugarten (Chicago: University of Chicago Press, 1968), 84: "Still in most lives, the reduction in vitality is not experienced as a negative affair, since a change from a more physical to a more mental life takes place and the second half of life takes on a more positive form. The ability to transpose oneself, to take on another attitude toward life is a character trait which is almost a necessity for success in life."

4. Winthrop D. Jordan, "Searching for Adulthood in America,"

in *Adulthood,* ed. Erik H. Erikson (New York: Norton, 1978), 192.

5. Bernice L. Neugarten, "The Awareness of Middle Age," in *Middle Age and Aging* (Chicago: University of Chicago, 1968), 94.

6. Bernice Hunt and Morton Hunt, *Prime Time* (New York: Stein and Day, 1975), 19.

7. Barbara Fried, *The Middle-Age Crisis,* rev. ed. (New York: Harper & Row, 1976); Elliot Jacques, "Death and the Mid-Life Crisis," *International Journal of Psychoanalysis* 46, no. 4 (1965): 502–14; Orville G. Brim, Jr., "Theories of the Male Mid-Life Crisis," in *Counseling Adults,* ed. Nancy K. Schlossberg and Alan D. Entine (Belmont, Calif.: Wadsworth, 1977), 1–18.

8. Edmund Bergler, *The Revolt of the Middle-Aged Man* (New York: Grosset and Dunlap, 1957).

9. Daniel J. Levinson, *The Seasons of a Man's Life* (New York: Knopf, 1978); Roger Gould, "The Phases of Adult Life: A Study in Developmental Psychology," *American Journal of Psychiatry* 129, no. 5 (1972): 521–31; Lois M. Tamir, *Men in Their Forties: The Transition to Middle Age* (New York: Springer, 1982), 122–123; Marjorie Fiske Lowenthal, Majda Thurnher, David Chiriboga, and Associates, *Four Stages of Life: a Comparative Study of Women and Men Facing Transitions* (San Francisco: Jossey-Bass, 1975); Klaus Riegel, "The Dialectics of Human Development," *American Psychologist,* October 1976, 689–699; George E. Vaillant, *Adaptation to Life* (New York: Aronson, 1977); Bernice Neugarten, *Personality in Middle and Late Life* (New York: Atherton Press, 1964); Bernice L. Neugarten, ed., *Middle Age and Aging* (Chicago: University of Chicago Press, 1968); Bernice Neugarten, "Adult Personality: Toward a Psychology of the Life Cycle," in *The Human Life Cycle,* ed. William C. Sze (New York, Aronson, 1975); Orville G. Brim, Jr., and Jerome Kagan, eds., *Constancy and Change in Human Development* (Cambridge, Mass.: Harvard University Press, 1980); Marjorie Fiske, "Changing Hierarchies of Commitment," in *Themes of Work and Love in Adulthood,* ed. Neil J. Smelser and Erik H. Erikson (Cam-

bridge, Mass.: Harvard University Press, 1980); Marjorie Fiske, "Tasks and Crises in the Second Half of Life: The Interrelationship of Commitment, Coping, and Adaptation," in *Handbook of Mental Health and Aging,* ed. James E. Birren and R. Bruce Sloane (Englewood Cliffs, N.J.: Prentice-Hall, 1980); Daniel Levinson, *The Seasons of a Man's Life* (New York: Knopf, 1978); Carol Gilligan, *In a Different Voice: Psychological Theory and Women's Development* (Cambridge, Mass.: Harvard University Press, 1982); Naomi Golan, *Passing Through Transitions* (New York: Free Press, 1981); Robert Kegan, *The Evolving Self: Problem and Process in Human Development* (Cambridge, Mass.: Harvard University Press, 1982); Robert Nemiroff and Calvin Colarusso, *The Race Against Time* (New York: Plenum Press, 1985).

10.   Quoted by Winthrop D. Jordan in "Searching for Adulthood in America," in Erik H. Erikson, ed., *Adulthood* (New York: Norton, 1978), 198.

11.   A cultural statement of the cyclical point of view can be found in Stephen Toulmin, *Cosmopolis: The Hidden Agenda of Modernity* (New York: Free Press, 1990).

Chapter Three

1.   Allen Wheelis, *How People Change* (New York: Harper & Row, 1973), 105.

2.   Frank J. MacHovec, trans. *I Ching: The Book of Changes* (Mount Vernon, N.Y.: Peter Pauper Press, 1971), 13, 38, 46–47.

3.   MacHovec, *I Ching,* 15, 25, 32–33, 35–36, 41.

4.   Guess Who, "Undun," *Undun,* RCA 0195, 1965.

5.   Stanley Keleman, *Living Your Dying* (New York: Random House, 1974), 51–52.

6.   MacHovec, *I Ching,* 29, 33–34, 53–54.

7.   The concept of "neutral zone" comes from the Dutch anthropologist Arnold Van Gennep, who wrote a classic essay on human change in the early years of the twentieth century. See Arnold Van Gennep, *The Rites of Passage,* trans. Monika B. Visedom and Gabrielle L. Chaffee (1908; reprint, Chicago:

University of Chicago Press, 1960). William Bridges describes the "neutral zone" as a part of adult transitions in his book *Transitions* (Reading, Mass.: Addison-Wesley, 1980).

8. MacHovec, *I Ching*, 15, 11, 22–23, 61.
9. For further reading on the adult "life course," see Daniel J. Levinson, "A Conception of Adult Development," *American Psychologist* 41, no. 1 (1986): 3–4; Daniel J. Levinson, "Conception of the Adult Life Course," in *Themes of Work and Love in Adulthood*, ed. Neil J. Smelser and Erik H. Erikson (Cambridge, Mass.: Harvard University Press, 1980), 265–290; John A. Clausen, "The Life Course of Individuals," in *Aging and Society*, vol. 3, ed. Matilda Riley, Marilyn Johnson, and Anne Foner (New York: Russell Sage Foundation, 1972). Charlotte Buhler, in Charlotte Buhler and Fred Massarik, eds., *The Course of Human Life* (New York: Springer, 1968), 2, writes that "to live a goal-directed life means to have the desire . . . to see one's life culminating in certain results." Then, she reasons, the life course is determined by four factors: the structure of human life, genetic factors, emotional factors, and sociocultural factors. Perhaps the most important scholar to articulate the life course was Henry A. Murray, whose life work was to "study the lives" of others as living wholes. See his article "Individuality: The Meaning and Content of Individuality in Contemporary America," *Daedalus* 87 (1958): 25–47.

Chapter Four

1. Dorothy Rowe, *The Construction of Life and Death* (New York: Wiley, 1982), 208–209.
2. Judith M. Bardwick, *The Plateauing Trap* (New York: AMACOM, 1986), 126–127.
3. Allan Bloom, *The Closing of the American Mind* (New York: Simon & Schuster, 1987), 201–202.
4. Henry David Thoreau, *Walden* (New York: New American Library, 1960) (originally published in 1854).
5. Oscar Wilde, *Lady Windermere's Fan*, act 3.
6. Harry Chapin, "Halfway to Heaven," *Verities & Balderdash* (Story Songs, 1973).

7. Bardwick, *The Plateauing Trap,* ix.

8. Robert Tannenbaum and Robert W. Hanna, "Holding On, Letting Go, and Moving On: Understanding a Neglected Perspective on Change," in *Human Systems Development: New Perspectives on People and Organizations,* Robert Tannenbaum, Newton Margulies, Fred Massarik, and Associates (San Francisco: Jossey-Bass, 1985), 108–109.

9. John W. Gardner, *Self-Renewal,* rev. ed. (New York: Norton, 1981), 15.

10. Ric Masten, "Not Exactly a Command Performance," in *Stark Naked* (Carmel, Calif.: Sunflower Ink, 1980), 70.

11. Erich Lindemann, *Beyond Grief* (New York: Aronson, 1979), 242. See also Judy Tatelbaum, *The Courage to Grieve* (New York: Harper & Row, 1980).

12. Elizabeth Kubler-Ross, *On Death and Dying* (New York: Macmillan, 1969), 2.

13. Mircea Eliade, *Myths, Dreams, and Mysteries,* trans. Philip Mairet (New York: Harper & Row, 1967), 80.

14. Arnold Van Gennep, *The Rites of Passage,* trans. Monika B. Visedom and Gabrielle L. Chaffee (1908; reprint, Chicago: University of Chicago Press, 1960).

Chapter Five

1. James Baldwin, *Nobody Knows My Name* (New York: Dial Press, 1961), 117.

2. Jimmy Carter and Rosalynn Carter, *Everything to Gain: Making the Most of the Rest of Your Life* (New York: Random House, 1987), 4, 7, 9, 26, 27, 30–34, 194.

3. Robert Tannenbaum first shared these ideas with me in many conversations and exchanges. See Robert Tannenbaum and Robert W. Hanna, "Holding On, Letting Go, and Moving On: Understanding a Neglected Perspective on Change," in *Human Systems Development: New Perspectives on People and Organizations,* Robert Tannenbaum, Newton Margulies, Fred Massarik, and Associates (San Francisco: Jossey-Bass, 1985), 95–121. A children's book describing this is E. B. White, *Charlotte's Web* (New York: Harper & Row, 1952); a book

describing how corporate heads depart is Jeffrey Sonnenfeld, *The Hero's Farewell: What Happens When CEOs Retire* (New York: Oxford University Press, 1988).

4. Hugh Prather, *There Is a Place Where You Are Not Alone* (New York: Doubleday, 1980), 39.

5. Quoted by Ellen Y. Siegelman, *Personal Risk: Mastering Change in Love and Work* (New York: Harper & Row, 1983), 38.

6. Siegelman, *Personal Risk*, 37.

7. Ann Kaiser Stearns, *Living Through Personal Crisis* (New York: Ballantine: 1989), 85–86.

8. Arnold R. Beisser, *A Graceful Passage: Notes on the Freedom to Live or Die* (New York: Doubleday, 1990), reported in the *Los Angeles Times*, Sunday, 8 Apr. 1990, section E, 1, 10.

9. Robert K. Greenleaf, *Servant Leadership: A Journey into the Nature of Legitimate Power and Greatness* (Mahwah, N.J.: Paulist Press, 1977), 327.

10. Most life transitions can be managed as developmental events by the people experiencing them. Useful references for managing a life transition effectively include Nancy K. Schlossberg, *Overwhelmed: Coping with Life's Ups & Downs* (Lexington, Mass.: Heath, 1989); William Bridges, *Transitions* (Reading, Mass.: Addison-Wesley, 1980); Ann Kaiser Stearns, *Living Through Personal Crisis* (New York: Ballantine, 1989); Nancy Datan and N. Lohmann, *Transitions of Aging* (Orlando, Fla.: Academic Press, 1980); Naomi Golan, *Passing Through Transitions* (New York: Free Press, 1981); Alan B. Knox, ed., *Programming for Adults Facing Mid-Life Change* (San Francisco: Jossey-Bass, 1979); G. D. Goldman and D. S. Milman, eds., *Man and Woman in Transition* (Dubuque, Iowa: Kendall-Hunt, 1978); Nancy K. Schlossberg and Lillian Troll, *Perspectives on Counseling Adults* (College Park: Umporium, University of Maryland, 1976); Nancy Schlossberg and Alan Entine, eds., *Counseling Adults* (Monterey, Calif.: Brooks/Cole, 1977); Thomas M. Skovholt and Others, eds., *Counseling Men* (Monterey, Calif.: Brooks/Cole, 1980); Lenore W. Harmon and Others, eds., *Counseling Women* (Monterey, Calif.: Brooks/Cole, 1978); Ann Howard

and Douglas W. Bray, *Managerial Lives in Transition* (New York: Guilford, 1988); Kathleen Adams, *Journal to the Self* (New York: Warner Books, 1990); Frederic Flach, *Resilience: Discovering a New Strength at Times of Stress* (New York: Fawcett, 1988); Bonnie Miller Rubin, *Time Out* (New York: Norton, 1987); G. A. Ford and Gordon L. Lippitt, *Planning Your Future: A Workbook for Personal Goal Setting* (San Diego, Calif.: University Associates, 1976); Genevieve D. Ginsburg, *To Live Again: Rebuilding Your Life After You've Become a Widow* (New York: Bantam Books, 1989); Richard E. Pearson and Albert J. Petitpas, "Transitions of Athletes: Developmental and Preventative Perspectives," *Journal of Counseling and Development* 69, no. 1 (1990) 7-10. Within a person's life cycle, some life transitions are "heavier" and more significant than others, depending on (1) the significance attributed to the life structure that one is leaving; (2) the inner strength of the present self to conduct the grieving and renewal processes and the ability of the self to manage loss and attachment to internal and external objects; (3) the deficits of the self resulting from character formation, past personal experience, and social disempowerment; (4) available social support, friendships, and a transitional environment; (5) a healthy body and mind, free of chronic unhappiness and clinical conditions; (6) the degree of emotional resistance to risk taking and exploring the unknown; (7) financial resources for investing in the transition process; and (8) capacities in the self to imagine and facilitate a fulfilling future. Jonathan Bloom-Feshbach, Sally Bloom-Feshbach, and Associates, in *The Psychology of Separation and Loss: Perspectives on Development, Life Transitions, and Clinical Practice* (San Francisco: Jossey-Bass, 1987), conclude their recent study of separation and loss with these words: "Human development and the course of life transitions confront the individual with many experiences of separation and loss, on both the practical and the symbolic level. These experiences spur growth in the relinquishing of the familiar and habitual and in the reaching forward to new possibilities. Developmentally appropriate and emotionally manageable separation experiences are healthy and growth-promoting while unexpected, severe, and developmentally asynchronous separations are psychologically problematic" (p. 558). Most adults are capable of managing life transitions by themselves through their normal support systems. However, those who have a previous history of emotional problems or find themselves incapable of managing the transition process on a day-to-day basis may need professional help and clinical interventions. For further reading on clinical aspects of adult development, see John G. Howells, ed., *Modern Perspectives in the Psychiatry of Middle Age* (New York: Brunner/Mazel, 1981); William H. Norman and Thomas J. Scaramella, *Midlife Developmental and Clinical Issues* (New York: Brunner/Mazel, 1980); Steven H. Zarit, *Aging and Mental Disorders* (New York: Free Press, 1980); Howard L. Millman, Jack T. Huber, and Dean R. Diggins, *Therapies for Adults: Depressive, Anxiety, and Personality Disorders* (San Francisco: Jossey-Bass, 1982); Edna I. Rawlings and Dianne K. Carter, eds., *Psychotherapy for Women: Treatment Toward Equality* (Springfield, Ill.: Thomas, 1977); Robert Allan Silverberg, *Psychotherapy for Men: Transcending the Masculine Mystique* (Springfield, Ill.: Thomas, 1986).

11.   Stanley Keleman, *Living Your Dying* (New York: Random House, 1974), 156.

12.   Arnold J. Toynbee, *A Study of History*, vols. 1 and 2 (1946; reprint, New York: Oxford University Press, 1957).

13.   Quoted in Jan Schmuckler, "Leadership and Followership in Changing Times: A Conversation with Bob Tannenbaum," *Vision/Action*, Winter 1990, 4.

14.   Bridges, *Transitions*, 90–104. Also see William Bridges, *Surviving Corporate Transitions* (New York: Doubleday, 1988).

15.   Mircea Eliade, *Myths, Dreams and Mysteries*, trans. Philip Mairet (New York: Harper & Row, 1967), 48.

16.   Clark E. Moustakas, *Loneliness and Love* (Englewood Cliffs, N.J.: Prentice-Hall, 1972), 21–22. Moustakas's main book on this topic is *Loneliness* (Englewood Cliffs, N.J.: Prentice-Hall, 1961). Considerable research has been conducted on adult loneliness, and one convenient summary can be found in Benedict T. McWhirter, "Loneliness: A Review of Current

Literature, with Implications for Counseling and Research,"
Journal of Counseling & Development 68 (March–April 1990):
417–422.

Chapter Six

1. Charles Garfield, *Peak Performers: The New Heroes of American Business* (New York: Avon, 1986), pp. 241, 83.

2. Hugh Prather, *There Is a Place Where You Are Not Alone* (New York: Doubleday, 1980), 201.

3. William Wordsworth, *The Prelude: The Complete Poetical Works of William Wordsworth* (London: 1950), p. 261.

4. Anthony Storr, *Solitude: A Return to the Self* (New York: Free Press, 1988), 12, 21, 29, 34–35. An excellent resource on the positive aspects of solitude is Jeffrey Kottler, *Private Moments, Secret Selves: Enriching Our Time Alone* (Los Angeles: Tarcher, 1990).

5. Richard E. Byrd, *Alone* (New York: Putnam, 1958), 7.

6. See Robert Kegan, *The Evolving Self: Problem and Process in Human Development* (Cambridge, Mass.: Harvard University Press, 1982); Daniel J. Levinson, *The Seasons of a Man's Life* (New York: Knopf, 1978), 209–44; John Bowlby, *Attachment and Loss*, vols. 1–3 (New York: Basic Books, 1958–1980); Erik H. Erikson, *Childhood and Society*, 2d ed. (New York: Norton, 1963), 219–31. This "redecision" process is described in Mary McClure Goulding and Robert L. Goulding, *Changing Lives Through Redecision Therapy* (New York: Brunner/Mazel, 1979).

7. Silvano Arieti, "Creativity and Its Cultivation," in *American Handbook of Psychiatry*, 2d ed. (New York: Basic Books, 1975), vol. 6, 230–50. Also see Silvano Arieti, *Creativity: The Magic Synthesis* (New York: Basic Books, 1976), 6; Rollo May, "The Nature of Creativity," in *Creativity and Its Cultivation*, ed. Harold H. Anderson (New York: Harper & Row, 1959), 55–68. This entire book is a valuable resource for understanding the creative process, with key articles by Erich Fromm, Carl Rogers, Abraham Maslow, Henry Murray, Margaret Mead, and

others. See also Rollo May, *The Courage to Create* (New York: Bantam Books, 1978).

8. Ellen Y. Siegelman, *Personal Risk: Mastering Change in Love and Work* (New York: Harper & Row, 1983), 126.

9. Louis A. Zurcher, Jr., *The Mutable Self: A Self-Concept for Social Change* (Newbury Park, Calif.: Sage, 1977), 215, 234; Mihaly Csikszentmihalyi, *Flow: The Psychology of Optimal Experience—Steps Toward Enhancing the Quality of Life* (New York: Harper & Row, 1990).

Chapter Seven

1. Madeleine L'Engle, *The Summer of the Great-Grandmother* (New York: Harper & Row, 1974), 52–53.

2. Daniel N. Stern, *The Interpersonal World of the Infant* (New York: Basic Books, 1985); Donald W. Winnicott, *The Maturational Processes and the Facilitating Environment* (New York: International Universities Press, 1965); Margaret S. Mahler, Fred Pine, and Anni Bergman, *The Psychological Birth of the Human Infant* (New York: Basic Books, 1975); Erik H. Erikson, *Childhood and Society*, 2d ed. (New York: Norton, 1963); Robert Coles, *The Spiritual Life of Children* (New York: Houghton Mifflin, 1990).

3. George E. Vaillant, *Adaptation to Life* (Boston: Little, Brown, 1977); Calvin A. Colarusso and Robert A. Nemiroff, *Adult Development* (New York: Plenum Press, 1981); William C. Sze, *Human Life Cycle* (New York: Aronson, 1975); Bernice Neugarten, ed., *Middle Age and Aging* (Chicago: University of Chicago Press, 1968); Carol B. Aslanian and Henry M. Brickell, *Americans in Transition: Life Changes as Reasons for Adult Learning* (Princeton, N.J.: College Entrance Examination Board, 1980).

4. Henry S. Maas and Joseph A. Kuypers, *From Thirty to Seventy: A Forty-Year Longitudinal Study of Adult Life Styles and Personality* (San Francisco: Jossey-Bass, 1974); Roger Gould, *Transformations* (New York: Simon & Schuster, 1978); Nancy Datan and N. Lohmmann, ed., *Transitions of Aging* (Orlando, Fla.: Academic Press, 1980); Neil J. Smelser and

Erik H. Erikson, eds., *Themes of Work and Love in Adult-hood* (Cambridge, Mass.: Harvard University Press, 1980); Robert Kegan, *The Evolving Self: Problem and Process in Human Development* (Cambridge, Mass.: Harvard University Press, 1982); Daniel J. Levinson, "A Conception of Adult Development," *American Psychologist* 41, no. 1 (1986): 3–4; Dorothy Rowe, *The Construction of Life and Death* (New York: Wiley, 1982); Martha Storandt and Gary R. VandenBos, eds., *The Adult Years: Continuity and Change* (Washington, D.C.: American Psychological Association, 1989); Marjorie Fiske and David A. Chiriboga, *Change and Continuity in Adult Life* (San Francisco: Jossey-Bass, 1990); Robert R. McCrae and Paul T. Costa, Jr., *Personality in Adulthood* (New York: Guilford Press, 1990).

5. For example, this book is addressed to Americans who are educated, entrenched in careers and intimacy commitments, and asking fundamental questions about their future options. Matilda White Riley, Ronald P. Abeles, and Michael S. Teitelbaum, eds., *Aging from Birth to Death*, vol. 1, *Interdisciplinary Perspectives* (Boulder, Colo.: Westview Press, 1981); Klaus F. Riegel, "Adult Life Crises: A Dialectic Interpretation of Development," in *Life Span Developmental Psychology: Normative Life Crises*, Nancy Datan and Leon H. Ginsberg, eds. (New York: Academic Press, 1975); Elizabeth J. Douvan, Jody Veroff, and R. Kulka, *A Study of Modern Living* (Ann Arbor: Institute for Social Research, University of Michigan, 1976); Andrew M. Mecca, Neil J. Smelser, and John Vasconcellos, eds., *The Social Importance of Self-Esteem* (Berkeley: University of California Press, 1989).

6. Some general references on gender issues throughout the life span include Bernice L. Neugarten, "Adult Personality: Toward a Psychology of the Life Cycle," in *Middle Age and Aging* (Chicago: University of Chicago Press, 1968); David C. Gutmann, "The Cross-Cultural Perspective: Notes Toward a Comparative Psychology of Aging," in *Handbook of the Psychology of Aging*, eds. James E. Birren and K. Warner Schaie (New York: Van Nostrand Reinhold, 1977). Carol Gilligan writes that "Conceptions of the human life cycle represent

different attempts to order and make coherent the unfolding
experiences and perceptions, the changing wishes and realities
of everyday life. But the nature of such conceptions depends
in part on the position of the observer. . . . When the observer
is a woman, the perspective may be a different sort. Different
judgements of the images of a man . . . to imply different ideas
about human development, different ways of imagining the
human condition, different notions of what is of value in
life." Carol Gilligan, *In a Different Voice: Psychological Theory and Women's Development* (Cambridge, Mass.: Harvard
University Press, 1982), 5. Robert Bly says much the same
about how maleness relates to the male journey through life.
Robert Bly, *Iron John: A Book About Men* (Reading, Mass.:
Addison-Wesley, 1990). Some salient references on women's
issues relating to adult development include Ruthellen Jossel-
son, *Finding Herself: Pathways to Identity Development in
Women* (San Francisco: Jossey-Bass, 1987); Mary C. Bateson,
Composing a Life (New York: Plume, 1990); Nancy J. Cho-
dorow, *Feminism and Psychoanalytic Theory* (New Haven,
Conn.: Yale University Press, 1989); Joan J. Zilbach, "In the
I: The Eye of the Beholder: Towards a Separate Line of De-
velopment in Women," unpublished lecture presented at the
Slavson Memorial Lecture American Group Psychotherapy
Association, Feb. 6, 1987. New Orleans, La.; Toni Bernay and
Dorothy W. Cantor, eds., *The Psychology of Today's Woman:
New Psychoanalytic Visions* (Hillsdale, N.J.: Analytic Press,
1986); Pamela D. McLean, "A Psycho-Social Analysis of the
Life Patterns of Five Hundred Educated Women" (Ph.D. dis-
sertation, Fielding Institute, 1980); Jean Baker Miller, *Toward
a New Psychology of Women* (Boston: Beacon Press, 1976);
Lillian B. Rubin, *Women of a Certain Age: The Midlife
Search for Self* (New York: Harper & Row, 1979); Martha C.
McBride, "Autonomy and the Struggle for Female Identity:
Implications for Counseling Women" *Journal of Counseling
and Development* 69, no. 1 (1990): 22–27; Elise Boulding,
Women in the Twentieth Century World (New York: Halsted
Press, 1977); Natalie Rogers, *Emerging Woman: A Decade of
Midlife Transitions* (Santa Rosa, Calif.: Personal Press, 1980);

"Women at Midlife and Beyond," *Psychology of Women Quarterly*, 14, no. 4 (1990): entire issue. Selected references on men's issues relating to adult development include Kenneth Clatterbaugh, *Contemporary Perspectives on Masculinity: Men, Women, and Politics in Modern Society* (Boulder, Colo.: Westview Press, 1990); Warren Farrell, *Why Men Are the Way They Are* (New York: McGraw-Hill, 1986); Michael P. Farrell and Stanley D. Rosenberg, *Men at Midlife* (Boston: Auburn House, 1981); Sam Keen, *Fire in the Belly: On Being a Man* (New York: Bantam, 1991); Shirley M. H. Hanson and Frederick W. Bozett, eds., *Dimensions of Fatherhood* (Newbury Park, Calif.: Sage, 1985); Stanley H. Cath, Alan Gurwitt, and Linda Gunsberg, eds., *Fathers and Their Families* (Hillsdale, N.J.: Analytic Press, 1989); Robert A. Lewis and Robert E. Salt, *Men in Families* (Newbury Park, Calif.: Sage, 1986); Samuel Osherson, *Finding Our Fathers: The Unfinished Business of Manhood* (New York: Free Press, 1987); Samuel Osherson and Steven Krugman, "Men, Shame, and Psychotherapy," *Psychotherapy* 27, no. 3 (1990): 327–39.

7.   Terrence E. Deal and Allen A. Kennedy, *Corporate Cultures* (Reading, Mass.: Addison-Wesley, 1982); Ichak Adizes, *Corporate Lifecycles* (Englewood Cliffs, N.J.: Prentice-Hall, 1988); Roy Lacoursiere, *The Life Cycle of Groups* (New York: Human Sciences Press, 1980); John R. Kimberly, Robert H. Miles, and Associates, *The Organizational Life Cycle: Issues in the Creation, Transformation, and Decline of Organizations* (San Francisco: Jossey-Bass, 1980); Tom Peters, *Thriving on Chaos: Handbook for a Management Revolution* (New York: Knopf, 1987); Ralph H. Kilmann, *Beyond the Quick Fix: Managing Five Tracks to Organizational Success* (San Francisco: Jossey-Bass, 1984); Donald Super, "Career and Life Development," in *Career Choice and Development: Applying Contemporary Theories and Practice*, Duane Brown, Linda Brooks, and Associates (San Francisco: Jossey-Bass, 1984); Edgar H. Schein, *Career Dynamics: Matching Individual and Organizational Needs* (Reading, Mass.: Addison-Wesley, 1978); Duane Brown, Linda Brooks, and Associates, *Career Choice and Development: Applying Contemporary Theories and*

Practice, 2d ed. (San Francisco: Jossey-Bass, 1990); Norman C. Gysbers and Associates, *Designing Careers: Counseling to Enhance Education, Work, and Leisure* (San Francisco: Jossey-Bass, 1984); Douglas T. Hall and Associates, *Career Development in Organizations* (San Francisco: Jossey-Bass, 1986); Barbara J. Berg, *The Crisis of the Working Mother* (New York: Summit Books, 1986); Uma Sekaran, *Dual-Career Families: Contemporary Organizational and Counseling Issues* (San Francisco: Jossey-Bass, 1986).

8. Elliot Jacques, "Death and the Mid-Life Crisis," *International Journal of Psychoanalysis* 46, no. 4 (1965): 502–14; Ernest Becker, *The Denial of Death* (New York: Free Press, 1973); Judith Viorst, *Necessary Losses* (New York: Simon & Schuster, 1986); Bernice L. Neugarten, "Time, Age, and the Life Cycle," *American Journal of Psychiatry* 136 (1979): 887–94; Robert Nemiroff and Calvin Colarusso, *The Race Against Time* (New York: Plenum Press, 1985).

9. Bernice L. Neugarten, "Adult Personality: Toward a Psychology of the Life Cycle," in *Middle Age and Aging* (Chicago: University of Chicago Press, 1968); Carl G. Jung, "Individuation," in *The Basic Writings of C. G. Jung,* ed. Violet Staub de Laszlo (New York: Modern Library, 1959), 143–57; F. A. Goldberg, ed., *Advances in the Psychology of the Self* (New York: International Universities Press, 1980); Herbert Fingarette, *The Self in Transformation* (New York: Basic Books, 1963); Henry A. Murray, "Individuality: The Meaning and Content of Individuality in Contemporary America," *Daedalus* 87 (1958): 25–47.

10. J. R. Kelly, *Leisure Identities and Interactions* (London: Allen & Unwin, 1983); Rhona Rapoport and Robert N. Rapoport, *Leisure and the Family Life Cycle* (London: Routledge & Kegan Paul, 1975); John Neulinger, *The Psychology of Leisure: Research Approaches to the Study of Leisure* (Springfield, Ill.: Thomas, 1974).

11. Stephen G. Holliday and Michael J. Chandler, *Wisdom: Explorations in Adult Competence* (New York: Karger, 1986); Vivian P. Clayton and James E. Birren, "The Development of Wisdom Across the Life Span: A Reexamination of an Ancient

Topic," in *Life-Span Development and Behavior,* vol. 3, ed. Paul B. Baltes and Orville G. Brim, Jr. (New York: Academic Press, 1980), 103–35; Erik H. Erikson, *The Life Cycle Completed* (New York: Norton, 1982); David L. Norton, *Personal Destinies: A Philosophy of Ethical Individualism* (Princeton, N.J.: Princeton University Press, 1976); Eugene C. Bianchi, *Aging as a Spiritual Journey* (New York: Crossroad, 1987); John Weir Perry, *The Heart of History: Individuality in Evolution* (Albany: State University of New York Press, 1987).

12.   Laurent A. Daloz, *Effective Teaching and Mentoring: Realizing the Transformational Power of Adult Learning Experiences* (San Francisco: Jossey-Bass, 1986); Robert K. Greenleaf, *Servant Leadership: A Journey into the Nature of Legitimate Power and Greatness* (Mahwah, N.J.: Paulist Press, 1977); John W. Gardner, *On Leadership* (New York: Free Press, 1990); Peter Block, *The Empowered Manager: Positive Political Skills at Work* (San Francisco: Jossey-Bass, 1987); Noel M. Tichy and Mary Anne Devanna, *The Transformational Leader* (New York: Wiley, 1986); Joseph L. Badaracco Jr., and Richard R. Ellsworth, *Leadership and the Quest for Integrity* (Boston: Harvard Business School Press, 1989).

13.   See Erik H. Erikson, *Identity: Youth and Crisis* (New York: Norton, 1968); Erik H. Erikson, *Identity and the Life Cycle* (1959); Carl Rogers, *On Becoming a Person* (Boston: Houghton Mifflin, 1961); James F. Masterson, *The Search for the Real Self* (New York: Free Press, 1988); Michael Polanyi, *Personal Knowledge* (Chicago: University of Chicago Press, 1958); Leona E. Tyler, *Individuality: Human Possibilities and Personal Choice in the Psychological Development of Men and Women* (San Francisco: Jossey-Bass, 1978); William Kilpatrick, *Identity and Society* (New York: Delta Books, 1975); Kathleen Adams, *Journal to the Self* (New York: Warner Books, 1990).

14.   See Charles Garfield, *Peak Performance* (Los Angeles: Tarcher, 1974); Stephen R. Covey, *The Seven Habits of Highly Effective People* (New York: Simon & Schuster, 1989); Perry Pascarella, *The New Achievers: Creating a Modern Work Ethic* (New York: Free Press, 1984); Ruth B. Kundsin, ed.,

Women & Success: The Anatomy of Achievement (New York: Morrow, 1974).

15. See Reuben Fine, *The Meaning of Love in Human Experience* (New York: Wiley, 1985); Kenneth S. Pope and Associates, *On Love and Loving: Psychological Perspectives on the Nature and Experience of Romantic Love* (San Francisco: Jossey-Bass, 1980); Willard Gaylin and Ethel Person, eds., *Passionate Attachments: Thinking About Love* (New York: Free Press, 1988); Shirley G. Luthman, *Intimacy: The Essence of Male & Female* (San Rafael, Calif.: Mehetabel, 1972); Sam Keen, *The Passionate Life: Stages of Loving* (New York: Harper & Row, 1983).

16. See Donald W. Winnicott, *Playing & Reality* (London: Tavistock, 1971); A. Reza Arasteh and Josephine D. Arasteh, *Creativity in Human Development* (New York: Schenkman, 1976); Silvano Arieti, *Creativity: The Magic Synthesis* (New York: Basic Books, 1976); Robert J. Sternberg, ed., *The Nature of Creativity* (New York: Cambridge University Press, 1988); Rollo May, *The Courage to Create* (New York: Bantam Books, 1978); Robert Grundin, *The Grace of Great Things: Creativity and Innovation* (New York: Ticknor & Fields, 1990).

17. See also Victor E. Frankl, *Man's Search for Meaning* (New York: Pocket Books, 1977); Rollo May, *The Discovery of Being* (New York: Norton, 1983); Paul Tillich, *The Courage to Be* (New Haven, Conn.: Yale University Press, 1952); Frances Vaughan, *The Inward Arc: Healing and Wholeness in Psychotherapy and Spirituality* (Boston: New Science Library, 1986); Althea Horner, *Being and Loving* (Northvale, N.J.: Jason Aronson, 1986); Stanislav Grof and Christina Grof, *The Stormy Search for the Self: A Guide to Personal Growth Through Transformational Crisis* (Los Angeles, Calif.: Teacher, 1990); Roger S. Gottlieb, *A New Creation: America's Contemporary Spiritual Voices* (New York: Crossroad, 1990).

18. Useful references for this topic are: Milton Mayeroff, *On Caring* (New York: Harper & Row, 1971); M. Scott Peck, *The Different Drum: Community Making and Peace* (New York: Touchstone, 1987); Arthur Simon, *Bread for the World* (Ramsey, N.J., and Grand Rapids, Mich.: Paulist Press and Eerd-

mans, 1975); Ralph E. White, ed., *Psychology and the Prevention of Nuclear War: A Book of Readings* (New York: New York University Press, 1986); Katherine Scholes, *Peace Begins with You* (Boston: Little, Brown, 1990); Joan Anzalone, ed., *Good Works* (New York: Dembner Books, 1985); Ram Dass and Paul Gorman, *How Can I Help?* (New York: Knopf, 1987).

19. See James Kavanaugh, *Search: A Guide for Those Who Dare to Ask of Life Everything Good and Beautiful* (New York: Harper & Row, 1985); Hugh Prather, *Notes to Myself: My Struggle to Become a Person* (New York: Bantam Books, 1970); Muriel James and Louis Savary, *A New Self* (Reading, Mass.: Addison-Wesley, 1977); Robert A. Johnson, *Inner Work: Using Dreams and Active Imagination for Personal Growth* (New York: Harper & Row, 1986); Ira Progoff, *At a Journal Workshop* (New York: Dialogue House, 1975); Kay Leigh Hagan, *Internal Affairs: A Journal-Keeping Workbook for Self-Intimacy* (New York: Harper & Row, 1990); Eric Shepherd and J. P. Watson, eds., *Personal Meanings: The First Guy's Hospital Symposium on the Individual Frame of Reference* (New York: Wiley, 1982).

20. See Susan M. Campbell, *The Couple's Journey: Intimacy as a Path to Wholeness* (San Luis Obispo, Calif.: Impact, 1987); Ellyn Bader and Peter Pearson, *In Quest of the Mythical Mate* (New York: Brunner/Mazel, 1988); Augustus Y. Napier, *The Fragile Bond: In Search of an Equal, Intimate and Enduring Marriage* (New York: Harper & Row, 1988); Harville Hendrix, *Getting the Love You Want; A Guide for Couples* (New York: Holt, Rinehart & Winston, 1988); George R. Bach and Peter Wyden, *The Intimate Enemy: How to Fight Fair in Love and Marriage* (New York: Avon, 1968); Roger W. Libby and Robert N. Whitehurst, *Marriage and Alternatives: Exploring Intimate Relationships* (Glenview, Ill.: Scott, Foresman, 1977); Betty Berzon, *Permanent Partners: Building Gay and Lesbian Relationships That Last* (New York: Dutton, 1988); Robert S. Weiss, *Marital Separation* (New York: Basic Books, 1975); Florence W. Kaslow and Lita L. Schwartz, *The Dynamics of Divorce: A Life Cycle Perspective* (New York: Brunner/Mazel,

1987); Melba Colgrove, Harold H. Bloomfield, and Peter McWilliams, *How to Survive the Loss of a Love* (New York: Bantam Books, 1976); Louise Montague, *A New Life Plan: A Guide for the Divorced Woman* (New York: Doubleday, 1978); Stephen R. Schuchter, *Dimensions of Grief: Adjusting to the Death of a Spouse* (San Francisco: Jossey-Bass, 1986).

21. See Michael Popkin, *Active Parenting* (New York: Harper & Row, 1987); Ellen Galinsky, *The Six Stages of Parenthood* (Reading, Mass.: Addison-Wesley, 1987); Rudolph Schaffer, *Mothering* (Cambridge, Mass.: Harvard University Press, 1977; Michael E. Lamb, ed., *The Role of the Father in Child Development*, 2d ed. (New York: Wiley, 1981); E. James Anthony and Therese Benedek, *Parenthood: Its Psychology and Psychopathology* (Boston: Little, Brown, 1970); Bruno Bettelheim, *A Good Enough Parent: A Book on Child-Rearing* (New York: Knopf, 1987); Alice S. Rossi, Jerome Kagan, and Tamara K. Hareven, eds., *The Family* (New York: Norton, 1978); Nicholas Hobbs et al., *Strengthening Families: Strategies for Improved Child Care and Parent Education* (San Francisco: Jossey-Bass, 1984); Elizabeth A. Carter and Monica McGoldrick, eds., *The Changing Family Life Cycle: A Framework for Family Therapy*, 2d ed. (Boston: Allyn & Bacon, 1990; Michael Lamb and Brian Sutton-Smith, eds., *Sibling Relationships: Their Nature and Significance Across the Lifespan* (Hillsdale, N.J.: Erlbaum, 1982); Francine S. Hall and Douglas T. Hall, *The Two-Career Couple* (Reading, Mass.: Addison-Wesley, 1979); Elizabeth Einstein, *The Stepfamily: Living, Loving & Learning* (New York: Macmillan, 1982); Emily B. Visher and John S. Visher, *Stepfamilies: A Guide to Working with Stepparents and Stepchildren* (New York: Brunner/Mazel, 1979); Elizabeth B. Goldsmith, ed., *Work and Family: Theory, Research, and Applications* (Newbury Park, Calif.: Sage, 1989).

22. See Robert Bell, *Worlds of Friendship* (Newbury Park, Calif.: Sage, 1981); Roger Fisher and Scott Brown, *Getting Together: Building Relationships as We Negotiate* (New York: Penguin, 1989); Lillian B. Rubin, *Just Friends: The Role of Friendship in Our Lives* (New York: Harper & Row, 1985).

23. See Zandy Leibowitz and Daniel Lea, eds., *Adult Career Development* (Washington, D.C.: National Career Development Association, 1986); Duane Brown, Linda Brooks, and Associates, *Career Choice and Development: Applying Contemporary Theories to Practice*, 2d ed. (San Francisco: Jossey-Bass, 1990); Dennis T. Jaffe and Cynthia D. Scott, *Take This Job and Love It* (New York: Fireside, 1988); Stan J. Katz and Aimee E. Liu, *Success Trap* (New York: Ticknor & Fields, 1990); Diane Fassel, *Working Ourselves to Death* (New York: Harper & Row, 1990); John D. Adams, ed., *Transforming Work* (Alexandria, Va.: Miles River Press, 1984); Samuel A. Culbert and John J. McDonough, *The Invisible War: Pursuing Self-Interests at Work* (New York: Wiley, 1980); Gifford Pinchot III, *Intrapreneuring* (New York: Harper & Row, 1985); Lyman Porter and Lawrence McKibbin, *Management Education and Development: Drift or Thrust into the 21st Century* (New York: McGraw-Hill, 1988); Harrison Owen, *SPIRIT: Transformation and Development in Organizations* (Potomac, Md.: Abbott, 1987); Robert Fritz, *The Path of Least Resistance*, revised edition (New York: Ballantine, 1989).

24. See Carl McDaniels, *Leisure: Integrating a Neglected Component in Life Planning* (Columbus, Oh.: National Center for Research in Vocational Education, 1982); Carl McDaniels, ed., *Leisure and Career Development at Mid-Life* (Blacksburg: Virginia Polytechnic Institute and State University, 1976); John M. Whiteley, ed., special issue on *The Counseling Psychologist*, 1981, *9* (3).

25. See Gordon L. Lippitt, Peter Langseth, and Jack Mossop, *Implementing Organizational Change: A Practical Guide to Managing Change Efforts* (San Francisco: Jossey-Bass, 1985); Manuel London, *Change Agents: New Roles and Innovation Strategies for Human Resource Professionals* (San Francisco: Jossey-Bass, 1988).

26. See Buckminster Fuller, *Ideas and Integrities* (New York: Collier Books, 1963); Robert Ornstein and Paul Ehrlich, *New World New Mind* (New York: Simon & Schuster, 1989); Kenneth E. Boulding, *The World as a Total System* (Newbury Park, Calif.: Sage, 1985); Urie Bronfenbrenner, *The Ecology*

of Human Development: Experiments by Nature and Design (Cambridge, Mass.: Harvard University Press, 1979); Carl Friedrich von Weizsacker, *The Unity of Nature,* trans. Francis J. Zucker (New York: Farrar, Straus & Giroux, 1980).

Chapter Eight

1. Theodore Lidz, *The Person: His Development Throughout the Life Cycle* (New York: Basic Books, 1968), 363 ff.
2. Frances Horn, *I Want One Thing* (Marina del Rey, Calif.: DeVorss, 1981), 31–34.
3. "The New Teens: What Makes Them Different," *Newsweek,* special edition, Summer–Fall 1990.
4. Dan Brown, "Thirtynothing," *Santa Barbara Independent,* 14 December 1989, 55. See also "The New Teens: What Makes Them Different."
5. Although the names and situations here have been purposively changed, this dialogue is based upon the real-life struggle quite typical of many thirtysomethings with whom I work.
6. Carl G. Jung, "Marriage as a Psychological Relationship," in *Collected Works of C. G. Jung,* vol. 17 (London: Routledge & Kegan Paul, 1954), 193.
7. Anton P. Tchekov, *Ivanov* (New York: Everyman's Library, No. 941).
8. William Bridges, *A Year in the Life* (New York: Bantam Books, 1982), inside front cover, 5, 15–16.
9. Descriptions of the midlife transition can be found in Daniel J. Levinson, *The Seasons of a Man's Life* (New York: Knopf, 1978), 191–305; Lois M. Tamir, *Men in Their Forties: The Transition to Middle Age* (New York: Springer, 1982); Herbert J. Freudenberger and Gail North, *Women's Burnout: How to Spot It, How to Reverse It, and How to Prevent It* (New York: Doubleday, 1985); Jeanne E. Gullahorn, *Psychology and Women: In Transition* (Washington, D.C.: Winston, 1979); A Chayes, "Disarmed at Middle Age," *Atlantic* 228 (November 1971): 72–73; Michael P. Nichols, *Turning Forty in the 80s: Personal Crisis Time for Change* (New York: Simon & Schus-

ter, 1986), 17–32. Two Jungian contributions are Peter O'Conner, *Understanding the Mid-Life Crisis* (New York: Paulist Press, 1988), and Daryl Sharp, *The Survival Papers: Anatomy of a Midlife Crisis,* (Toronto: Inner City Books, 1988). See also Solomon Cytrynbaum et al., "Midlife Development: A Personality and Social Systems Perspective," in *Aging in the 1980s: Psychological Issues,* ed. Leonard W. Poon (Washington, D.C.: American Psychological Association, 1980), 463–74.

Chapter Nine

1. Henry David Thoreau, *Walden* (1854; reprint, New York: New American Library), 10, 66.
2. Carol Gilligan, *In a Different Voice: Psychological Theory and Women's Development* (Cambridge, Mass.: Harvard University Press, 1982), 63.
3. Marvin Bansky is a businessman and a professional working with young adults in Santa Barbara, California.
4. Marilyn Mosley is a professional educator in Ojai, California.
5. Bernice Neugarten, "The Awareness of Middle Age," in *Middle Age and Aging* (Chicago: University of Chicago Press, 1968), 93–98. There are a number of useful references on midlife: Janet Zollinger Giele, *Women in the Middle Years* (New York: Wiley, 1982); see footnote 6, chapter 7 for a discussion of gender issues; Ralph LaRossa and Maureen M. LaRossa, *Transition to Parenthood: How Infants Change Families* (Newbury Park, Calif.: Sage, 1981); Henry S. Maas and Joseph A. Kuypers, *From Thirty to Seventy: A Forty-Year Longitudinal Study of Adult Life Styles and Personality* (San Francisco: Jossey-Bass, 1974); Judith M. Bardwick, "Middle Age and a Sense of Future," *Merrill-Palmer Quarterly* 24, no. 2 (1978); 129–38; Stanley H. Cath, "Individual Adaptation in the Middle Years: A Testing of Faith in Self and Object Constancy," *Journal of Geriatric Psychiatry* 9 (1976): 19–40; Lillian E. Troll, *Early and Middle Adulthood* (Belmont, Calif.: Wadsworth, 1975); Lois M. Tamir, *Men in Their Forties: The Transition to Middle Age* (New York: Springer, 1982); Ross

Goldstein with Diana Landau, *Fortysomething* (Los Angeles: Tarcher, 1990); Pierre Mornell, *Passive Men, Wild Women* (New York: Ballantine, 1979); Michael P. Farrell and Stanley D. Rosenberg, *Men at Midlife* (Boston: Auburn House, 1981); Lillian E. Troll, Joan Israel, and Kenneth Israel, *Looking Ahead: A Woman's Guide to the Problems and Joys of Growing Older* (Englewood Cliffs, N.J.: Prentice-Hall, 1977); Marilyn R. Block, Janice L. Davidson, Jean D. Grambs, *Women over Forty* (New York: Springer, 1981).

6. Carl G. Jung, *Modern Man in Search of a Soul*, trans. W. S. Dell and Carry F. Baynes (1933; reprint, New York: Harcourt Brace & World, 1983); on "individuation" and "self," see Jolande Jacobi, "Complex/Archetype/Symbol in the Psychology of C. G. Jung" (New York: Bollingen Foundation, 1959), 113–16, 186; 65, 179, 64, 194n; and 114–15, respectively.

7. Bob Sipchen, "The Inner Warrior," *Los Angeles Times* 19 March 1991, E1, E5.

8. Herant Katchadourian, *Fifty: Midlife in Perspective* (New York: W. H. Freeman, 1987), 6. An excellent book for understanding adult development in this decade and after is Janet K. Belsky, *Here Tomorrow: Making the Most of Life After Fifty* (Baltimore: Johns Hopkins University Press, 1988).

9. Since his late twenties, Richard Haid had been an insurance executive in Hamilton, Ohio. He is now a Ph.D. student at the Union Institute and a consultant for family business executives.

10. Marie Dressler, *My Own Story* (Boston: Little, Brown, 1934), chap. 4.

11. Anne Morrow Lindbergh, *Gift from the Sea* (New York: Vintage, 1977), 84.

12. Germaine Greer, "Letting Go," *Vogue,* May 1986, 141–43.

13. David C. Gutmann, "The Post-Parental Years: Clinical Problems and Developmental Possibilities," in *Mid-Life: Developmental and Clinical Issues*, ed. William H. Norman and Thomas J. Scaramella (New York: Brunner/Mazel, 1980), 44. See also David Gutmann, *Reclaimed Powers* (New York: Basic Books, 1987).

Chapter Ten

1. Lillian E. Troll, *Early and Middle Adulthood* (Belmont, Calif.: Wadsworth, 1975), 143.
2. Larry L. King, "What, Me Sixty?" *Parade Magazine*, 5 November 1989, 4–9. The celebration of his sixtieth birthday in 1989 prompted author and playwright Larry L. King to reassess his attitudes about aging. Reprinted with permission from Parade, copyright © 1989.
3. "Suddenly 60," *USA WEEKEND*, 9–13 June 1989, 23.
4. See Laurent A. Daloz, *Effective Teaching and Mentoring: Realizing the Transformational Power of Adult Learning Experiences* (San Francisco: Jossey-Bass, 1986); Daniel J. Levinson, *The Seasons of a Man's Life* (New York: Knopf, 1978), 97–101. Levinson writes, "What are the various functions of the mentor? He may act as a teacher to enhance the young man's skills and intellectual development. Serving as sponsor, he may use his influence to facilitate the young man's entry and advancement. He may be a host and guide, welcoming the initiate into a new occupational and social world and acquainting him with its values, customs, resources and cast of characters. Through his own virtues, achievements and way of living, the mentor may be an exemplar that the protege can admire and seek to emulate. He may provide counsel and moral support in time of stress. . . . The mentor has another function, and this is developmentally the most crucial one: to support and facilitate the realization of the Dream. The true mentor, in the meaning intended here, serves as an analogue in adulthood of the "good enough" parent for the child. . . . The mentor is not a crypto-parent. His primary function is to be a transitional figure" (pp. 98–99). Grandparenting is a form of mentoring. See Arthur Kornhaber and Kenneth L. Woodward, *Grandparents/Grandchildren: The Vital Connection* (New York: Doubleday, 1981); Vern L. Bengtson and Joan F. Robertson, eds., *Grandparenthood* (Newbury Park, Calif.: Sage, 1985); Lillian E. Troll, "Grandparenting," in *Aging in the 1980s: Psychological Issues,* ed. Leonard W.

Poon (Washington, D.C.: American Psychological Association, 1980).

5. Phillip L. Berman, ed. *The Courage to Grow Old* (New York: Ballantine, 1989), 72. Born in 1918, Robert Lee has coauthored some of the great contemporary classics for the American theater, including *Inherit the Wind* and *Auntie Mame*. He teaches advanced playwriting at UCLA.

6. Berman, *The Courage to Grow Old*, 187–89. Sarah McClendon operates her own news bureau in Washington, D.C. During her career, she has been a reporter, news service executive, and television and radio analyst.

7. Berman, *The Courage to Grow Old*, 260–61. Malcolm Muggeridge was a British journalist, social critic, and theologian. He died in 1990.

8. Larry Porter, "A Conversation with Bob Tannenbaum," *OD Practitioner*, September 1990, 13. See also Eugene C. Bianchi, *On Growing Older: A Personal Guide to Life after 35* (New York: Crossroad, 1986).

9. Erik H. Erikson, *Identity: Youth and Crisis* (New York: Norton, 1968), 140–41. See also Erik H. Erikson, *The Life Cycle Completed* (New York: Norton, 1982); Erik H. Erikson, Joan M. Erikson, and Helen Q. Kivnick, *Vital Involvement in Old Age* (New York: Norton, 1986); and Helen M. Luke, *Old Age* (New York: Parabola Books, 1987).

10. See Walter M. Bortz II, *We Live Too Short and Die Too Long* (New York: Bantam Books, 1991); Lissy F. Jarvik, ed., *Aging into the Twenty-First Century: Middle-Agers Today* (New York: Gardner Press, 1978); Paul Homer and Martha Holstein, eds., *A Good Old Age?* (New York: Touchstone, 1990); Warren A. Peterson and Jill Quadagno, eds., *Social Bonds in Later Life: Aging and Interdependence* (Newbury Park, Calif.: Sage, 1985); Robert C. Atchley, *The Social Forces in Later Life*, 3d ed. (Belmont, Calif.: Wadsworth, 1980).

11. Simone de Beauvoir, *The Coming of Age* (New York: Putnam's Sons, 1972), 378.

12. Arnold R. Beisser, *A Graceful Passage: Notes on the Freedom to Live or Die* (New York: Doubleday, 1990), quoted in the *Los Angeles Times*, 8 April 1990, E-10. See also Ardath H.

Rodale, *Climbing Toward the Light: A Journey of Growth, Understanding, and Love* (Emmaus, Pa.: Good Spirit Press, 1989); Stephen Levine, *A Gradual Awakening* (New York: Anchor Books, 1989).

Chapter Eleven

1. Further inquiry into this point of view might include a study of the writings of Sigmund Freud and Carl Jung. An easy but profound beginning point would be Donald W. Winnicott, *Human Nature* (New York: Schocken Books, 1988).
2. See Jerry Gerber et al., *Lifetrends: The Future of Baby Boomers and Other Aging Americans* (New York: Macmillan, 1989).
3. See Nancy Smith, "In the Shadow of the Boomers: Post-Boom," *Oregonian*, 29 July 1990, D3–D4, which suggests that the current twentysomethings can be characterized as ambivalent, indecisive, seeking to define themselves through their work. "Our lives are so open, the choices endless. We need to make decisions but don't want to leave anything out. We are grown-up children, wearing the suit but keeping the ponytail. We are migrants in search of a more perfect home. We are seriously unserious. We are confident neurotics. We are undecided, leaving the doors open. We are pending."
4. See Bernice L. Neugarten, "The Awareness of Middle Age" and "Adult Personality: Toward a Psychology of the Life Cycle," in *Middle Age and Aging* (Chicago: University of Chicago Press, 1968). See also Robert Peck, "Psychological Developments in the Second Half of Life," in *The Human Life Cycle*, ed. William C. Sze (New York: Aronson, 1975).
5. See the Foreword to this book.
6. See, for example, Urie Bronfenbrenner, *The Ecology of Human Development* (Cambridge, Mass.: Harvard University Press, 1979); Klaus Riegel, "Adult Life Crises: A Dialectical Interpretation of Development," in *Life-span Developmental Psychology: Normative Life Crises*, ed. Nancy Datan and Leon H. Ginsberg (Orlando, Fla.: Academic Press, 1975); Matilda White Riley, Ronald P. Abeles, and Michael S. Teitel-

baum, eds., *Aging from Birth to Death*, vol. 2, *Sociotemporal Perspectives* (Boulder, Colo.: Westview Press, 1981).

7.   See Frederick Towne Melges, *Time and the Inner Future* (New York: Wiley, 1982); Joseph E. McGrath and Janice R. Kelly, *Time and Human Interaction: Toward a Social Psychology of Time* (New York: Guilford Press, 1986); Robert Grundin, *Time and the Art of Living* (New York: Ticknor & Fields, 1982); Marilee Zdenek, *Inventing the Future* (New York: McGraw-Hill, 1987); Howard F. Didsbury, Jr., ed., *The Future: Opportunity Not Destiny* (Bethesda, Md.: World Future Society, 1989).

Chapter Twelve

1.   In Robert Ornstein and Paul Ehrlich, *New World New Mind* (New York: Simon & Schuster, 1989), 200, 264–65.

2.   Edward E. Sampson, "The Debate on Individualism," *American Psychologist*, 45, no. 1 (1988), 15–22.

3.   Andrew M. Mecca, Neil J. Smelser, and John Vasconcellos, eds., *The Social Importance of Self-Esteem* (Berkeley: University of California Press, 1989), xi.

4.   Rainer Marie Rilke, "The Ninth Elegy," *Duino Elegies*, Trans. C. F. MacIntyre (Berkeley, Calif.: University of California Press, 1965), pp. 71–73.

5.   From an unpublished article, "Surfing, a Radical Yoga" (1974), by Richard Heckler, provided to me by an ardent surfer from San Diego, Mark Tourteilote.

6.   Jack London, *The Cruise of the Snark* (1907; reprint, New York: Macmillan, 1939).

7.   James Gleick, *Chaos: Making a New Science* (New York: Penguin Books, 1987); Gery Taubes, "The Body Chaotic," *Discover*, May 1989, 63–67.

8.   Harry Hurt III, *For All Mankind* (New York: Atlantic Monthly Press, 1988), 325–26.

9.   Suzanne Berger, et al., "Toward a New Industrial America," *Scientific American* 260, no. 6 (1989): 47. Other writings that support this way of thinking include Tom Peters *Thriving on Chaos: Handbook for a Management Revolution* (New York:

Knopf, 1987); William Bridges, *Surviving Corporate Transitions* (New York: Doubleday, 1988); Robert H. Waterman, Jr., *The Renewal Factor* (New York: Bantam Books, 1987); Donald L. Kirkpatrick, *How to Manage Change Effectively: Approaches, Methods, and Case Examples* (San Francisco: Jossey-Bass, 1985); and Burt Nanus, *The Leader's Edge: The Seven Keys to Leadership in a Turbulent World* (New York: Contemporary Books, 1989).

10. Willis Harman, *Global Mind Change: The Promise of the Last Years of the Twentieth Century* (Indianapolis, Ind.: Knowledge Systems, 1988), 132.

Chapter Thirteen

1. Mihaly Csikszentmihalyi, *Flow: The Psychology of Optimal Experience—Steps Toward Enhancing the Quality of Life* (New York: Harper & Row, 1990), 213.

2. Dag Hammarskjold, *Markings* (New York: Knopf, 1964), 55.

3. Charlotte Buhler and Fred Massarik, eds., *The Course of Human Life* (New York: Springer, 1968), 2.

4. Anthony Storr, *Solitude: A Return to the Self* (New York: Free Press, 1988), 34–35.

5. Hammarskjold, *Markings*, 13.

6. Anne Morrow Lindbergh, *Gift From the Sea* (New York: Vintage, 1977), 80, 84–85.

7. Hilary Appelman, *Santa Barbara News-Press*, 4 February 1991, C4.

8. See, for example, Barbara F. Okun, *Working with Adults: Individual, Family, and Career Development* (Monterey, Calif.: Brooks/Cole, 1984); David N. Ulrich and Harry P. Dunne, Jr., *To Love & Work: A Systematic Interlocking of Family, Workplace, and Career* (New York: Brunner/Mazel, 1986); John F. Nussbaum, ed., *Life-Span Communication: Normative Processes* (Hillsdale, N.J.: Erlbaum, 1989); FM-2030, *Are You A Transhuman? Monitoring and Stimulating Your Personal Rate of Growth in a Rapidly Changing World* (New York: Warner Books, 1989).

9. Carl Jung, *Modern Man in Search of a Soul*, trans. W. S. Dell

and Carry F. Baynes (1933; reprint, New York: Harcourt Brace & World, 1983), 108.

10. See Morris T. Keeton and Associates, *Experiential Learning: Rationale, Charactertistics, and Assessment* (San Francisco: Jossey-Bass, 1976); Malcolm S. Knowles, *Self-Directed Learning: A Guide for Learners and Teachers* (Chicago: Follett, 1975); Alan M. Thomas, *Beyond Education: A New Perspective on Society's Management of Learning* (San Francisco: Jossey-Bass, 1991); Stephen D. Brookfield, *Developing Critical Thinkers: Challenging Adults to Explore Alternative Ways of Thinking and Acting* (San Francisco: Jossey-Bass, 1987); Trevor A. Williams, *Learning to Manage Our Futures: The Participative Redesign of Societies in Turbulent Transition* (New York: Wiley, 1982); Hugh J. Lurie, "Life Planning: An Educational Approach to Change," *American Journal of Psychiatry* 134 no. 8 (1977): 878–82.

11. Mortimer J. Adler, *Reforming Education: The Opening of the American Mind* (New York: Macmillan, 1990), 328. Adler goes on to say, "To the extent that the great books constitute the monuments of our culture, the substance of our intellectual tradition, the more individuals who in any degree actually possess some of that culture through the reading and discussion of the great books, the more favorable are the conditions for its transmission and progress."

12. Perry Pascarella, *The New Achievers: Creating a Modern Work Ethic* (New York: Free Press, 1984), 13, 110, 137, 169.

13. Peter M. Senge, "The Leader's New Work: Building Learning Organizations" *Sloan Management Review* 7 (Fall 1990): 7–23. See also Peter M. Senge, *The Fifth Discipline: The Art and Practice of the Learning Organizaton* (New York: Doubleday, 1990); Victoria J. Marsick and Karen E. Watkins, *Informal and Incidental Learning in the Workplace* (New York: Routledge, 1990).

14. Seymour B. Sarason and Elizabeth Lorentz, *The Challenge of the Resource Exchange Network: From Concept to Action* (San Francisco: Jossey-Bass, 1979), 226–27.

15. Alvin Toffler, *Future Shock* (New York: Random House, 1970), 429.

16.   See Harry C. Boyte and Frank Riessman, eds., *The New Populism: The Politics of Empowerment* (Philadelphia: Temple University Press, 1986); Harry C. Boyte, *Citizen Action and the New American Populism* (Philadelphia: Temple University Press, 1986). The classic for understanding this model of innovation and change is John W. Gardner's *Self-Renewal* (rev. ed. New York: Norton, 1981). Speaking in simple language, Gardner describes the personal and social renewal process with great clarity. Gardner's new book *On Leadership* (New York: Free Press, 1990) expands on his earlier ideas. Also see Joseph N. Pelton, *Future Talk: Global Life in the Age of Telepower* (Boulder, Colo.: Cross Communications Press, 1990).

17.   Robert K. Greenleaf,, *Servant Leadership: A Journey into the Nature of Legitimate Power and Greatness* (Mahwah, N.J.: Paulist Press, 1977).

Name Index

Subject Index

A